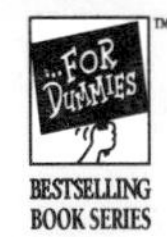

Cascading Style Sheets For Dummies

Basic Style Structure in an HTML Document

```
<HEAD>
<STYLE type="text/css">
   .rule   {
      property: value;
   }
</STYLE>
</HEAD>
```

The CSS Top 15 Properties

Property	
:link	font-weight
:visited	padding
background	position
border	text-align
color	text-decoration
font-family	visibility
font-size	z-index
font-style	

HTML Elements That Should Get Default Styles

BODY	H2
P	H3
DIV	TABLE
SPAN	TR
H1	TD

For Dummies: Bestselling Book Series for Beginners

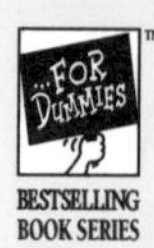

Cascading Style Sheets For Dummies®

Cheat Sheet

CSS Length Units

CSS Length Unit Syntax

Unit	Style Representation	Example
inches	in	margin-left: 1.0in
centimeters	cm	margin-top: 3cm
millimeters	mm	line-height: 7mm
points	pt	font-size: 12pt
picas	pc	font-size: 2pc
pixels	px	font-size: 10px
em	em	font-size: 2em
x-height	ex	font-size: 10ex

Colors and Their Values

Named Colors and Their RGB Values

Named Color	Percentage	RGB Value	Hexadecimal
Black	(0%, 0%, 0%)	(0, 0, 0)	#000000
Green	(0%, 50%, 0%)	(0, 128, 0)	#008000
Silver	(75%, 75%, 75%)	(192, 192, 192)	#C0C0C0
Lime	(0%, 100%, 0%)	(0, 100, 0)	#00FF00
Gray	(50%, 50%, 50%)	(128, 128, 128)	#808080
Olive	(50%, 50%, 0%)	(128, 128, 0)	#808000
White	(100%, 100%, 100%)	(255, 255, 0)	#FFFFFF
Yellow	(100%, 100%, 0%)	(255, 255, 0)	#FFFF00
Maroon	(50%, 0%, 0%)	(128, 0, 0)	#800000
Navy	(0%, 0%, 50%)	(0, 0, 128)	#000080
Red	(100%, 0%, 0%)	(255, 0, 0)	#FF0000
Blue	(0%, 0%, 100%)	(0, 0, 255)	#0000FF
Purple	(50%, 0%, 50%)	(128, 0, 128)	#800080
Teal	(0%, 50%, 50%)	(0, 128, 128)	#008080
Fuchsia	(100%, 0%, 100%)	(255, 0, 255)	#FF00FF

Cheat Sheet $2.95 value. Item 0871-7.
For more information about Hungry Minds, call 1-800-762-2974.

Hungry Minds™

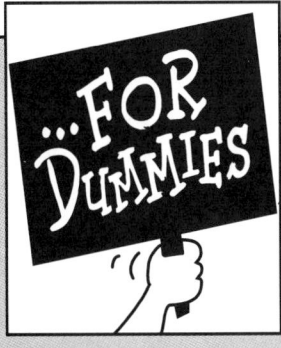

Cascading Style Sheets FOR DUMMIES®

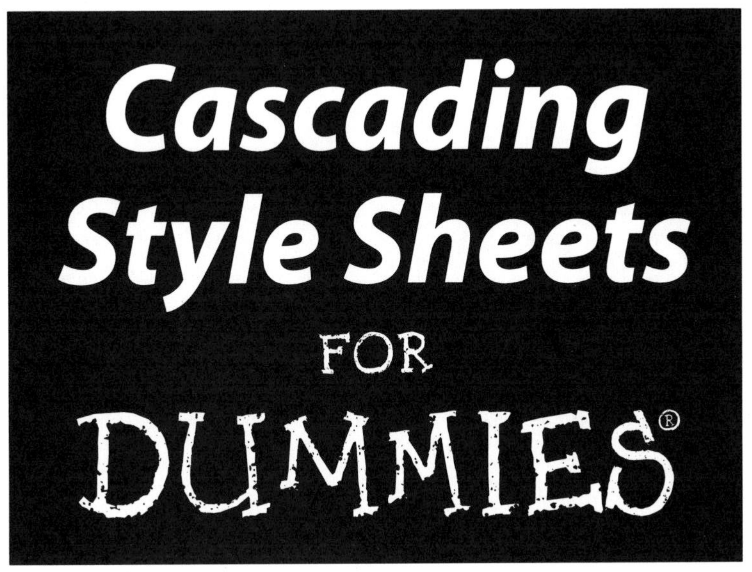

Cascading Style Sheets For Dummies

by Damon Dean

Best-Selling Books • Digital Downloads • e-Books • Answer Networks • e-Newsletters • Branded Web Sites • e-Learning

New York, NY ◆ Cleveland, OH ◆ Indianapolis, IN

Cascading Style Sheets For Dummies®

Published by
Hungry Minds, Inc.
909 Third Avenue
New York, NY 10022
www.hungryminds.com
www.dummies.com

Library of Congress Control Number: 2001089344

ISBN: 0-7645-0871-7

Printed in the United States of America

10 9 8 7 6 5 4 3 2 1

1B/RU/QY/QR/IN

Distributed in the United States by Hungry Minds, Inc.

Distributed by CDG Books Canada Inc. for Canada; by Transworld Publishers Limited in the United Kingdom; by IDG Norge Books for Norway; by IDG Sweden Books for Sweden; by IDG Books Australia Publishing Corporation Pty. Ltd. for Australia and New Zealand; by TransQuest Publishers Pte Ltd. for Singapore, Malaysia, Thailand, Indonesia, and Hong Kong; by Gotop Information Inc. for Taiwan; by ICG Muse, Inc. for Japan; by Intersoft for South Africa; by Eyrolles for France; by International Thomson Publishing for Germany, Austria and Switzerland; by Distribuidora Cuspide for Argentina; by LR International for Brazil; by Galileo Libros for Chile; by Ediciones ZETA S.C.R. Ltda. for Peru; by WS Computer Publishing Corporation, Inc., for the Philippines; by Contemporanea de Ediciones for Venezuela; by Express Computer Distributors for the Caribbean and West Indies; by Micronesia Media Distributor, Inc. for Micronesia; by Chips Computadoras S.A. de C.V. for Mexico; by Editorial Norma de Panama S.A. for Panama; by American Bookshops for Finland.

For general information on Hungry Minds' products and services, please contact our Customer Care Department within the U.S. at 800-762-2974, outside the U.S. at 317-572-3993, or fax 317-572-4002.

For sales inquiries and reseller information, including discounts, premium and bulk quantity sales, and foreign-language translations, please contact our Customer Care Department at 800-434-3422, fax 317-572-4002, or write to Hungry Minds, Inc., Attn: Customer Care Department, 10475 Crosspoint Boulevard, Indianapolis, IN 46256.

For information on licensing foreign or domestic rights, please contact our Sub-Rights Customer Care Department at 212-884-5000.

For information on using Hungry Minds' products and services in the classroom or for ordering examination copies, please contact our Educational Sales Department at 800-434-2086 or fax 317-572-4005.

For press review copies, author interviews, or other publicity information, please contact our Public Relations Department at 317-572-3168 or fax 317-572-4168.

For authorization to photocopy items for corporate, personal, or educational use, please contact Copyright Clearance Center, 222 Rosewood Drive, Danvers, MA 01923, or fax 978-750-4470.

About the Author

Damon Dean is the author of *Web Channel Development For Dummies*, *FrontPage 2000 For Dummies Quick Reference*, and *ACT! 2000 For Dummies Quick Reference*, all published by Hungry Minds, Inc. He's also the author of *A Pocket Tour of Multimedia on The Internet* (published by Sybex), and a ton of magazine articles.

During the day, when he's awake, Damon is the Director of Solutions for 415 Inc., a Web development firm in San Francisco. Really, his title is a just a fancy term for the guy who solves problems and figures out what to build. In his free time, Damon makes films, snowboards, hikes, enjoys a stiff martini, and is looking for the next big thing to occupy his time.

Dedication

For Chris, my partner in crime, as well as life, I promise to come to bed at a reasonable hour now that the book is complete . . . and of course, I love you.

Author's Acknowledgments

No man is an island, unless . . . well, never mind. The point is that nobody makes a book all by himself. Well, he could, but if nobody read it, would it really exist?

Okay, enough babbling! There are quite a few people that I want to stop and thank for helping me get this book out to you, the reader. In particular, I'd like to thank one of my best friends — Ryan Clifford — who took time off from his busy schedule of relaxing after getting the all-to-common 2001 layoff call to help craft a couple of the chapters in this book. I'd also like to thank Bethel Simone Kusz who was instrumental in pulling out a chapter on tables (her headlines are quite clever) near the very end of the process. I give a big thank you to my good friend and co-worker Scott Zucca for providing some good technical consulting on the XML chapter. Lastly, thanks to everyone at 415 for being so supportive in this endeavor.

At Hungry Minds, I want to thank Shirley Jones, my editor, for consistently staying on top of the project throughout the process, and providing the attention that any writer needs. Teresa Artman did a fantastic job of copy editing, and seemingly always knew right where to throw in a smiley face after tearing apart my writing! Thanks also to tech editor Rob Shimonski. It's always nice to have someone else looking at your code! Of course, there's also a big crew of people at Hungry Minds who worked to put together the book, and while I haven't seen a copy of it at the time of this writing, I'm sure it's going to look grand, so thank you.

Finally, I want to give a big shout out to Steve Hayes, who made this whole experience happen in the first place. It was good to hear your voice again.

To all my friends — I swear, I'll be in touch again soon!

Publisher's Acknowledgments

We're proud of this book; please send us your comments through our Hungry Minds Online Registration Form located at www.dummies.com.

Some of the people who helped bring this book to market include the following:

Acquisitions, Editorial, and Media Development

Project Editor: Shirley A. Jones

Senior Acquisitions Editor: Steve Hayes

Copy Editor: Teresa Artman

Technical Editor: Robert J. Shimonski

Editorial Manager: Leah Cameron

Senior Permissions Editor: Carmen Krikorian

Media Development Specialist: Megan Decreane

Media Development Coordinator: Marisa Pearman

Media Development Manager: Laura VanWinkle

Media Development Supervisor: Richard Graves

Editorial Assistant: Jean Rogers

Production

Project Coordinator: Nancee Reeves

Layout and Graphics: Jackie Nicholas, Jeremey Unger

Proofreaders: John Greenough, TECHBOOKS Production Services

Indexer: TECHBOOKS Production Services

Special Help:
Rebecca Senninger

General and Administrative

Hungry Minds, Inc.: John Kilcullen, CEO; Bill Barry, President and COO; John Ball, Executive VP, Operations & Administration; John Harris, Executive VP and CFO

Hungry Minds Technology Publishing Group: Richard Swadley, Senior Vice President and Publisher; Mary Bednarek, Vice President and Publisher, Networking and Certification; Walter R. Bruce III, Vice President and Publisher, General User and Design Professional; Joseph Wikert, Vice President and Publisher, Programming; Mary C. Corder, Editorial Director, Branded Technology Editorial; Andy Cummings, Publishing Director, General User and Design Professional; Barry Pruett, Publishing Director, Visual

Hungry Minds Manufacturing: Ivor Parker, Vice President, Manufacturing

Hungry Minds Marketing: John Helmus, Assistant Vice President, Director of Marketing

Hungry Minds Production for Branded Press: Debbie Stailey, Production Director

Hungry Minds Sales: Michael Violano, Vice President, International Sales and Sub Rights

◆

The publisher would like to give special thanks to Patrick J. McGovern, without whom this book would not have been possible.

◆

Contents at a Glance

Cartoons at a Glance

By Rich Tennant

"Give him air! Give him air! He'll be okay. He's just been exposed to some raw HTML code. It must have accidently flashed across his screen from the server."

page 279

"Maybe it would help our Web site if we showed our products in action."

page 265

page 5

"Oh, we're doing just great. Philip and I are selling decorative jelly jars on the Web. I run the Web site and Philip sort of controls the inventory."

page 203

"So far our Web presence has been pretty good. We've gotten some orders, a few inquiries and nine guys who want to date our logo."

page 41

"You know, it dawned on me last night why we aren't getting any hits on our Web site."

page 171

Cartoon Information:
Fax: 978-546-7747
E-Mail: richtennant@the5thwave.com
World Wide Web: www.the5thwave.com

Table of Contents

Introduction

Shortly after the folks at Hungry Minds asked me to write this book, I found myself at a cocktail party — a reasonably frequent occurrence — where a friend asked me what I was up to. I told him that I was about to write a new *For Dummies* book, and naturally, he asked the title's name. My reply, "*Cascading Style Sheets For Dummies,*" was immediately met with one of those blank stares that says, "I'm sorry . . . you've suddenly started speaking a language that means nothing to me, and I simply have no response to you. I've got to get out of this conversation as soon as I possibly can. Good night."

Try not to glaze over like my party friend. Cascading Style Sheets (CSS) are way cool critters — they are for Web designers, after all. Hang with me though this book as I walk you through the basics, throw in a little history on the way, and then kick it up a notch or two to discover the ultra-cool things you can create with CSS. Bear in mind, too, that even though some of the best CSS features aren't fully browser supported yet, you'll have a leg up when they are.

About This Book

You could choose to read this book from end to end, and if I were being paid by the page, I'd certainly encourage that. But this book, like all *For Dummies* books, is modular — okay, that's just a fancy word meaning that you can hop in and out wherever you want. You don't have to read Chapter 2 to understand Chapter 5. Gear your reading toward your individual needs and desires. Check out the table of contents and plan your journey accordingly. If you start at the beginning, you can be assured of getting some very . . . yawn . . . interesting history about the development of Cascading Style Sheets. Find the meaty stuff in the middle of the book, where I drill you on the whole idea of putting the *style* back into Cascading Style Sheets.

Toward the back of the book you'll find some resource materials, such as where to find editors, great Web sites for ideas, and reference appendixes. And don't forget to explore what's on the attached CD-ROM; I put a lot of toys on there for you.

Peruse, flip, scan, and otherwise jump around this book. I stay focused so you don't have to.

How This Book Is Organized

Organized? Who said anything about being organized? Is that in my contract? Oh, it is . . . darn.

For those readers who require a little reinforcement, you can read *Cascading Style Sheets For Dummies* anyway you'd like. Back to front, top to bottom, even upside down if that works for you. Should you decide, though, to read it from front to back, here's how it'll look:

Part I: Welcome to the Web Design Jungle

Grab a stout grapevine and come in swingin'. Read through this part to discover how to become a better Web designer and to creatively and efficiently use the design tools at your disposal. In this part, I provide you a look at the current Web development landscape, and tell you how Cascading Style Sheets fit in. If you're new to Web design, I recommend starting here because I include some shocking revelations about who uses style sheets and why. It's true. I've seen an advance version of the script, and no late comers will be seated after the beginning of the presentation.

Part II: Parlez-Vous CSS?

Like French, CSS acts like a language. Unlike French, CSS is not very guttural, nasal, or otherwise disposed to heavy cream sauces and beef. In Part II, I break down the Cascading Style Sheet syntax, properties, and elements, and also show you how these items are used to establish different graphical properties on a Web page. In this part, I also demystify that whole *cascading* thing once and for all.

Part III: Putting CSS to Work for You

With any language, you have to practice it to really understand it. The same approach applies to CSS. In Part III, you don your sweats and tee shirts and take CSS out for a bit of a workout. Here you find out what it really feels like to build style sheets, see how you can use more than one style sheet in a site, and explore the unthinkable: converting your existing Web content with Cascading Style Sheets.

Part IV: Getting Your Advanced CSS Degree

Time to get super stylish — or dare I say, *sassy*. CSS is cool enough when being used for text and layout, but it really begins to hum when you add JavaScript and my good ol' friend, Document Object Model (DOM). Read along here to discover how to generate content, build tables, and work in a little eXtensible Markup Language (XML). And listen up: In this part, I also introduce you to Aural Style Sheets. You heard me: aural!

Part V: The Part of Tens

This just wouldn't be a *For Dummies* book with The Part of Tens. No really, it wouldn't. You can't be a writer for Hungry Minds unless you include this section. Whipcrackers. So, for your feasting pleasure, I include lists of great Web sites that use CSS (I'm not above spying) and resources for discovering more about CSS.

Part VI: Appendixes

Not so fast! I got more good stuff! In this kind-of-dry-but-useful part, check out the resources I give you. Part VI includes a CSS syntax chart, a look at how a number of the more popular HTML editors incorporate CSS, and a preview of the contents on the CD-ROM that comes with this book. Hey — I even put most of the code you see in this book on the CD for your convenience.

Icons Used in This Book

Along the way, I may want to point out something that is particularly *cascading*, especially *stylish*, or even something downright *sheet*-y. (Think that last one will make it past my relentless copy editor? — she's a pit bull with a keyboard.) When I want to draw your attention to something, I use one of the following icons.

Even if you ignore everything else I say in this book, when you see one of these little puppies, sit up and take notice. Here's something that's going to make your life a whole lot easier.

Would I let you wear plaid pants with a velour striped shirt and Converse high tops? Well, maybe, if you were trying to start yet another '70s cover band . . . but in general, certainly not! That's what the Warning icon is for: to help you avoid pitfalls and trouble spots along the way.

If you're more of the technically proficient type, take note when you see this icon. It simply means that I'm about to detour from the super stylish, and let my Geek Guard down just long enough to let you know how or why something works the way it does. Of course, if it's too painful, you can just close your eyes until it's over.

Every now and then, everyone needs to be reminded of something. Right now, I can't remember what it is I wanted to say here, so you see, if I had one of these icons here with a reminder, it wouldn't have been a problem.

Seeing this little fellah lets you know that whatever product, script, style sheet, or Web page I'm discussing is also included on the accompanying CD.

About the CD

All *For Dummies* books are all about info, fun, and value, and that means tossing in a CD-ROM for good measure. On the accompanying CD, you'll find a host of utilities, including HTML editors, CSS editors, CSS validators (tools that check to make sure your CSS syntax is correctly defined), plus all the materials that are used for explanation purposes in the book.

Anything Else before You Dive In?

Take a big deep breath, sit back, and relax. Remember, Cascading Style Sheets are supposed to be fun, and easy to learn . . . not to mention, *stylish*. If at any point during the book, you find that your fun, ease, or style appears to be waning, move on to a different topic. Or take a break. No need to beat yourself senseless and take the fun out of something this cool. Go surf the Web a little. You'll probably come across some styles that appeal to you, and then you can return here to discover how to make the magic behind the mouse.

Part I

Welcome to the Web Design Jungle

In this part . . .

The Web is growing up, and at any second will hit puberty and introduce us to those notorious teenage raging hormones. Ask yourself whether you're really truly ready for the power of the Internet — data around every corner, multiple platforms of development, handheld devices, accessibility requirements, rich media — and the list goes on. Oh, it gives me a headache just thinking about it.

The good news is that Cascading Style Sheets (CSS) are built for design. Sometimes it may not seem that way; CSS may seem like more of a programming language, but style sheets truly give Web designers unprecedented flexibility. This part first takes a look at the history of style sheets and answers the burning question, "How did we end up here, anyway?" by taking a look at the past, present, and future of the CSS specification.

I also give you a brief overview of CSS in action. Sort of an appetizer, if you will. Nothing too heavy, just a taste of what CSS can do for you — sometimes, on certain browsers, in the summer, on every third Tuesday of the month . . . .

Finally, I bear down, glaze over all the rules, and show you how to quickly create a Style Sheet (give or take the twenty minutes it takes you to read the chapter). After you breeze through this part, you'll be ready to talk cogently about style sheets at cocktail parties, board meetings, and those ever-so-tricky client rendezvous!

Chapter 1

Cascading Style Sheets 101

In This Chapter

- Discovering Cascading Style Sheets and their origins
- Watching Cascading Style Sheets Level 1 grow into Level 2
- Understanding how Cascading Style Sheets work
- Deciphering browser support for Cascading Style Sheets
- Looking ahead to Cascading Style Sheets Level 3

Buried deep in the bowels of major universities and military installations, scientists and programmers labored to create a network that would allow the simple and easy communication of data through a structured language across any number of computers. Decades later, their prized creation — the Internet — has changed the way we communicate, learn, and interact with one another.

If you look underneath the hood of the Internet, though — even just a little — you can pretty well surmise that if you been right alongside the founders of the Internet at the beginning, you never would have heard the following question:

"Hey, what if someone wants to make this stuff look pretty?"

Although HyperText Markup Language (HTML) is a great language for structuring documents and creating linkages between documents, it has no mechanism for making things looking prettier or pleasing to the eye. Since the release of the National Center for Supercomputing Applications (NCSA) Mosaic browser, it's been apparent that HTML lacks a little something — okay, a big something — when it comes to design. Heck, the very first version of HTML didn't even include bold or italic tags. Instead, its design tools were limited to changing header sizes and sporadic use of the `<STRONG>` tag, which worked basically like a bold tag.

In addition to the font limitations, the early versions of HTML didn't support tables. This was a serious limitation because tables today provide the basic foundation for creating Web page structure and layout. With no mechanism for creating any kind of layout except to have text run down the page, most of the original early Web pages left a lot to be desired graphically.

HTML: The little language that couldn't

Original HTML was nothing if not efficient — and I really do mean *nothing*, as you can see in the figure in this sidebar.

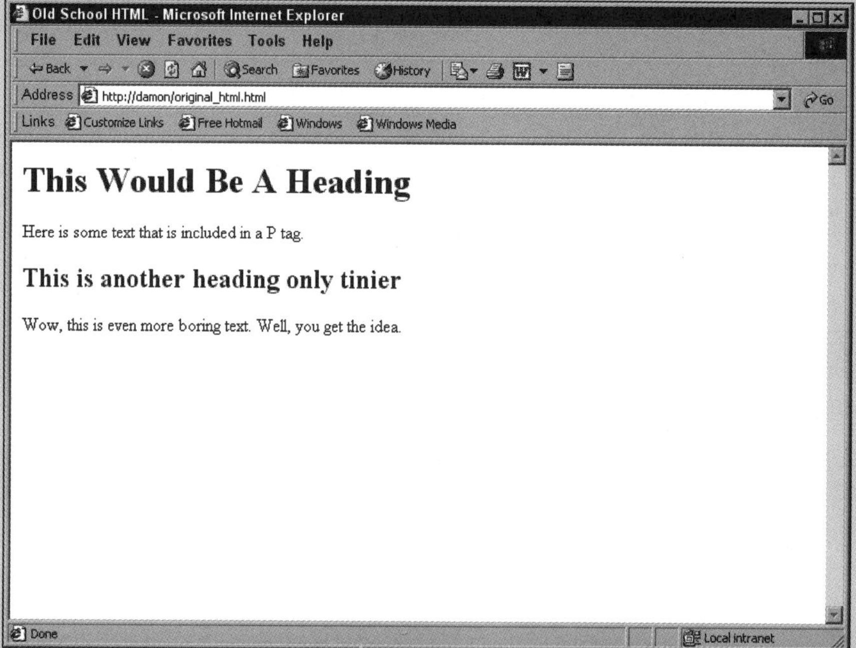

When you consider that there were no defined standards, no governing bodies, and no browsers at the time when HTML was first developed, you can understand its shortcomings. After all, this was pioneering stuff! Many of the first attempts to develop browsers had a novel concept. With HTML, you at least had a language that did a nice job of structuring data. Rather than mess that up, many software developers attempted to create a clean separation between the data and how it displayed through a browser.

Then Mosaic (the first widely distributed graphical browser for the World Wide Web) came along. Unlike other browsers, Mosaic relied on HTML alone for both data and display. Mosaic delivered a big time score on the data side, and well, if its display didn't look good . . . too bad! Add in the booming expansion of the Web, and a generation of really ugly Web sites was born.

Subsequent versions of HTML have all included upgrades that enable a greater degree of design flexibility . . . although calling it *sexy* (techie-talk for *cool beans*) would be a bit of a stretch. HTML has evolved to include basic text formatting, table structures, some basic positioning properties, and embedded graphics. These features have been met with wide acceptance, making Web design possible — but still frustrating.

Such design and layout problems were solved when the World Wide Web Consortium (W3C) introduced Cascading Style Sheets (CSS). With these standardized style sheets for HTML elements, Web designers could now use CSS syntax to attach styles to specific HTML elements, such as margins, font, color, and positioning. In this chapter, you'll discover the basics of CSS and how to use them to your advantage.

The Dawn of CSS

Using HTML alone to design content rich, graphically interesting Web sites is a very messy process — kinda like eating soup with a fork. Including a variety of font styles requires that a designer use large numbers of font tags, and creating interesting layouts on a page usually involves creating tables within tables within tables within more tables. Add to that an unusually large number of HTML features — including embedding background images in tables that work differently in different browsers — and you've really taken quite a few steps toward giving yourself one big design headache.

Consider the mid-'90s as the Dark Ages of Web Development. HTML was still in its infancy, Mosaic was giving way to Netscape Navigator as the browser of choice, and Microsoft was just beginning to realize how far behind it was. Everyone was screaming for change. "Make HTML more designer friendly!" they cried. And the Web community listened . . . eventually. The answer was Cascading Style Sheets, a simple mechanism for adding font, color, positioning, and other basic design features to HTML elements.

Late in 1996, the W3C made Cascading Style Sheets a recommendation and defined specifications for Web developers. These style sheets, similar to templates used in desktop publishing applications, contain simple styling language for attaching styles to HTML elements. These style sheets are *cascading* because certain style definitions override others in a cascading, or waterfall, sequence.

Although Microsoft claimed that it would support CSS in Internet Explorer (IE) 3.0, in reality, the browser supported little more than the very basic CSS properties. True support on the part of both Microsoft and Netscape for CSS Level 1 came in the 4.0 versions of their browsers. And with that, a new age in Web development and design was, ahem, born.

For more fascinating history of CSS, check out the W3C site at `www.w3.org`.

Over the course of five or so years, Cascading Style Sheets have gone though two iterations. The Cascading Style Sheets Level 1 Specification (CSS1), which the W3C recommended in late 1996, covered all the hard stuff. CSS1 laid the foundation for the way in which style sheets would operate, providing the framework within HTML. CSS1 also introduced the concepts of inheritance and cascading of attributes, as well as a host of formatting properties. The major features introduced in CSS1 are in Table 1-1.

Table 1-1 Major Features of CSS1

Feature	*Description*
Containment	Describes how browsers, through HTML, must enable CSS to be called in the HTML page as well as through external linking
Cascading and Inheritance	Describes parent and child relationships of styles as they relate to document elements, and how the document elements styles will be applied
Pseudo-classes and Pseudo-elements	Enables the designer to prescribe a variety of different effects on hypertext anchors
Text and Font Properties	Enables users to change both the specific fonts used in an HTML document, as well as a host of text properties associated with those fonts
The Box Model	Enables the user to manipulate such things as margins, borders, padding, and the positioning of various elements on the page

CSS Level 2 (CSS2) became a W3C recommendation in 1998, offering more bang and better special effects than CSS1. CSS2 includes a host of additions to the base set of properties introduced in CSS1, such as pseudo-elements and generated content. CSS2 also included some sweeping changes to the notion of decoupling content from the display of that content. In the initial CSS1 specification, the primary User Agent — sounds like a spy's name, doesn't it? — was the Web browser.

A *User Agent* is just a tool that can either process or generate CSS. The most common User Agent is a Web browser. Similarly, though, a tool that creates styles to use in a Web page — an HTML editor such as Dreamweaver and FrontPage, for example — is also a considered a User Agent.

In CSS2, however, the whole notion of User Agents changed. Peering into their crystal balls and seeing an Internet that was more accessible (and perhaps looking beyond the browser itself), the builders of CSS2 extended its reach to a whole host of different User Agents that included aural browsers (browsers that talk), TV-based browsers, handheld devices such as Palm Pilots, and even TTY (teletypewriter).

Because of this futuristic and ambitious outlook — one that may eventually be realized — Microsoft and Netscape (the two main browser powerhouses) have vastly improved their CSS1 implementations. Both are well on the way to completing their CSS2 work. The integration with other User Agents remains one of the largest pieces of unfinished work in the area of Cascading Style Sheets.

Style Sheets Rule — How They Work

It should come as no surprise that CSS — like a lot of things on the Web — is a teeny weenie bit of an oxymoron. Surprise! Cascading Style Sheets doesn't really have much to do with sheets at all. In fact, CSS is a language, a very simple scripting language with a simple structure and whole lot of commands. Okay, now before you toss the book aside and head off on that rafting trip, let me explain just how this all fits together.

Think of Cascading Style Sheets as a collection of *design properties* and the *values* for those properties. An example of a design property is color, and the value of that property could be red. Or, you may assign font-family as a property and the name of the font as the value for that property. Similarly, you could have font-size and then the size the font.

The combination of a property and its value is a *declaration.* After you compile a collection of these declarations, you've got yourself a rule. One or more rules can make up and entire style sheet. In the following code snippet, the property is `font-family`, and the value of this property is `Arial, Helvetica, sans-serif;`. A simple but typical style might look a little something like this:

```
.arialblack11 {
   font-family: Arial, Helvetica, sans-serif;
   font-size: 11px;
   font-style: normal;
   color: #000000;

}
```

Don't be overwhelmed by all the things going on in this code snippet. Trust me, I'll be covering them all throughout this book — but for now, you should just try to get the feel for the way these things look and the characters that are involved in creating a rule. Here's a cool feature that's worth mentioning right off the bat: You can name your styles pretty much whatever you like (with some restrictions that I cover in Chapter 4).

Finding Your Own Style

If you've looked at an HTML file lately (I know I can't get through a Friday without browsing scads of HTML files myself), then you've very likely seen a style sheet in some form. CSS, although a robust language in its own right, is wholly reliant on two things to make it work: HTML and the Web browser. Created as part of the ratification of HTML 3.2 in 1996 by the W3C, the STYLE element is essentially a container within HTML. All this elements does is throw whatever is in the container directly to the Web browser with the understanding, "Hey, pal, you deal with this as you see fit."

You'll find three different representations of the STYLE element within HTML, which correspond to the three different places you can find a style sheet:

- Inside the HEAD element
- Inside the BODY element
- From an external file

Inside the HEAD element

In the HEAD element of an HTML document, the STYLE element is represented as a tag, just like any other good old-fashioned HTML tag. With the STYLE element, you specify the kind of style you're going to be passing to the browser, and then within the open and close tags, you can specify any number of styles. The code below shows what a typical style for 11-point Arial black type would look like inside the <HEAD> of an HTML document.

```
<STYLE type="text/css">
.arialblack11 {
   font-family: Arial, Helvetica, sans-serif;
   font-size: 11px;
   font-style: normal;
   color : #000000;

}
</STYLE>
```

Inside the BODY element

Inline styles are also permitted, though they use slightly different syntax than the STYLE element. When the STYLE element is used in the HEAD element, you can specify as many styles as you like. When you call a style from within a given <P> (paragraph) tag, for example, you're limited to only one style.

Building on the 11-point Arial black type example from earlier in this chapter, you can specify a style for an individual <P> tag with the following snippet of code.

```
<P style="font-family : Arial, Helvetica, sans-serif;
        font-size : 11px; font-style : normal;
        color : #000000">
```

See what text styled with the <P> tag looks like in Figure 1-1.

From an external file

In addition to being able to call a style from within an HTML file, you can also use HTML to point to an external text file that includes various styles. Again, this little piece of magic happens within the HEAD element, but you use the LINK element rather than the STYLE element. When you use the LINK element, you still have to specify that the external document is a style sheet, and you also need to include the location of that style sheet.

When the HTML page is processed, the styles are processed along with the HTML. Using the following example, the code would look like this:

```
<LINK rel="stylesheet" href="mystyles.css" type="text/css">
```

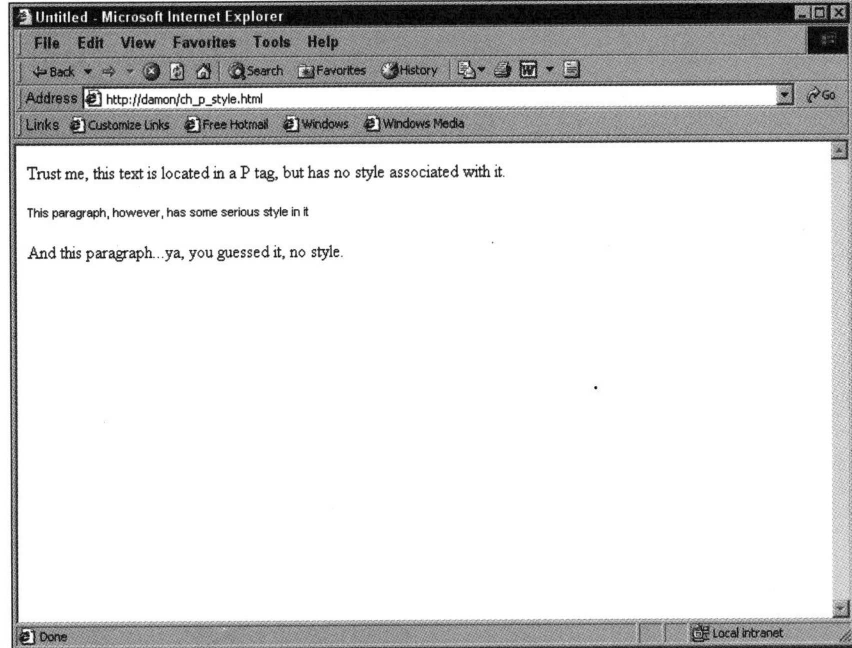

Figure 1-1: You can call a style from within a paragraph tag.

Even though you're specifying an external document to define a style in the `LINK` element, that doesn't mean that your work is done. In that external text file, you have to define your styles; and yes, they do need to include the `STYLE` element as I describe in the earlier section "Inside the HEAD element."

Can I Get a Little Support Here?

Perhaps the most frustrating thing about Cascading Style Sheets is that they need the support of a Web browser for them to work. You can write script until the cows come home, but if the browser can't process the style sheet . . . well, then, you'll be writing script for a very, very long time. If a single common implementation standard existed for Web browsers, this compatibility issue really wouldn't be much of a problem. Unfortunately, that's certainly not the case.

Today, Microsoft (Internet Explorer, or IE) and Netscape (Navigator) own nearly all the browser market, but not every person owns the latest versions of either. Moreover, the Microsoft and Netscape implementations are not equivalent. In the best-case scenario, you always have to take at least these two browsers into account. However, because of the differing numbers of browser versions in use today — as well as the various hardware platforms — the average Web developer may need to consider seven or eight different browsers in his or her Web site development.

For this reason, I'm limiting the browser discussion in this book to versions Internet Explorer 4.0 and above and Netscape Navigator 4.0 and above. Internet Explorer 3.1 for the PC was the only browser below a 4.0 version that supported CSS (and that was CSS1, the predecessor to today's standard CSS2); that browser represents less than 1 percent of all browsers on the market, according to Web-trending service StatMarket.

You'll need to know which browsers support which CSS functions and on which hardware platforms. To help you with this, I've included a chart in Appendix A of this book of all CSS functions and which browsers support them on the various hardware platforms. From this chart, you can reference element compatibility for the following browsers for Windows 95/98/NT:

- IE 3.01, 4.0, 5.0, and 5.5
- Navigator 4.6 and 6.0
- Opera 3.6, 4.02, and 5.0

And for Macintosh platforms, use this chart for these browser versions:

- IE 3.02, 4.5, and 5.0
- Navigator 4.5 and 6.0

Singing the sweet sounds of Opera

Being the little guy in a two-man town is darn tough — just ask the folks at Opera Software. Pretty much under the consumer radar since its inception, Opera has managed to produce one of the best — if not *the* best — browser on the market. So what's the hitch? Simple: Nobody knows about it.

Opera is faster than both IE and Netscape, is a smaller download, includes a more complete integration of CSS Level 2, and is available for nearly every platform. The only glaring glitch I find is a rather annoying ad banner feature that is persistent within the browser itself in Version 5.0, which launched late December 2000. This is really the only flaw in the program, save some crash bugs caused by the integration of the ICQ messenger. If you want the version without the ad banner, you can get it — but it'll cost you about $40.

So why hasn't Opera really taken off? It still may, given time and its ability to compete against Microsoft and Netscape (Netscape is now owned by AOL/Time Warner), which is a very tall order. Opera's big claim to fame today is speed, and the fact that it uses open standards in the development of its browser. The downside to that, however, is that most end-users don't care too awful much about open standards; and, with the rapidly growing DSL and cable modem market, bandwidth is becoming less and less of an issue.

For more element/browser details, check out Eric Meyer's Master Compatibility Chart on the WebReview.com site (`www.webreview.com/style/css1/charts/mastergrid/shtml`). Here you can read how whether certain combinations of elements, browser, and platforms are viable, won't work, work partially, are buggy, are quirky, or unknown.

The Processing Line Starts Here

Conceptually, browsers process style sheets in the same fashion, according to the CSS Level 2 specifications established by the W3C. Notice that I intentionally write *conceptually*. In reality, the details, which are guaranteed to put you to sleep no matter how much coffee you drink late at night, basically delineate the following:

- **The browser must support at least one of the CSS media types.** You'll find nine media types in the CSS2 specification, including
  - Text for computer monitors
  - Aural styles for visually impaired readers
  - Handheld for handheld devices

Notice the big problem brewing here: Even today, browsers don't have to conform to all the media types, but just one! Refer to the browser support guide in Appendix A.

- **For each document (usually an HTML document), the browser must attempt to retrieve all associated style sheets for that document.** In other words, a browser can't chose to ignore a pointer to an external style sheet.
- **The browser must parse a style sheet according to the CSS Level 2 specification for those media types that the browser supports.** Parsing a style sheet means that it's read and then displayed on the screen. Although this concept seems reasonable enough, a browser can interpret the specification by a number of different ways — and if the browser does not support a certain media type, it can just ignore elements in the style sheet that apply to those unsupported media types.
- **The browser must assign the correct style to the correct object in the source document according to the rules of cascading and inheritance laid out in the CSS specification.** Here's another way to think about this rule: If you tell the browser to make that paragraph have pink text with a picture of an orangutan in a tutu in the background, then it better work that way.
- **If two possible style sheets are used through HTML 4.0's alternate tag, for example, then the browser must let the user select from the available style sheets and then apply the selected one.** This rule really applies mostly in cases when you're designing for multiple environments, such as for TTY (teletype) readers or possibly for TV-based browsers such as WebTV. Check out the path for this selection process in Figure 1-2.

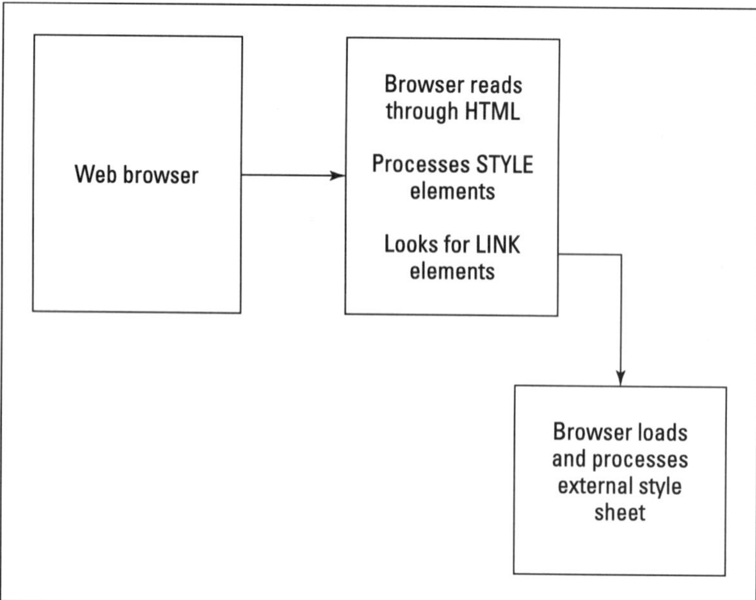

Figure 1-2: The basic processing model for style sheets within a Web browser.

You Will Conform . . . Eventually

Here's my latest geek fantasy. I'm a nervous but eager contestant on the TV quiz show *Who Wants to Be a Millionaire?*, Regis has laughed at all my jokes, I'm out of lifelines, I really need the cash to pay off those pesky student loans, and I'm up to the million-dollar question, which reads:

Which of the following Web browsers implements CSS Level 2 completely? Is it:

A Internet Explorer Version 5.5

B Netscape Navigator Version 6.0

C AOL Version 6.0

D None of the above

Come on now, no lifelines! Work with me here! If you chose Answer D (None of the above) as I did, you are correct — but I'll keep the cash and the fame. Not one of the major Web browsers has fully implemented CSS Level 2, let alone CSS Level 1. You would assume that because both Microsoft and Netscape are members of the W3C that they helped make the specification, right? You are correct again, and although both claim to be heading toward a full implementation, neither company has committed to a completion date.

Just how much of the CSS specifications have the browsers implemented to date? Close your eyes if you're easily spooked — the answer may scare you.

The truth is that, pretty much without exception, the two major browsers have gotten better with each successive release. Internet Explorer 4.*x* (*x* being different versions of IE 4) was the first major release of a browser with a broad array of CSS Level 1 features.

Netscape is still struggling with its CSS implementation even today. Complicating its initial buggy CSS introduction is the large number of successive releases to the Version 4.0 browsers on both the Mac and the PC, resulting in upwards of 15 distinct iterations, all of which have differing degrees of support for CSS.

Looking Ahead: CSS3

Like so many other things on the Web, CSS is still evolving. Good thing, eh? — that's what keeps us Web developers in business. Web browsers are getting upgrades about once a year. The wireless generation is just beginning to take off, XML is a standard, and Cascading Style Sheets is heading into its third iteration, CSS3.

You don't have to worry that CSS3 will be a wholesale change to how style sheets work. True, it's been nearly three years since the CSS2 specification was made a recommendation, and to put it mildly, a lot has changed. For the first time, style sheets will take a serious role in styling an XML document, for example. Similarly, the role of CSS in styling content on mobile devices will be made more explicit. You can also expect some enhancement with CSS3 that extends the internationalization of style sheets to be used more easily with the character-based languages such as Japanese or Chinese.

Ideally, all these enhancements will make the job of a Web designer that much easier. But until CSS3 is made a recommendation, you need to live in the present and use the tools you have now. Read through the chapters of this book to discover how.

Chapter 2

Shopping for Sheets with Style

In This Chapter

- Choosing fonts for fun and effect
- Positioning text for layout and emphasis
- Designing for better visibility
- Inserting links for user friendliness
- Using box models to define the size of an element

An essential part of planning a new Web page, or redesigning an existing page, is to decide how you want it to look. Maybe you already have a rough idea for the look and feel you're going for, or you know that certain text or graphics need to be presented in a prominent way. Maybe you just want to snazz things up a bit, or make your page more formal.

What better way to see ideas in action than to browse active Web sites for ideas — as well as to see what really works and what really doesn't. By checking out other Web sites, you'll get an idea how CSS can jazz yours up. Two, your comparative shopping will drive home the realization that HTML can only give you so much, and CSS can give you so much more.

In this chapter, I show you some of the magic behind some of the meat-and-potatoes elements (like text) and some pretty nifty things others have done using CSS, and how to achieve what you see.

Throughout this chapter, I refer to some sites out there on the Internet. For copyright purposes, however, I can't show screen shots of many of the sites. I recommend that you settle in next to your trusty computer and Internet connection while you read through this chapter and follow along to the sites that I mention in the chapter. That way, you can see in practice the visual effects that I describe. Remember to bookmark those pages so they're easy to come back to in the future!

This Is Font-astic!

In Chapter 1, I discuss some of the limitations of HTML, including the lack of control you have over setting font and text properties. CSS provides you with a range of font and text properties that enable you to set font families (Times, Arial, and so forth), font styles (italics, bold, outline), as well as text decoration (small caps, underlining, strikethrough). Together, these properties give you as much control over your font and text styles as you'd have using a word processor such as Microsoft Word.

Consider the online home of ESPN at `espn.go.com`. Whether or not you're a sports fan, the ESPN Web site can give you an idea of how to use CSS to your advantage. Most everything on this site is created using the CSS font properties, including (but not limited to) its menus, headlines, captions, body copy, pull quotes, and statistics. Take a look at the following code snippet from the ESPN home page:

```
<DIV CLASS="TOPCOPY">The writing was on the wall in the
            fourth quarter of Game 6 in the East finals. Allen
            Iverson broke loose for 26 points that quarter,
            and he never slowed down in Game 7, scoring 44
            Sunday to lift the Sixers past the Bucks 108-91.
            It marks the first time the 76ers have been to the
            NBA Finals since 1983. The Sixers face the
            defending champion Lakers, starting Wednesday in
            L.A.</DIV>
```

This code shows the main feature story from the site. The `DIV` element, using the `class` function, is being used to call a style rule called `topcopy`. `topcopy` includes the font size, weight, and style values for that text block. Such a style rule might look as follows:

```
.mywannabeESPNstyle{
font-family: Arial;
font-size: 12px;
}
```

I realize that some of these things may look a little foreign at the moment, and that's okay. In Chapter 3, I show you how to make a style rule and use it in a Web page in just ten minutes. I cover style rule structure in Chapter 4, and using those font and text properties in Chapter 6.

Want to see the HTML code? Using Internet Explorer, choose View⇨Source from your browser's menu. With Netscape, choose View⇨Page Source.

Fonts are usually the first, and one of the most important, considerations when designing your Web pages. When you find a font you like, check out the HTML code at that site to determine which fonts are used and how that designer used CSS to call them.

Also consider how large you want the font to appear, which you also call using CSS.

For added emphasis and fun, you can also decorate your text with nuances such as boldface, italics, colors, small caps . . . the list is darn near endless. And CSS provides you with lots of ways to dress text.

Designing Your Pages Your Way with Positioning

The CSS positioning properties are designed to enable you to take any piece of content and place it wherever you want on the screen. With the different positioning schemes in CSS, you can make your site run faster, and make it easier to maintain. No more messing with ugly HTML table structures, and tables embedded within tables. These design considerations will make your site more attractive, more consistent, and most important, not irritate a visitor so much that he leaves your site!

Take a look at the `415.com` site in Figure 2-1. This site shows some great examples of using absolute positioning. The site uses the CSS positioning scheme to control the size and location of the navigation elements you see across the top of the page.

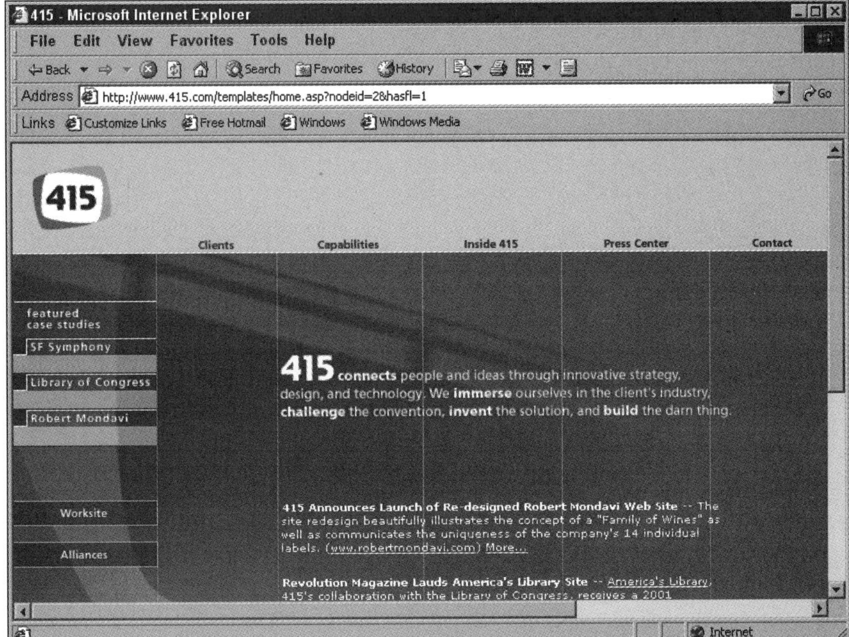

Figure 2-1: The 415.com site is a good example of the CSS positioning properties.

Consider the following style rules, which come directly from the 415.com Web site:

```
.clientsnav   {
position: absolute;
      left: 131px;
      top: 83px;
width:112px;
      z-index: 75;}
   .capabilitiesnav {
position: absolute;
      left: 242px;
      top: 83px;
width:135px;
      z-index: 75}
   .insidenav {
position: absolute;
      left: 376px;
      top: 83px;
width:128px;
      z-index: 75}
   .pressnav {
position: absolute;
      left: 503px;
      top: 83px;
width:139px;
      z-index: 75}
   .contactnav {
position: absolute;
      left: 641px;
      top: 83px;
width:118px;
z-index: 75}
```

Each of the rules defined in the above code snippet — `clientsnav`, `capabilitiesnav`, `insidenav`, `pressnav`, and `contactnav` — sets the physical location on the screen for a navigation rollover. Set this location by using the `position` property, as well as the `left` and `top` properties. In addition to setting the position, these style rules also set the width of the elements, as well as their depth position on the screen (represented by the `z-index` property).

Find more detail about all CSS positioning properties in Chapter 9. Turn to Chapter 7 for more on the `z-index` and `width` properties.

Now You See Me, Now You Don't

One of the coolest things CSS enables you to do is to set whether you want a content element to be visible. With the use of some relatively simply Dynamic

HTML, this will enable you to do things such as create drop-down menus that appear when you roll over them with your cursor and magically disappear when the cursor is no longer over them.

Look at the two examples from the Bay Area Rapid Transit (BART) Web site. (This is a public transportation system for the San Francisco area.) If you place your mouse cursor so that the little hand graphic goes over a menu item, then the menu drops down (as shown in Figure 2-2). When you move the hand away from the menu (Figure 2-3), the drop-down menu disappears. This simple behavior is a perfect example of how you can use CSS to define the characteristics of visibility. Simply put, you instruct CSS: "Drop down this menu when this happens, and the rest of the time keep it hidden."

A typical style rule using the `visibility` property in CSS might look as follows:

```
.menu {
position: absolute;
left: 222px;
width:126px;
top: 0px;
visibility: hidden;
}
```

I cover the `visibility` property in depth in Chapter 7.

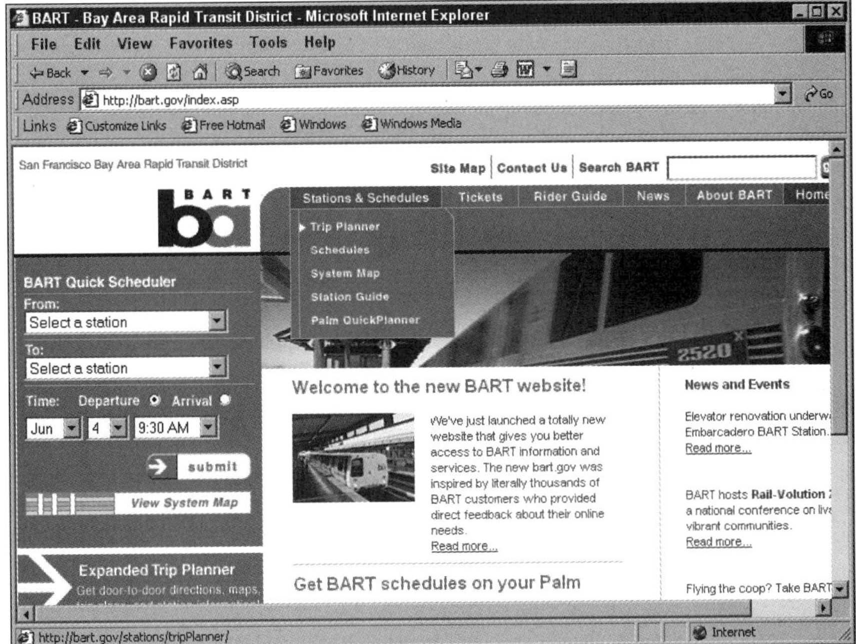

Figure 2-2: Now you see it . . .

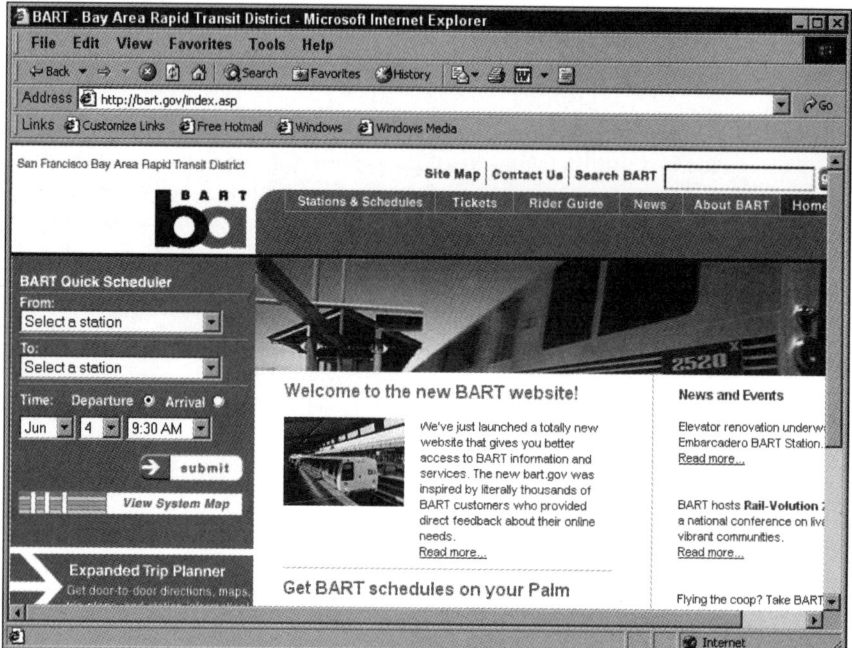

Figure 2-3: . . . and now you don't!

The Missing Link

Are too many hyperlink underlines undermining your site? Do you want to make them all just go away? De-clutter your site by eliminating these eye-sores with CSS.

Hop on over to the MSNBC site at `www.msn.com` for a great example of how CSS can be used to give a new style to your links. Check out the hand that's placed over an active link: Where's the line you usually see with a link? The designers of the MSNBC site used CSS to remove the underlines, while keeping the text an active link.

This is all handled by some very sexy elements in CSS called pseudo-elements. These elements enable you to take control over the `A` element in HTML and to prescribe different properties based on the state of the `A` element (`link`, `active`, `visited`, `hover`). I describe pseudo-elements in more detail in Chapter 4 — but just to whet your appetite, here's what the style rules would look like to get rid of those annoying underlines:

```
A:link {text-decoration: none}
A:visited {text-decoration: none}
A:hover {text-decoration: none}
```

The Box Model Defines the Size of an Element

I have to admit, though, the term *box model* makes me think of fabulously beautiful boxes sashaying down the catwalk and posing in swimsuits on the beach, or maybe some of those saucy kraft numbers (aah, the corrugated ones!) in FedEx commercials and U-Haul ads.

In the world of CSS, the box model is the physical size of a content element on the screen. As I noted in a previous section, positioning tells you where an element goes on the screen. The box model, in contrast, specifies just how large that element should be. To calculate the size of an element, you need to consider:

- The **amount of content** within the element
- The **amount of padding** you apply around the content (using the CSS padding properties)
- The **size of the border** you put around the content (using the CSS border properties)
- The **size of the margins** you put around the content (using the CSS margin properties)

A good site to check out to see the box model (in all its glory) is Virgin, at `www.virgin.com`. Although most of the style rules are linked, click over to something like the House and Home section and look at the source code. You'll see that the site uses a lot of Dynamic HTML, and the styles in the Web page use the CSS border, padding, and margin properties.

For a more in-depth review of all the box model properties in CSS, check out Chapter 7.

Chapter 3

Down and Dirty: Building a Style Sheet in Ten Minutes

In This Chapter

- Deciding what you want to create
- Setting up your style sheet
- Determining the needed styles
- Creating the styles
- Assigning properties and values
- Calling your styles in HTML
- Testing your styles

Here's where the rubber hits the road! Time to get busy and get started using style sheets! With that in mind, in this chapter I give you a quick and dirty introduction to putting style sheets to work in your Web site. I won't throw any fancy curve balls at you; this is just using good old wholesome Cascading Style Sheets to do the easy stuff to make your development life easier. First, I show you how you can include styles in your HTML, and from there, I show you how to build a style. Finally, I show you how to apply those newly created styles to some basic HTML elements.

So sit back in that fancy ergonomic chair of yours, crack this book open, bring up your favorite HTML editor, and take a deep breath, because this is where the magic begins to happen.

If you don't have an HTML editor, you can check out the CD accompanying this book for trial versions of some of the Internet's most popular HTML editors. And you can always visit `www.download.com` and search for HTML editors there.

Some Questions to Ask Yourself First

Before you start creating style sheets all willy-nilly, review some of the key questions you should be asking yourself about the Web site you're about to create or edit. These questions may seem a tad bit on the obvious side, but having a clear understanding of them will help you to make the right decisions about how to design your style sheets. Think of it this way: You can't get where you want to go if you don't know how to get there.

With these questions, I'm trying to give you an idea of the kinds of things you need to think about when building style sheets, like the scope of your projects and how fancy you need to be. Read through these questions first, keeping them in the back of your mind when you're ready to take on adding CSS to your site.

How many pages do I need?

The first question you're going to need to ask yourself is just how many pages you need to manage with your style sheet. If you're thinking about adding a style to a single page, then you might as well just include the style in the HTML document itself. If, however, you want to apply the style to a number of different parts to a number of different pages, then you're better off creating an external style sheet so that if you need to change the style at a later date, you only need to change it once.

How is the Web site organized?

What does Web site organization have to do with style sheets? Depending upon the complexity of the site, site organization can be quite important. For example, larger sites with a wide variety of sections using different graphical look-and-feels may call for more than one style sheet. Alternatively, if your site has a lot of different text styles on different pages, then a style sheet may be for you. Style sheets can get long and cumbersome if you try to consolidate them all into one external sheet. Segmenting them can give you a way to easily define styles that are both global to the site and then specific to an individual section, making it easier to maintain and update over time.

I see some hands in the back there! Yes, you can have more than one style sheet in a page. Good question! I walk you through the whole idea of cascading and inheritance in Chapter 9. Stick with me here first, though, and practice crawling before walking.

What do I need to apply styles to?

You can apply a style to almost anything, such as text and graphics. Beware the temptation to apply a style in every way that you can. You can get a lot out of styles, but as a general rule, you should be judicious in their use. In HTML, if you go hog wild creating tables within tables within tables, you can easily find yourself in a situation where making even the smallest of changes can mess up the whole page. The same rules of simplicity apply to CSS: Use style sheets when it makes sense, not just because you can.

Here's what you can apply a style to, including (but certainly not limited to):

- **Text:** You can apply style attributes to body text, headlines, headers, footers, links, and the rest of the text gang.
- **Graphics:** Some styles, such as the positioning attributes, apply to location on the screen, as opposed to text formatting.
- **Page elements:** This fancy term means that you can give a style to an element within HTML, and it will then be applied equally to the items contained within that element. If I apply a style to a <P> tag, give it a position on the page, and include both text and graphics within that tag, they'd all be given the same style. Check out Figure 3-1 to see how this works.

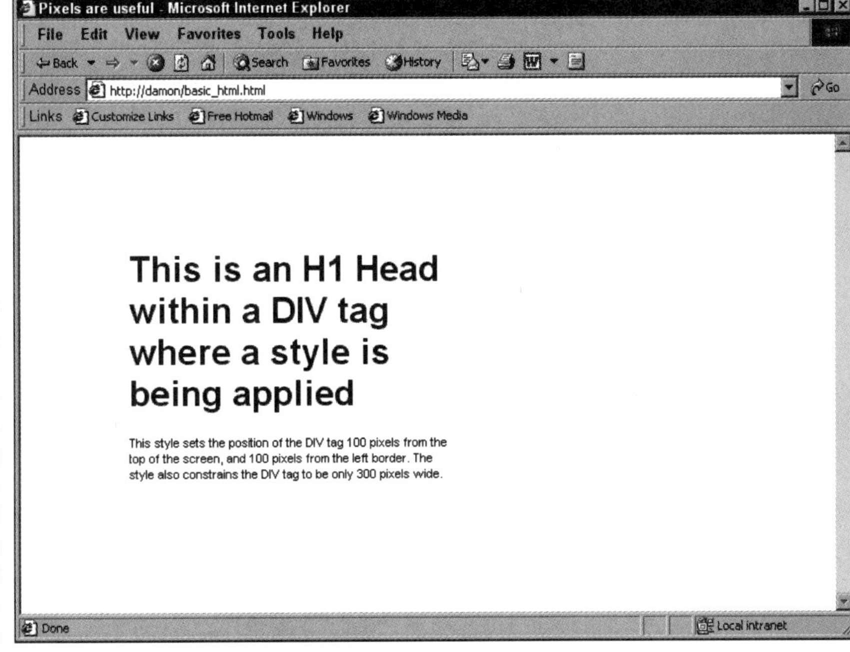

Figure 3-1: Applying a style to a page element applies the style to all the contents in that element.

What are my browser requirements?

I hate to say it, but even with style sheets, you need to plan for compatibility issues. What's the big deal about browsers? Browsers behave differently, both against one another and on different platforms, so you need to be attentive and stringent when defining your style sheets. (See Chapter 1 for more on this, and see Appendix A for a browser compatibility chart.)

In addition to your constant awareness of these issues, you must also plan for Web-enabled e-mail clients, such as Microsoft Outlook or Outlook Express, Netscape Mail, and Eudora Mail if you want to send Web-enabled mail.

Keep these questions in mind when considering the browsers and mail clients:

- Are you building for Explorer, Navigator, or both?
- Are you building for browsers above version 4.0, or do you need to degrade gracefully to the 3.0 browsers as well?
- Are you building for PC or Macintosh platforms?
- Will any of your content eventually be viewed through Web-enabled e-mail in conjunction with any of the above browsers and platforms?

You'll mainly encounter Internet Explorer (IE) and Netscape (Navigator) browsers and PCs and Mac platforms. That should honestly cover about 95 percent of the scenarios that you'd ever be using style sheets in.

Building Your First Style Sheet

Like any good TV chef, the first step to building your style sheet is to put all your content out there on the kitchen counter for the cameras to get a good look at. Bam! I have some ingredients — I mean, content — here that I will put into a very simple Web page featuring a recipe. The recipe, from my favorite cookbook, is for a fennel and mushroom salad. I've sectioned the recipe into four elements: the recipe name, ingredients, preparation instructions, and a picture.

If I had already put this content into an HTML document (`recipes.html`) with no style applied to it whatsoever, it would do nothing but look ugly, a lot like this:

```
<html>
<head>
```

```
<title>My Recipes</title>
</head>

<body>
<P>Fennel and Mushroom Salad</P>

<p>4 large field mushrooms<br>
2 tablespoons butter, melted<br>
1 tablespoon oil<br>
150g (5oz) baby English spinach leaves<br>
1 tablespoon sage leaves<br>
1 tablespoon shredded lemon rind<br>
2 baby fennel bulbs, thinly sliced<br>
1/2 cup marinated green olives<br>
cracked black pepper<br>
2 tablespoons balsamic vinegar<br>
</p>

<p>
Wipe mushrooms clean and trim stems. Brush mushrooms with
           butter and oil, and place on a hot preheated
           grill. Cook mushrooms for two minutes on each
           side. To serve, place a pile of baby spinach
           leaves on each serving plate. Scatter sage leaves
           and lemon rind over spinach and top with a
           mushroom. Top with fennel, olives, and pepper.
           Drizzle balsamic vinegar over salad and serve with
           warm sourdough bread.
</p>

<img src="/images/fennel_mushroom_salad.gif" width="200"
           height="200" border="0" alt="Fennel and Mushroom
           Salad">

</body>
</html>
```

Sounds tasty, doesn't? But styling (or not styling) it this way is pretty ugly, as shown in Figure 3-2. For such a great recipe, I want to spend the time to make it look as good online as it tastes!

Setting up your style sheet

If this were the only recipe on your site, perhaps just having the style in HTML would be easier. Conversely, if you've got a whole bunch of recipes on a site and you want to tell the world about them, set up your styles so that you can use them again and again. Either way is fine!

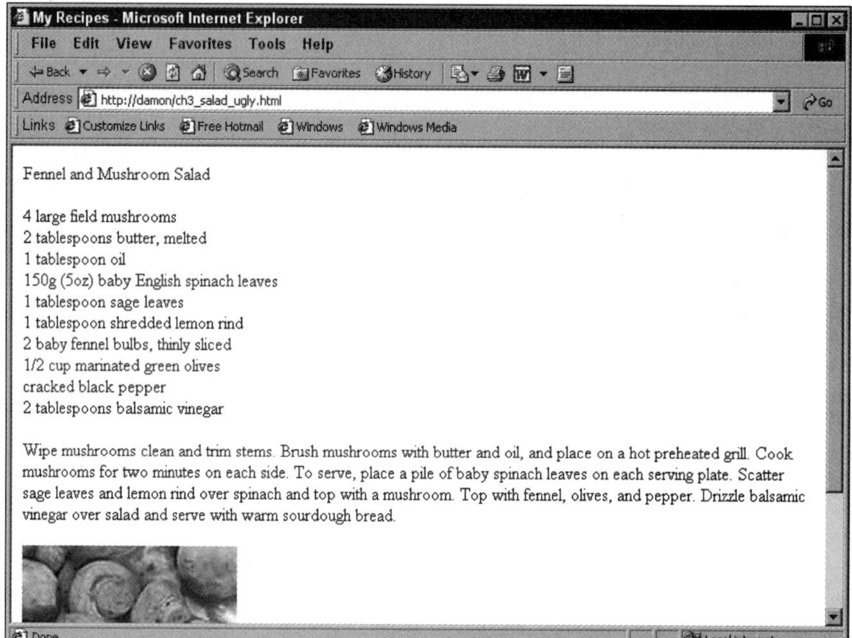

Figure 3-2: Sounds good . . . looks ugly.

To set up your style sheet in the HTML document, you need only add the following snippet of code to be contained within the <HEAD> element, as follows:

```
<head>
<title>My Recipes</title>
<style type="text/css"></style>
</head>
```

The default for the <STYLE> element in the HTML specification — `type=@”text/css"` — simply specifies that you're using a CSS style sheet, as opposed to some other kind of style.

If you want to go the route of using an external style sheet, just follow these steps:

1. **Add a <LINK> element to the <HEAD> element in your HTML document, as follows:**

   ```
   <head>
   <title>My Recipes</title>
   <LINK>
   </head>
   ```

2. **Using the <LINK> element attributes, specify the location of the style in relation to the source HTML document and specify what the link is to (in this case, a style sheet).**

The resulting link should look like this:

```
<LINK href="recipes.css" rel="stylesheet"
        type="text/css">
```

3. **Create a text document (**`recipes.css`**) using a text editor such as Notepad (PC) or SimpleText (Mac) in the same directory as your HTML document.**
4. **Within** `recipes.css`**, add the same** `<STYLE>` **you would have added if you were working directly in the HTML.**

   The result looks like this:

```
<style type="text/css"></style>
```

Regardless of whether you're building the style sheet with the HTML document or external to the HTML document, the styles themselves will always go within the `<STYLE></STYLE>` tag, as you'll see in the next section.

Determining the needed styles

The TV chef magically pulls the casserole out of the oven, not having lifted a finger, and the creation looks as if Matisse himself had painted it. Of course, you know that perfection is never that easy. Work had to go on behind the scenes while the rest of the world refilled snacks and took bio-breaks during the commercials. And the same is true here, too.

When creating a style, the first step is to decide how you want the page to look because that will help you to determine just how many styles you need and what they should look like. For kicks, suppose you want to have a headline at the top, a bold listing of the ingredients and the picture positioned side-by-side, and the directions underneath. Figure 3-3 conceptually demonstrates what this would look like.

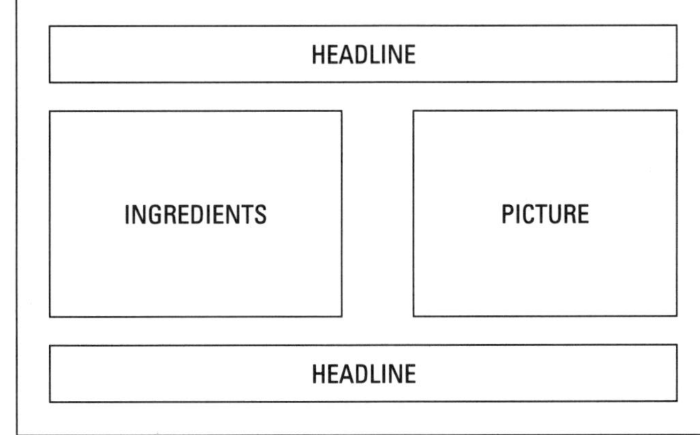

Figure 3-3: Create a block diagram for an idea of what the final look should be.

Based on this block diagram, creating three styles will probably take care of this recipe: one each for the headline, the ingredient list, and the directions text. For the graphic (the picture), just let that be a part of the HTML table you'll need to create the basic structure of the diagram.

You could totally eliminate the need for an HTML table here, but rather than complicate this example with the tedium of figuring out pixels widths and the like, I'll keep this simple. For a more advanced discussion on positions, hop over to Chapter 8.

Now you need to decide how you want your styles to look. To make it stand out, the headline style should probably be larger than the other styles. The ingredients need to be bold, and should perhaps be a bit larger than the directions for clarity. Consider making the directions italic to make them stand apart from the ingredient list. Check out Table 3-1 to get an idea of what those properties look like for this example.

Table 3-1 Recipe Styles

Style Name	*Font*	*Type Size*	*Other Features*
Headline	Arial	18 points	Color is blue
Ingredients	Arial	11 points	Bold
Directions	Times	11 points	Italicized and justified

Creating your styles

Creating a style is nothing more than defining the variables that it comprises. For example, you need to give it a name (`stylename`), and define what it contains, such as properties and values. *Properties* are descriptors that specify things such as the font name, the font size, or the font color. The *values* are the numeric or character variables for those properties.

The basic format of a style is as follows:

```
.stylename {
property: value;}
```

Not too bad so far, right? Not too much to keep track of yet. Of course, you can make it more complicated, but that's where the cool stuff comes in. Keep these basic rules in mind when building styles, including:

- Style names cannot include spaces.
- Brackets { } must follow the name of the style and encapsulate all the style's properties and values.

- Properties and values must be separated by a colon (:).
- Individual property and value combinations must be separated by a semi-colon (;).
- All styles that do not specify a default style for an HTML document element (such as `<H1>`, `<H2>`, or `<P>` elements) must have a period (.) that precedes the `stylename`.

What's the deal with that period before the `stylename`, anyway? For those of you who are geek averse, just look away now. The period represents the location of the style in the document hierarchy. Styles can be applied to document elements in general. For example, if I were to create the following style `P {font-family: Arial, Helvetica, sans-serif}`, then all the `<P>` elements in the document would use Arial, Helvetica, or sans-serif as their default font. When adding the period (.) before a style, you are then going one layer deeper into the document structure and specifying a style for that part of the element, or the entire element.

The CD at the back of this book includes the HTML and styles for this exercise, in all their various forms from start to finish.

Armed with all those rules and regs (you're now entitled to techie slang: Say, "Regulations"), you can finish creating the style sheets for the recipe. Follow these steps:

1. **Name your styles and put them in the `<STYLE>` tag.**

   For the sake of simplicity, call these styles `headline`, `ingredients`, and `directions`. The empty styles, then, would look as follows in the `<STYLE>` tag.

   The `<STYLE>` tag may be in the HTML or in the external text file, depending upon how you initially set it up.

```
<style type="text/css">
.headline {
}

.ingredients {
}

.directions {
}

</style>
```

2. **Find the correct properties and value combinations for the styles you've created.**

   To make the text styles as outlined in the previous section, you need six CSS properties. Table 3-2 includes the style attributes and the corresponding CSS property, as well as the value variables used to describe that property.

Table 3-2 CSS Properties Needed for the Recipe Style Sheet

Text Attribute	*CSS Property*	*Value Variable(s)*
font	font-family	This must be the name of a font, such as Arial or Times New Roman.
font size	font-size	Size can be described in a number of ways; for absolute sizes, integers represents pixel size. The integer must be followed by *px* in order to denote pixels.
italics	font-style	The font style can be normal, italic, or oblique (tilted to the right).
bold	font-weight	Use font-weight to set varying degrees of boldness on a font.
justified	text-align	The basic options here are left, right, center, and justify.
font color	color	Color is a hexadecimal value, just like in HTML, representing a color. You can also use the default name values for colors, such as red, black, or white.

3. **Put the property and value combinations with their correct styles.**

   Using the CSS properties that I define in Table 3-2, adding the correct interpretation of the value form the original text attributes, your style sheet should look like this:

```
<style type="text/css">
.headline {
   font-family: Arial, Helvetica, san-serif;
   font-size: 18 px;
   color: #000099;
   }

.ingredients {
   font-family: Arial, Helvetica, san-serif;
   font-size: 11 px;
   font-weight: bold;
   color: #000000;
   }

.directions {
   font-family: Times, Times New Roman;
   font-size: 11 px;
   font-style: italic;
   text-align: justify;
   color: #000000;
   }
</style>
```

Much like with HTML, you should always include the PC, Mac, and other platform equivalents for the `font-family` property. For example, when you set a sans-serif font, specify Arial for the PC, Helvetica or Geneva for the Mac, and san-serif for other platforms.

Calling your styles in HTML

The behind-the-scenes magic continues. This is some long commercial break before the chef pulls out his perfected creation, isn't it? (Must be an infomercial for the George Foreman grilling machine.) After your style sheet is set up, switch your attention back to the HTML document. The following HTML gives you the layout as I describe previously in Figure 3-3 (I've included HTML comments to guide you in the code):

```
<table width="400" border="0" cellspacing="0"
          cellpadding="0">
<!-- This row locks down the table so I can use Colspans for
          the headline and directions-->
<tr>
   <td width="200"><img src="images/spacer.gif" width="200"
          height="1" border="0"></td>
   <td width="200"><img src="images/spacer.gif" width="200"
          height="1" border="0"></td>
</tr>
<!-- This row includes the headline -->
<tr>
   <td colspan="2">HEADLINE</td>
</tr>
<!-- This row includes the ingredients and the picture -->
<tr>
   <td valign="top" align="left" width="200">INGREDIENTS</td>
   <td valign="top" align="left">PICTURE</td>
</tr>
<!-- This row includes the directions-->
<tr>
   <td align="left" class="directions"
          colspan="2">DIRECTIONS</td>
</tr>
</table>
```

The goal now is to put the content into its proper place in the HTML and then call the appropriate style. When the browser processes the HTML page, all the styles are processed right along with it and made available to be called from within the HTML itself. You can call the styles from within HTML in a number of different ways, but because the content is surrounded in `<P>` elements early on, do it from there. This minimizes the amount of extra work you have to do. Plus, IE and Netscape prefer this method, so that's a benefit working in your favor.

IE and Netscape both refer to styles as a *class,* not to be confused with Java classes, cooking classes, or that debutante-coming-out-party kind of class. When you want to apply a style to a particular element on a Web page, use the following code syntax:

```
class="stylename"
```

For each of those <P> elements in the HTML content from the previous example, go ahead and add the proper class name to the tag. For the recipe, the three style calls would look like this:

```
<P class="headline">Fennel and Mushroom Salad</P>
<p class="ingredients">4 large field mushrooms<br>
2 tablespoons butter, melted<br>
1 tablespoon oil<br>
150g (5oz) baby English spinach leaves<br>
1 tablespoon sage leaves<br>
1 tablespoon shredded lemon rind<br>
2 baby fennel bulbs, thinly sliced<br>
1/2 cup marinated green olives<br>
cracked black pepper<br>
2 tablespoons balsamic vinegar<br></p>
<p class="description"> Wipe mushrooms clean and trim stems.
           Brush mushrooms with butter and oil, and place on
           a hot preheated grill. Cook mushrooms for two
           minutes on each side. To serve, place a pile of
           baby spinach leavs on each serving plate. Scatter
           sage leaves and lemon rind over spinach and top
           with a mushroom. Top with fennel, olives, and
           pepper. Drizzle balsamic vinegar over salad and
           serve with warm sourdough bread.</p>
```

After you complete this task, you just need to put the content into the proper place in the HTML table, and voilà!, you created and used a style sheet! See what the final page should look like in Figure 3-4.

Testing your styles

Now's the time to test your styles. You need to test the HTML, and then check that your styles are viable on different browsers and platforms.

Got a bad code?

This is the easy part. To check your HTML, all you really need to do is grab a browser and check out your page. Of course, the more browsers you check it on, the better your chances for having awesome CSS code!

Did your styles work for you the very first time you tried? If so, super! If not, then you need to go back to your HTML editor and review your code to see if you missed anything from the exercise above.

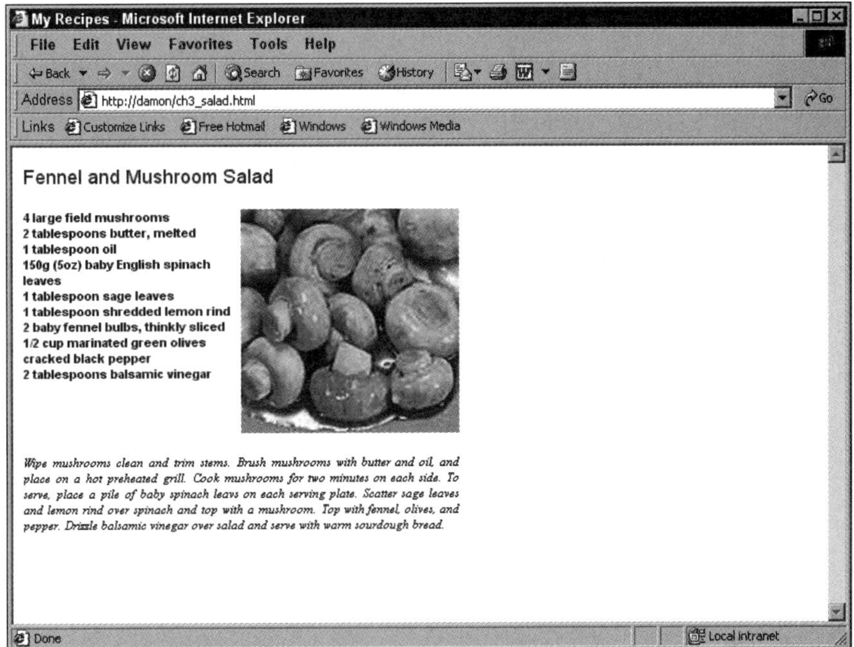

Figure 3-4: Now this page is as pretty as your salad!

Just browsin'

Another critical part of testing your styles is to check them on different browsers. This is the toughest part because not everyone just happens to have every Web browser on all platforms dating back to 1998 just hanging around the house or office.

Here are some things that you can at least do to give your styles the best chances for success.

- **Install the latest versions of IE and Navigator on your machine, regardless of what platform you're on.**

  Microsoft and Netscape are getting better and stricter with their CSS implementations, so if your styles work on the newest browser, you're going to be okay in most cases. Also, because people tend to upgrade their systems over time, the older 4.0 browsers are becoming more and more obsolete. If you can only install one browser, though, choose Navigator 6.01 because Netscape tends to be stricter with both its HTML and CSS implementations.

- **Use a CSS validation tool.**

  You'll find a great CSS validator from the W3C at `http://jigsaw.w3.org/css-validator/`. You can download the validator from this site or use the tools there to validate your style sheets, testing for well-formedness (that's a fancy term for making sure your CSS is written properly), and validity.

The CD accompanying this book also includes the CSS validator from the W3C.

- **Showing your pages to your friends and coworkers.**

  This suggestion may sound odd, but your friends and coworkers could have different browsers or platforms than you do. Have them take a look at your pages first, before you show them to the rest of the world.

However you choose to check your styles, your chances of them working right increase when you check them on different browsers before you show off that final creation.

Part II

Parlez-Vous CSS?

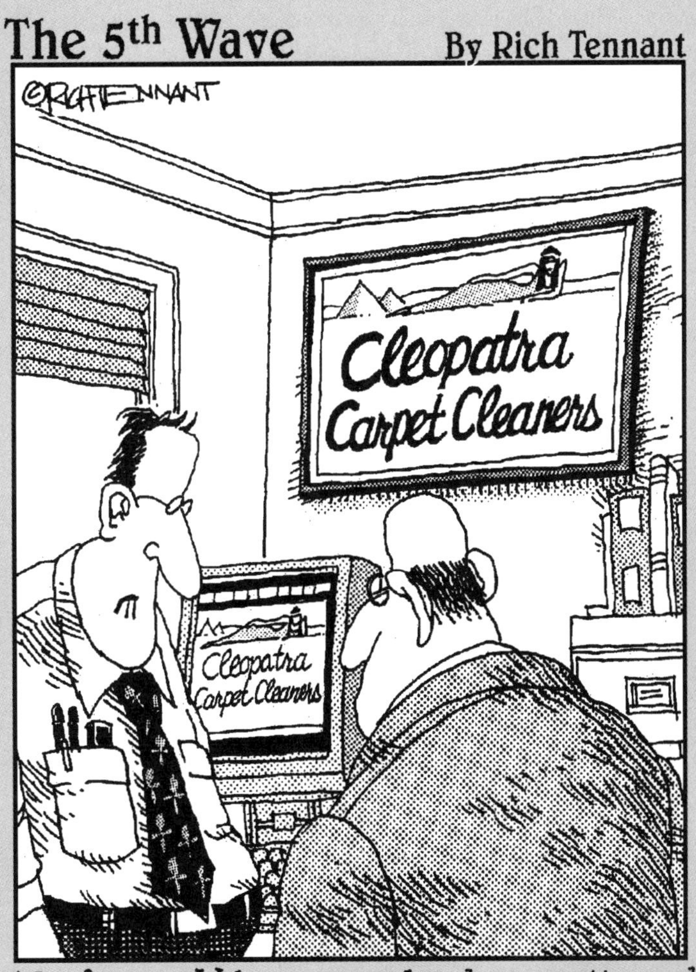

"So far our Web presence has been pretty good. We've gotten some orders, a few inquiries and nine guys who want to date our logo."

In this part . . .

This part of the book throws a lot of information your way, from basic Cascading Style Sheet syntax to the specifics of individual properties. A lot of it is quite intuitive, so you should have no problem picking it all up lickety-split. I begin with the basics: selectors, rules, declarations, and other ominous words that strike fear in the hearts of Web developers everywhere. Read here while I demystify these terms for you.

Then I move on to the text properties, and progress through boxes and positions. Finally, I jet-set through the cascades to show you what the rarely used and rarely understood part, *cascading*, in Cascading Style Sheets really means.

After you peruse this part, you'll be ready to flex your CSS muscles and jump into some of the really challenging stuff — like using CSS in your own site! For more on that, sally forth to Part III.

Chapter 4

I Declare: Who Selected These Rules Anyway?

In This Chapter

- Understanding the difference between selectors and rules
- Declaring yourself with style
- Grouping your declarations together
- Specifiying with class and ID selectors
- Putting real pseudo-elements to work

In Chapter 3, I quickly walk you through what makes style sheets work in order to make a style sheet in ten minutes or less. Here in Chapter 4, I give you a closer look at the foundations of Cascading Style Sheets. Specifically, I detail the structure of a style sheet and its elements, and how these elements work together to enable you to add styles to elements in your HTML documents. This is the foundation for styles everywhere, and these rules will be your guiding principles when creating styles now and in the future!

The Anatomy of a Rule

Style *rules* comprise a style sheet, instructing a browser how to present a document. Each rule is made up of a *selector,* which contains one or more *declarations*. A *declaration* is defined by different *properties*, and each property takes a *value*. You can see their relationships in Figure 4-1.

Here's a basic style rule:

```
selector { property: value }
```

Look at this example with the selector, property, and value defined.

```
H1 { font-size: large }
```

For this style rule, the selector names the element (H1), the property identifies font-size, and the value (large) further defines the property.

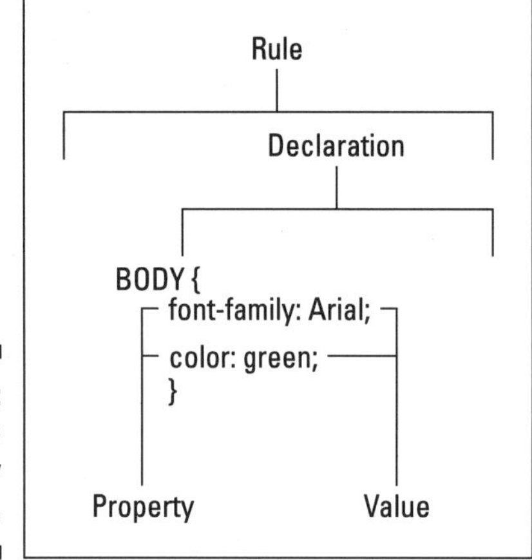

Figure 4-1: The anatomy of a rule.

As a bit of a primer, check out Table 4-1 to see a number of common HTML elements and their basic usage.

Table 4-1 Commonly Used HTML Document Elements

Element	*Common Usage*
BODY	Describes the *BODY* of an HTML document
P	Sets a *P*aragraph of text
H1 To H6	Specifies a *H*eadline weight 1 to 6 (6 is the smallest)
A	Specifies an *A*nchor point in the document
EM	Indicates *Em*phasis by using italics
STRONG	Indicates more emphasis by using bold
LI	Creates a *Li*st item

As I'm sure you already know (but I just want to double check and make sure), when working with HTML, you're very likely to come across an element encased in a greater-than and a less-than symbol, like this: <P>. I call those *tags*.

Here's where the first great thing about style sheets comes into play! Suppose that you've got a 100-page Web site that uses Times New Roman as the main font (black in color). Early one Monday morning, before you have your requisite mocha beverage, you decide that you want the whole site to use Arial as the font instead, and you want to change the font color to green. To accomplish this change, you'd have to go through the entire site and specify Arial green in every single page in the BODY element. Ick — who wants to make 100 replacements? That's tedious, and just plain dumb.

By simply changing a style rule in your style sheet, you can very easily take control over common — and not so common — HTML elements and consolidate them into a single statement. In the previous example, you can control all the <BODY> tags with a single global style (rather than change 100 tags) if you use an externally linked style sheet for all those pages. Your new rule would look like this:

```
BODY {font-family: Arial; color: green;}
```

This rule goes one step further than the one I earlier show you in this section. Note that this rule has two properties (font-family and color) and a value for each (Arial and green).

When put together and encompassed within a <STYLE> tag, rules collectively make up a style sheet.

Selectors on the Left

As I mention in the previous section, a style rule is made up of a selector. If you were to crack open the CSS specification (you know, to put yourself to sleep at night), you'd see that it lists a number of different selectors. These selectors can include HTML elements, names you come up with yourself, or even wildcards, which are symbols that have a predefined meaning, such as the asterisk (*) character (which means *select all*). Generally speaking, the selectors fall into four different types, as follows:

- **Type selectors:** These selectors apply a rule to an HTML element, such as a P or DIV element. An example of this kind of selector is:

  ```
  TD {font-family: Arial;}
  ```

- **Class selector:** These selectors have a specific name that you (the author) create and then call using the class value in an HTML element. An example of this kind of selector is:

  ```
  .mystyle {font-family: Arial;}
  ```

- **ID selectors:** These selectors are designed to identify a unique element in the HTML document and are identified using the ID value in HTML. An example of this kind of selector is:

  ```
  TD#1234 {font-family: Arial;}
  ```

- **Universal selector:** These selectors are designed to identify all the elements in an HTML document. An example of this kind of selector is:

```
* {font-family: Arial;}
```

I describe each of these selectors in more detail in the upcoming sections of this chapter.

Type selectors

Type selectors represent an element in the document. (No, type doesn't mean clacking your fingers on a keyboard; rather, it's a *type of* element.) Type selectors match all instances of the element type in the document. In the following rule, all H1 elements are matched in its document;

```
H1 { font-family: Arial }
```

All the elements in Table 4-1 are considered type selectors for the HTML language. What if, though, you weren't using HTML? If you were using XML instead, you'd have a document structure that looks like the following:

```
<room type="living" width="10" length="15" >
   <furniture name="couch" type="leather"/>
   <furniture name="chair" type="recliner"/>
   <furniture name="coffee table" type="oak" />
   <wall type="stucco" />
   <floor type="hard wood">
   <description> Don't I have a really boring living room?
         </description>
</room>
```

In the XML code block above, ROOM, FURNITURE, WALL, FLOOR, and DESCRIPTION are all type selectors. You could apply styles to those selectors the same way that you can apply a style to a BODY element in HTML.

XML and CSS get more face time together in Chapter 14.

Making your content CLASSy

The class selector is a pretty clever little tool that makes CSS incredibly powerful. Suppose that you want to apply a style to some text within a document element, such as a <P> tag. If you could only apply styles to the <P> tag itself, then you'd basically be stuck. Or, use this selector to set different styles for the same element — to apply a particular style to some <P> tags, but not others.

The CLASS attribute in HTML applies to nearly all elements within HTML, but it's used most commonly in the following elements:

- BODY
- P
- DIV
- SPAN
- H1 through H6

To illustrate how class selectors work, look at these snippets of HTML text:

```
<p>That's one small step for man...</p>
<p>One giant leap for mankind</p>
```

If the only rule for the <P> tags in this style is

```
P {
font-family: Arial, Helvetica, sans-serif;
font-size: 10px;
   }
```

then the page that you'd see onscreen would apply the rule equally to both paragraphs of content. See the results in Figure 4-2.

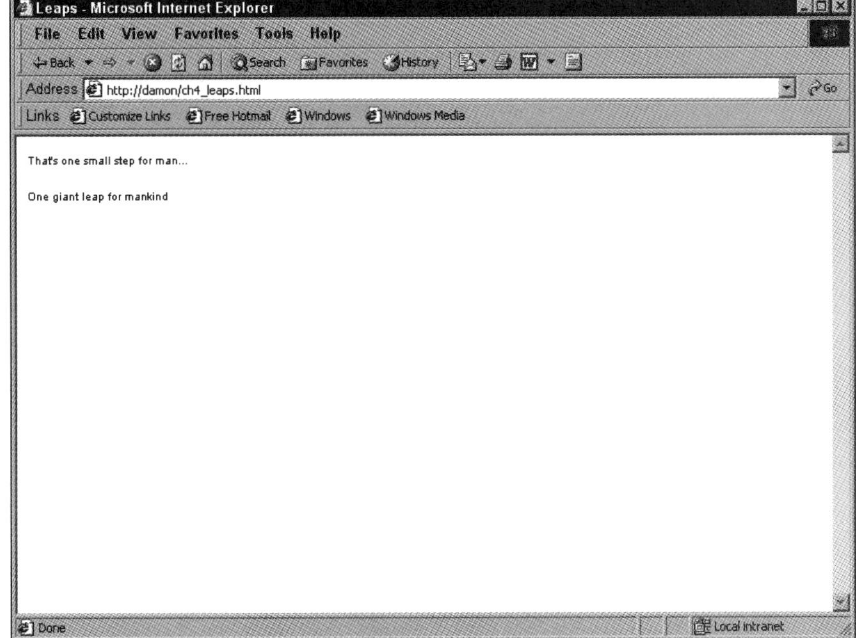

Figure 4-2: Both paragraphs are rendered with the same rule.

To identify a style that's going to be applied to a specific HTML element — in this case, the <P> tag — you first have to define a style for that individual element. After that's complete, you can call it through the CLASS attribute in HTML.

The syntax for creating the class selector is almost identical to that of any other selector, with one major difference. Class selectors must be preceded by a period (.) when creating the rule. If you want to put some huge emphasis on the text *One giant leap for mankind*, you could create a rule that looks like this:

```
.huge {
font-size: 36px;
font-weight: bold;
      }
```

This rule can be called from any of the HTML elements that support the CLASS attribute. To apply it to the second paragraph of text, use the following HTML:

```
<p class="huge"> One giant leap for mankind</p>
```

Note that the initial period is dropped when calling the style from the CLASS attribute. The huge rule would then be applied to the second paragraph instead of the default <P> rule. The first paragraph, however, would get the default <P> rule because no specific style was being called for it. The resulting page looks like Figure 4-3.

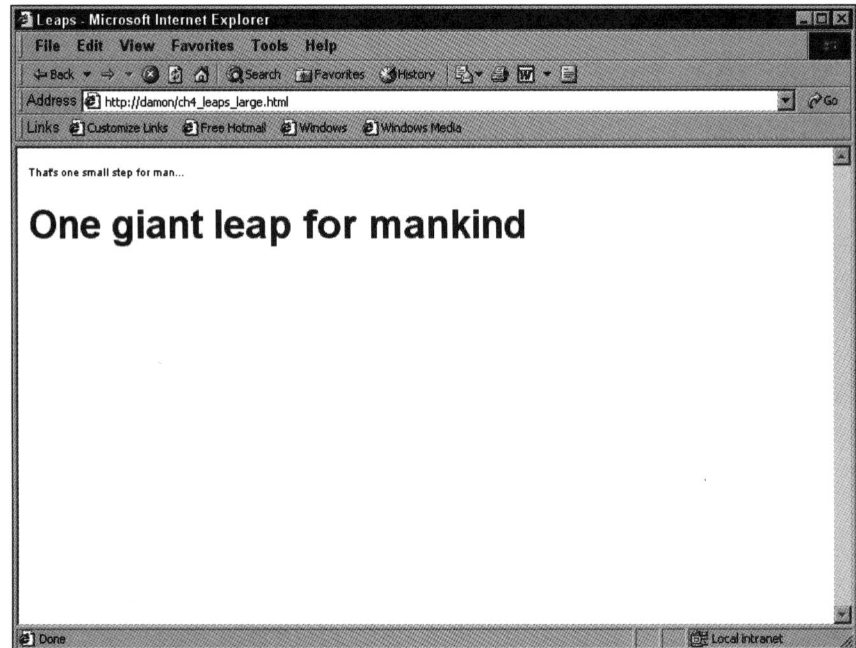

Figure 4-3: Rendering the second paragraph with the huge rule.

Another way to conceptualize the class selector is as a child to the universal selector (see more on the universal selector in the section "Universal selectors" later in this chapter). You could actually add the * as a precedent to the huge rule (*.huge is the syntax), and it would process the rule just the same. Similarly, you could also decide that the huge rule only applies to certain P elements, and not to the DIV, SPAN, or H1 elements. To do that, name the rule P.huge, and only P elements with the name CLASS attribute of huge would apply the style. You can read more on inheritance in Chapter 9.

You can get even deeper into the document by using the SPAN element. Suppose you want to make just the word *mankind* have the huge style. In the following code, check out how to use the SPAN element to isolate one word for the huge style.

```
<p>That's one small step for man...</p>
<p>One giant leap for <span class="huge">mankind</span></p>
```

See the result in Figure 4-4.

You got some ID for that selector?

Now, what if you really, really, *really* want to identify something very specific in an HTML document? Not just some crummy piece of content in a <DIV> element, but perhaps a whole class of content that, while similar to another class of content, is definitively unique in its own right. In HTML, you can make just such a distinction with the ID attribute, and you can use style sheets to apply a style to that individual ID.

Suppose you're the head of a major news media conglomerate, MegaNews Company, and your main newspaper is the *Daily Journal*. One day, you point your managerial finger at your under-appreciated Web design team, and exclaim, "Okay, you slackers! Today's big scoop is about a man chased down by a comet! To make it really stand out, I want the whole story to show up in italics, not that boring regular stuff we always use! I don't care what it takes — just do it!"

The ID selector will save your bacon on this one. First look at the headline and the text.

```
<H1 class="headline">Man Chased By Renegade Comet</H1>
<DIV class="story_body">The Defense Department reported today
          that a man was chased across five states by a
          renegade comet. Officials from Jupiter, where the
          space rock originated, could not be reached for
          comment. <a href="comet_full_story.html">More</a>
</DIV>
```

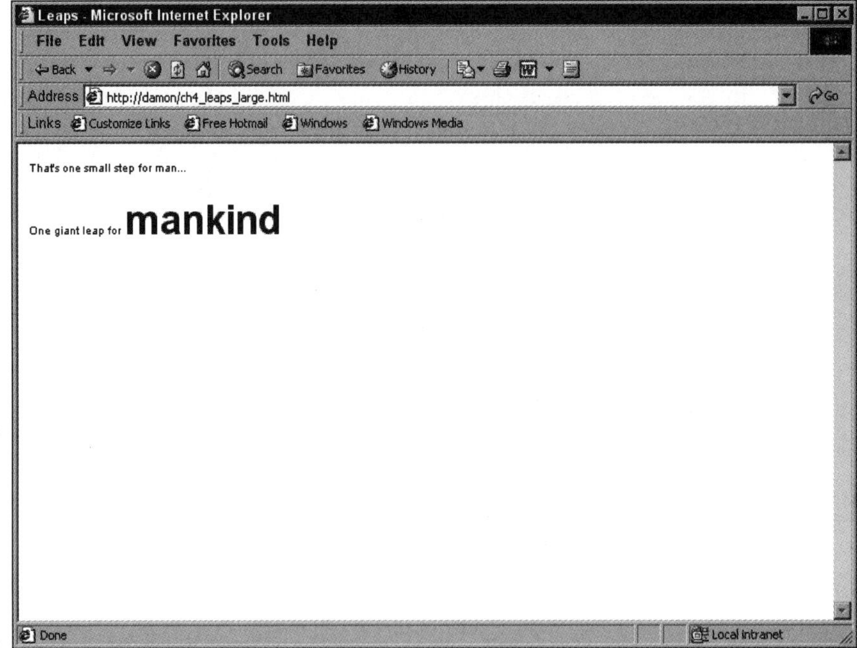

Figure 4-4: Applying the huge rule using a SPAN element.

In the style sheet, you've also got references to the following style rules for headlines and body copy:

```
.headline  {
   font-family: Arial, Helvetica, san-serif;
   font-size: 18 px;
   color: #000099;
   }
.story_body {
Font-Family: Arial, Helvetica, sans-serif;
   font-size: 11 px;
color: black;
}
```

Under normal circumstances, the story, although a tad ugly, would look something like Figure 4-5.

To create a style that would apply italics to that single news story, follow these steps:

1. **Create an ID selector within the `<DIV>` tag for the comet story.**

   For the sake of simplicity, call the story `"comet_promo"`. The resulting `<DIV>` tag would be:

   ```
   <DIV id="comet_promo">
   ```

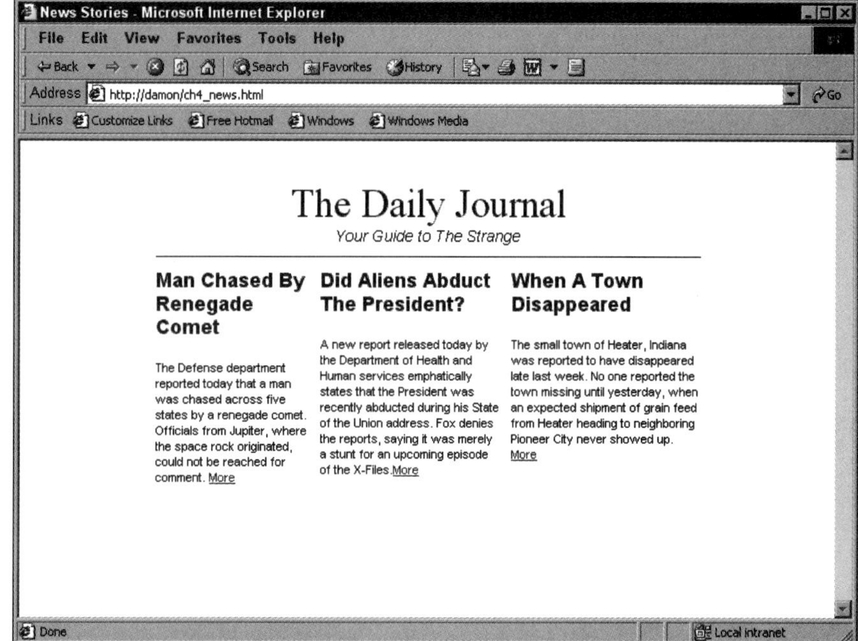

Figure 4-5: Your story, pre-italics.

2. **In your style sheet, create a rule called** `DIV#comet_promo`**.**

   Like the `CLASS` selector, the `ID` selector uses a divider between the HTML element and the name of the style. In this case, the divider is the pound sign (#). Like the period (`.`), the pound sign is required for `ID` selectors.

   If you don't want to apply the rule to a particular HTML element, you could drop the `<DIV>` precursor, and the rule `#comet_promo` would still work on most other elements in the HTML document.

3. **Add the italics declaration (**`font-family: italic;`**).**

The resulting style sheet and HTML look like the following:

```
<html>
<head>
<title>News Stories</title>
<style type="text/css">

.headline   {
   font-family: Arial, Helvetica, san-serif;
   font-size: 18 px;
   color: #000099;
   }
.story_body {
```

```
Font-Family: Arial, Helvetica, sans-serif;
   font-size: 11 px;
color: black;
}

DIV#comet_body   {
font-style: italic;
}

</style>
</head>
<body>
<H1 class="headline">Man Chased By Renegade Comet</H1>
<DIV class="story_body" id="comet_body">The Defense
           Department reported today that a man was chased
           across five states by a renegade comet. Officials
           from Jupiter, where the space rock originated,
           could not be reached for comment. <a
           href="#">More</a>
</DIV>
</body>
</html>
```

In Figure 4-6, you can see how the browser then displays the text in italics while the other text keeps its default styles:

Universal selectors

The *universal selector*, just like its name implies, selects everything in the document. Syntactically, the universal selector is called by using the asterisk (*) as the selector in a rule. If you want every single element in your document to be lovely froggy Arial green, then use the universal selector like this:

```
* {font-family: Arial; color: green;}
```

Ribbet.

I Declare!

Selectors find the elements in a document, and *declarations* describe how the element should behave after it's found. Declarations are defined by properties and values. *Properties* are all the things that the CSS specification enables you to modify or control, and the *values* are the variables that you can apply to those modifiable properties.

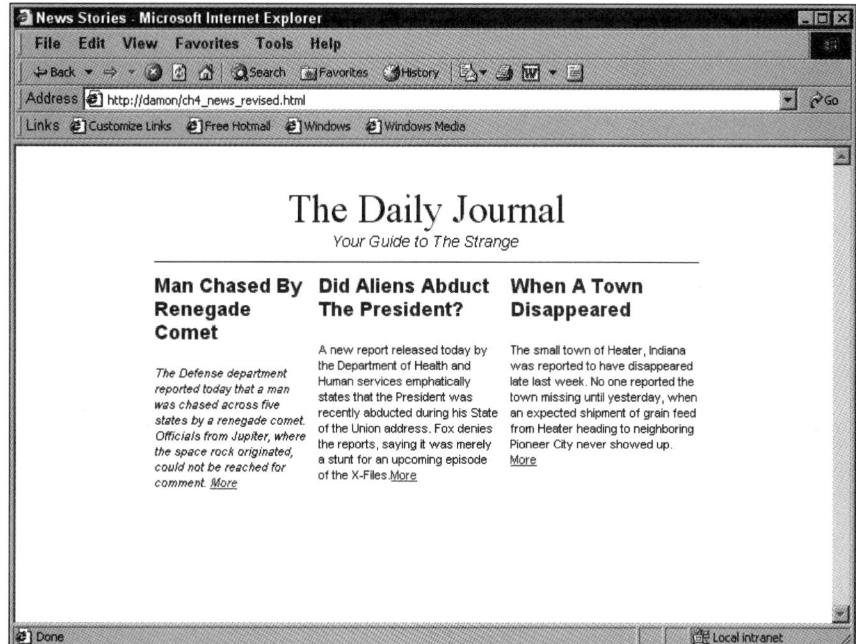

Figure 4-6: Here's the comet story italicized.

In Chapter 3, I mention some rules of syntax for properties and values. Syntax errors in a property or a value are supposed to be ignored by the browser, but following these rules carefully is a good idea.

- **Properties and values must be separated by a colon (:), as follows:**

```
property: value
```

- **Property and value combinations must end with a semi-colon (;) when there's more than one declaration, as follows:**

```
property: value;
property: value;
```

If you've only got one declaration in a rule, then you don't need to have the semi-colon (;) at the end of the value.

- **Property and value combinations are case insensitive — mostly!**

You can mix and match cases in CSS if that's allowable in the language you choose for your document. For example, element type names in HTML are *not* case sensitive; conversely, they *are* case sensitive in XML.

In addition, some browsers like Netscape are also notoriously case sensitive; regardless of what the CSS Level 2 specification says, you really should try to keep your styles consistent when it comes to case.

- **Some properties support having more than a single value.**

  For example, the `font-family` property allows you to specify more than one font, as follows:

  ```
  font-family: Arial, Geneva, Helvetica;
  ```

- **Some properties support multiple units of measurement.**

  For example, the `font-size` property allows you to specify font size using pixels, picas, or inches as follows:

  ```
  font-family: 18px
  ```

  I discuss units in more detail in Chapter 5.

In CSS2, you can modify about 100 different properties through a rule. Most declarations consist of a property that enjoys a one-to-one relationship with its value partner: that is, a property that is modified by one value. Some declarations, however, can have more than one value assigned to a property. The following sections highlight some of these unique cases.

Passing multiple values

With some properties, such as `font-family`, you can pass more than one value to a property. This can be exceptionally handy when you're trying to create styles for different platforms — and you'll run into this situation frequently. For example, Arial is a default Windows font, and Helvetica is a default Mac font. Theoretically, you'd need two styles (one for the PC and one for the Mac) — bummer! Thankfully, though, because the `font-family` property supports multiple values, you can simply create one style that includes both fonts, and the browser will read them in the order in which they were received, and apply the first one that's installed on the user's system. The declaration would look like this:

```
font-family: Arial, Helvetica;
```

Note that some multiple values, such as those used for the `margin` property, use a space (and not a separating comma) to distinguish between values. Use this property to (hmmm) specify the left, top, right, and bottom margins for a specific piece of content. For example, to put a 3-pixel margin around the content, your declaration would look like this:

```
margin: 3px 3px 3px 3px
```

Passing multiple properties and values

Some declarations can contain multiple values and properties. To accomplish this slick trick, use a shorthand property, which can process multiple properties and values in one property-value combination. Talk about convenient!

Suppose you have the following collection of properties:

```
font-weight: bold;
font-size: 11 px;
font-family: Arial, Helvetica, san-serif;
```

By using the `font` shorthand property (which can set `font-style`, `font-variant`, `font-weight`, `font-size`, `line-height`, and `font-family` values all at once), you can wrap all those values into one single statement. Note the internal separating by spaces, and not commas.

```
font: bold 11px Arial;
```

Watch out, though, for this catch: The font property can't just read any random collection of values thrown at it. It has to read values in a specific order for it to appropriate the proper value with its corresponding property. How do you know the correct order? Well, you could read it at `www.w3.org` (yuk). I also highlight these critters throughout this book, reminding you about the ordering requirement. For reference, though, here's a list of all the shorthand properties in CSS (you can also see these in Appendix A):

- `background`
- `border`
- `font`
- `list-style`
- `outline`

Group Hug!

Grouping is another handy feature of CSS, and you can apply it to both selectors and declarations. Suppose that you want every HTML element on a Web page to be green. You could create a group of rules that looks like this:

```
BODY { color: green;}
P { color: green;}
H1 { color: green;}
A { color: green;}
```

Wow, by this point, the page would pretty much be green from top to bottom! Nevertheless, with CSS, this same set of rules can easily be represented — much more simply — with this one single rule:

```
BODY, P, H1, A { color: green;}
```

The same concept applies to declarations. A single rule may have multiple property and value combinations applied to it. In this case, the semi-colon at the end of a declaration serves to separate it from the subsequent declaration. The following example shows how grouping declarations works:

```
P {    font-weight: bold;
   font-size: 11 px;
   font-family: Arial, Helvetica, san-serif;
  }
```

Those Selectors Aren't Real — Just Pseudo!

I just love the CSS specification for its amazing ability to say something and nothing all at the same time. Here are two of my favorite gems:

- Pseudo-elements create abstractions about the document tree beyond those specified by the document language.
- Pseudo-classes classify elements on characteristics other than their names, attributes, or content.

In essence, you'll eventually need something a little more granular than a big old <P> tag in HTML. Pseudo-elements and pseudo-classes are designed to give you that flexibility, even if you can't immediately tell that from their descriptions.

Small but mighty — the pseudo-element

A pseudo-element is not a real HTML element. Rather, it's an element that CSS creates dynamically from an existing HTML element in order to apply a style rule to it. Pseudo-elements are designed for those times when you need to change just a bit of an HTML element, and not the whole thing. Using a pseudo-element you can apply a specific style to only part of that element (usually a block element, such as a `P` element).

Why not just use a `SPAN` element? Why all the complexity? Simplicity, that's why. If I can apply a style to all the first lines or first paragraphs of a document with only one command, then that's the obvious route to take!

Even though they're way cool, pseudo-elements are not the best supported of CSS properties. Most of them are just now gaining adoption in Internet Explorer (IE 5.5) and above, and Netscape has sort of supported them since the later version 4.0 browsers. Netscape 6.0 and above, however, does have good support for the pseudo-elements.

I'm the first line!

The `first-line` pseudo-element is probably the most often used in this family. Use it to apply a style to the first sentence in a block element, such as a <P> tag. Using the comet story from earlier, you can make its first line italicized with the following rules:

```
P   {
   font-family: Arial, Helvetica, san-serif;
   font-size: 12 px;
   color: #000099;
   }
P:first-line {font-style: italic;}
```

The `first` rule defines the default style for a <P> element. Notice that pseudo-elements use a colon (`:`) as a divider that follows the selector. This is the case for all pseudo-elements. When applied to the following bit of HTML, the first line of text becomes italic, as shown in Figure 4-7.

```
<P>The Defense Department reported today that a man was
           chased across five states by a renegade comet.
           Officials from Jupiter, where the space rock
           originated, could not be reached for comment. <a
           href="full_story.html">More</a></P>
```

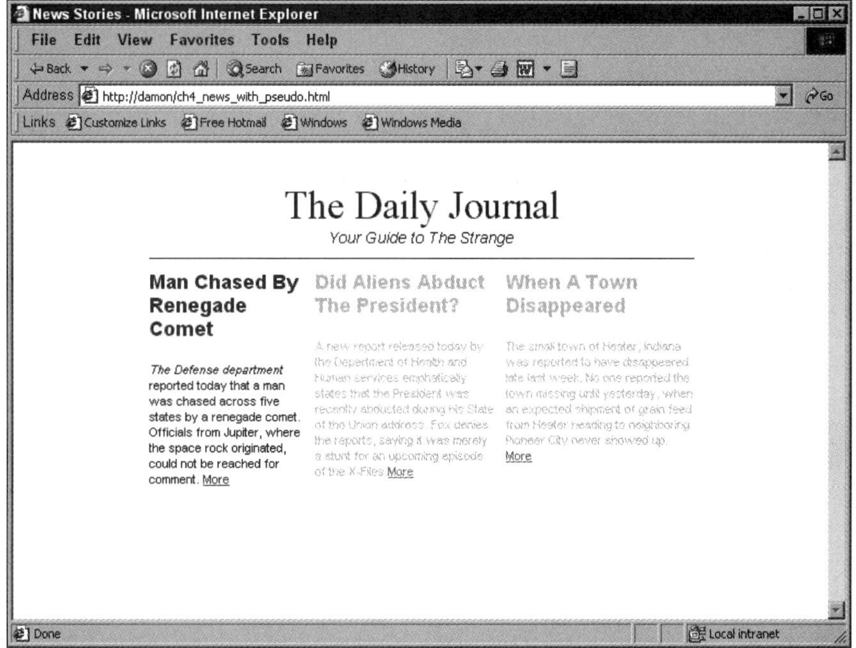

Figure 4-7: Using the first-line pseudo-element.

First in line!

Flip back to the first page of this chapter, and look at where the text starts after the chapter title. Check out how different that first character (called a drop-cap) looks; it's way big and way bold to set it apart. By using the `first-letter` pseudo-element, you can do exactly the same thing, and make the first character in a text block look different. If I add the following rule to the style sheet above,

```
P:first-letter {font-size: 50px;}
```

then the lead character in my text block really stands out, as shown in Figure 4-8. The observant ones in the crowd will notice that I combined both `first-line` and `first-letter` pseudo-elements together. CSS is so accommodating!

Go to CLASS; take your ID

You can also use pseudo-elements with the `CLASS` and `ID` attributes to extend your reach even further into the document elements and give you more control over the styles being applied to elements. For example, the following rule

```
P.yippee:first-letter   {
   font-family: Arial, Helvetica, san-serif;
   font-size: 60 px;
   color: #000099;
   }
```

would create a 60-pixel high, blue Arial character when the `CLASS="yippee"` was called from a `P` element in HTML. Similarly, this rule

```
P#lookatme:first-line   {
   font-family: Arial, Helvetica, san-serif;
   font-size: 60 px;
   color: #000099;
   }
```

would create a 60-pixel high, blue Arial sentence when `ID="lookatme"` was called from a `P` element in HTML. And a big beautiful blue line it would be!

I want to stress that these features are not well supported in many browsers, and although they might work conceptually (and even in the latest browsers), the desired effect you're striving for could end up being lost on a large number of site viewers.

Before and after

Here are two more powerful pseudo-elements — `:before` and `:after` — you can add to the `first-line` and `first-letter` pseudo-elements. It's a very small leap from using virtual styles to change the way content looks to using virtual styles to generate content dynamically, which is precisely what these elements are designed to do. Delve into more detail about `:before` and `:after` in Chapter 12.

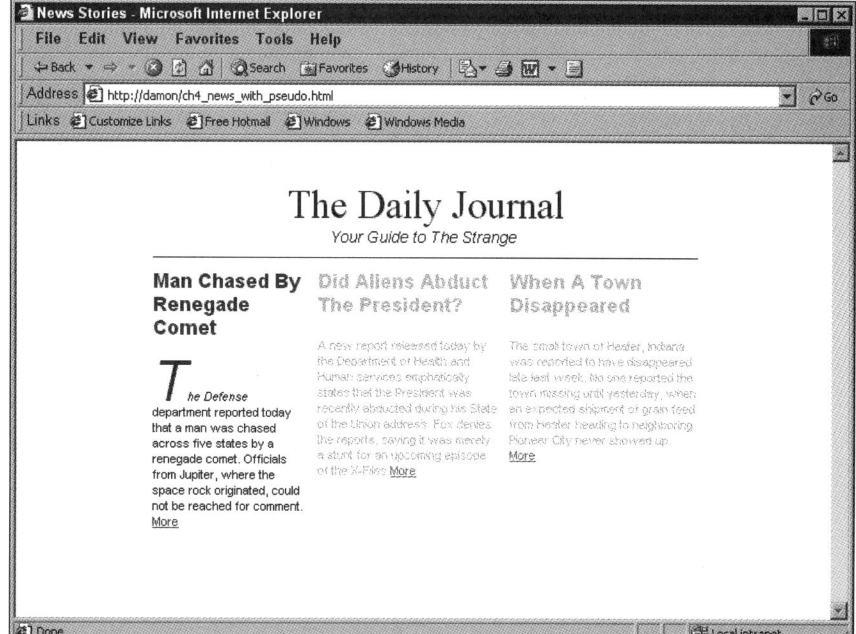

Figure 4-8: The first-line and first-letter combo platter.

You ain't got real class, just pseudo-class

Pseudo-classes, like their pseudo-element brethren, are a tad bit of a mystery. Roughly defined, *pseudo-classes* mess with content that may or may not be defined in the document structure. (Wow, that doesn't sound much better than what's written in the CSS specification.) Regardless, Web designers can truly benefit from some of these unique CSS features.

Getting rid of that annoying underline

One of the most annoying features in HTML — probably because it's so pervasive — is the underline on hyperlinks. Sure, it's functional, but wouldn't you like to get rid of those underlines every now and then? That's exactly the point behind what the `:link` and `:visited` pseudo-classes can help you do, along with a few other things.

If I want to get rid of the underline, I create a rule with the following syntax

```
a:link {text-decoration: none;}
```

and bingo! No more underline on rollover text. To eliminate the underline on a link that's been clicked, create a similar rule using `:visited`, that looks like this:

```
a:visited {text-decoration: none;}
```

If you set `text-decoration` to `none`, include in the rule a different color than the default text color for the link and visited states for the anchor.

The `:link` and `:visited` pseudo-classes are really designed only to be used with the `<A>` element because that's the one designed for links. In addition, don't be afraid to use other declarations on the `:link` and `:visited` pseudo-classes. Just be aware that because of differences in browsers, they may render things such as changes to text sizes and the like in different and sometimes unforeseen ways!

Some pseudo-classes are dynamic!

Some pseudo-classes are just designed for fun, and the dynamic pseudo-classes are just such a category. You'll find three pseudo-classes in this category: `:hover`, `:active`, and `:focus`.

`:hover` and `:active` work like `:link` and `:visited`, with the following features:

- **`:hover`:** In an interactive User Agent (browsers apply), using `:hover` will change styles when the user rolls over a given object (for example, an `<A>` element in HTML).
- **`:active`:** In that same interactive user agent (and yes, browsers still apply), using the `:active` pseudo-element will change styles when the user clicks the given element.

Figure 4-8 shows both `:hover` and `:active` in action on a Web page!

Again, much like the some of the pseudo-elements, `:hover` and `:active` can be dangerously temperamental in browsers. Be sure to tread carefully and check out the browser compatibility chart in Appendix A before going too far with these pseudo-classes.

`:focus` is a bit different than the others; it's a tad more specialized and designed to work with keyboard or mouse events, which are simply inputs from your keyboard or mouse (like the Enter button or a mouse click). Ideally, you'd use this pseudo-class to create a style when a keyboard input is passed. The implementation of this pseudo-class is not good. Netscape 6 supports it, and IE 5 on the Mac evidently supports it, but I could not confirm that. The following rule, when used in Netscape 6, will change an `A` element from its default size to 50 pixels high when clicked with a mouse:

```
A:focus {font-size: 50px;}
```

Other pseudo-classes waiting in the wings

A few more pseudo-classes are briefly worth mentioning here. Like `:focus`, they're a tad more obscure. The `first-child` pseudo-class can be an exceptionally useful function when you want to apply a style to the first child of an element within a document structure. This has great potential for other languages than HTML because the `parent:child` relationship in HTML is fairly limited. XML is a great example of a language that could use `first-child` for styling in very effective ways.

If you've ever maintained a site in multiple languages, you know just how tedious dealing with different languages can be. The `:lang` pseudo-class is designed to address some of the concerns of the common multilingual site, such as content length. Again, when combined with other languages such as XML, the applications of the `:lang` pseudo-class become more robust and exciting.

A potential problem with the pseudo-elements is that because they were created with the CSS Level 2 Specification, they haven't had time to be fully adopted yet by the browsers. As such, there's very little point in diving too deeply into them. I spend more time in this book discussing those that are well (or better) supported. To read more about the more obscure pseudo-elements, please visit the W3C at `www.w3.org`.

Chapter 5

Where There's a Property, There's a Unit

In This Chapter

- Color units any way you like them
- The six different length units and how to use them
- Other standard units and values

An integral part of defining a property is defining its value. This makes the declaration complete. And as much as you may wish, you can't give a property just any old number or text string. Well, let me clarify that statement. You *can* give a property any value you want, but unless you give the correct value (in most cases), the property won't work. You can't call a size value to a `font-family` property, for example. Moreover, the concept of error handling, or telling you what you did wrong, doesn't really exist in Cascading Style Sheets (CSS).

To define the value of a property, CSS supports a number of different unit systems. These *unit systems* apply to a number of different properties, giving designers a tremendous amount of flexibility in how they can style a page. In this chapter, I give you an overview of these unit systems so that you can have some idea about how much flexibility you have when you work with properties. For more on individual properties and the values that they can accept, peruse Appendix A.

Although CSS has a number of different units you can use, not all properties require a unit for the value. Fonts are a great example. There's no unit designation for a font type, nor is there one for font style (italic, oblique, and so forth). But, for things like font size, you definitely need to use units of measurement. This chapter only applies to those properties that actually require a value with a unit requirement, such as color, length, and size.

Color Your World

Color units in CSS will look shockingly familiar to you if you've ever added color to a font in HTML. That's because the color units are essentially the same in both HTML and CSS. Hey — something to celebrate! A consistency between Web technologies! Somebody break out the champagne!

With HTML, you can specify color in two basic ways: through a set of base colors, and through RGB (red/green/blue) values. CSS works in the same fashion when using the `color` property in a style rule, which I describe in the following two sections.

Naming your color

HTML and CSS allow for a set of 16 base colors that can be expressed by using a name as the value for the color. This is a handy and easy way to throw color into your styles and not have to worry about those pesky RGB values. So how can a name be a unit? Okay, you got me . . . it's a tad fuzzy. Even though the value is a named color, the browser will still convert that name to its proper RGB value and then render it to the screen. So, even though the value is technically a name, it's still using the RGB units. They're sneaky, those engineers who make this stuff.

The property for including a named color is simple and will probably look awfully familiar to you. For example, to set *black* as the named color, use the following:

```
color: black
```

Beautifully simple, no? The named colors in the HTML 4.0 specification — and therefore available in Cascading Style Sheets — include aqua, black, blue, fuchsia, gray, green, lime, maroon, navy, olive, purple, red, silver, teal, white, and yellow.

Here's something to keep in mind about named colors. Even though you may give something the named color of red, the result may not look like the same red on all machines. Differences in monitors can introduce variations in the colors when they appear onscreen. Remember that if you're working in a group environment, always be sure to check out your named colors on another machine, preferably on a different platform.

Seeing red . . . and green and blue

If you've ever been on an airplane or in a sports bar, you've probably seen the big honking projectors that are used for showing movies and TV programs.

You know, the ones that look like they'd really, really hurt if they ever came crashing down on your head. Look at one of these machines closely, and you'll see that it has a red, a green, and a blue lens. These lenses provide varying intensities of red, green, and blue light to create literally millions of different colors. A computer monitor does exactly the same thing. With CSS, you can specify exactly what the values of those three colors are gonna look like to create virtually any color you want! Now that, my friends, is power!

How does it all work? ***Hint:*** This is where the unit part comes into play. Just like playing with finger paints, you have to add certain amounts of this or that to get the color you want. When specifying an RGB value in CSS, you use the same concept. You have to specify how much red or green or blue you want for each color value you set.

No matter what unit scheme you're using, you always present the red values first, followed by the green values, and then the blue values because . . . well, that's just the way it's done. In CSS, you can specify RGB colors through the `color` property using one of three different unit schemes:

- **Percentages:** You can use percentages ranging from 0–100 percent for each of the red, green, and blue bands to produce the color you desire. For example, if you wanted solid red, create it like this

  ```
  color: rgb(100%, 0%, 0%)
  ```

  where the `100%` is the solid red, with no green or blue added.

  You can also use decimals in your percentages, so values such as 12.5 and 44.9 are also acceptable.

  Values above and below the 0 to 100 range are just tossed out by the browsers and reassigned to the nearest correct value. For example, a –20 value would be reassigned as 0, and a 5,000 value would be reassigned as 100.

  Although you can use decimals in percentage values, not all browsers support this equally. In some versions of Netscape, the browser will just drop the decimal point, creating absurdly large values, which then get reassigned to 100. So, it's generally best to avoid decimal points where possible.

- **RGB values:** In addition to percentages, here's another unit system for representing red, green, and blue values that uses integers between 0 and 255. This is the common system that is used in the printing world, and can be found in products such as a Photoshop. Take at look at these values in Table 5-1.

  Using solid red again as an example, the format would be as follows:

  ```
  color: rgb (255, 0, 0)
  ```

  where the `255` is the solid red, with no green or blue added.

Like when using percentages, values outside the 0 to 255 range are reassigned to their closest valid value. Unlike percentages, though, you can't use decimal places in this unit system.

Converting from percentages to the RGB value units is a snap. Just take your percentage value and multiply it by 255. Then round it up or down to the next closest integer and yee-ha!, instant conversion. To convert 45% red to an RGB value, multiple .45 x 255, which gives you 114.75. Round that answer up to 115 and you have your RGB value. (Or, you could just check out Table 5-1 below to get you started.

- **Hexadecimal:** Okay, so the geeks raise their ugly heads once again. If you've done some Web development in the past, you've probably seen the hexadecimal color scheme. This is not going to be intuitive to the average person who's never programmed or worked in a base 16 language before. If you'd like to know more about it, though, check out the sidebar "What the heck is hexadecimal?" elsewhere in this chapter.

  The basic syntax for hexadecimal RGB values looks like this:

  ```
  #RRGGBB
  ```

  where the # sign is the indicator that tells a browser that a hexadecimal value is heading that way. The RR, GG, and BB pairs are numbers or letters representing base 16 equivalents for red, green, and blue values.

  Using solid red as an example, the rule would look as follows:

  ```
  color: #FF0000
  ```

  Notice that in the hexadecimal format, the `rgb` that preceded the individual color units in the other two formats is dropped, as well as the parentheses.

Calling your colors

You've got a lot of options when it comes to choosing how you call your colors. Hexadecimal colors are perhaps the most common because they've been in use since the first version of HTML, but that's not necessarily a good reason to keep using them. I prefer RGB values and percentages because they're basically interchangeable, and they are also way more standardized when compared with other media, such as print and television. If you're building a site from scratch, you may consider using one of these other methods.

For reference, and more importantly to get you started, I've included a number of common colors and their values in Table 5-1 below. The order in this table is how you'll find them in the CSS specification.

What the heck is hexadecimal?

Here's a lesson in how to count with a combination of numbers and letters. When you and I count from one to ten, we're counting using base 10. This is a simple way to define working with ten numbers — in this case, the numbers 0 to 9 (after you get to nine, you start all over again with 0). Computers use base 2, only using 0s and 1s. Hexadecimal uses base 16, which uses 16 numbers and also letters.

Here's how to count in base 16 (hexadecimal):

00, 01, 02, 03, 04, 05, 06, 07, 08, 09, 0A, 0B, 0C, 0D, 0E, 0F

10, 11, 12, 13, 14, 15, 16, 17, 18, 19, 1A, 1B, 1C, 1D, 1E, 1F

20, 21, 22, 23, 24, 25, 26, 27, 28, 29, 2A, 2B, 2C, 2D, 2E, 2F

and so forth.

Convert base 16 to base 10, and this is what you get:

Base 16: 00, 01, 02, 03, 04, 05, 06, 07, 08, 09, 0A, 0B, 0C, 0D, 0E, 0F

Base 10: 00, 01, 02, 03, 04, 05, 06, 07, 08, 09, 10, 11, 12, 13, 14, 15,

Here's an easy, although not the most precise, way to convert a hexadecimal RGB value to a percentage.

- Take your RGB value and divide it by 16 (I'll use 131 for my RGB value).
- Dividing 131 by 16 gives you approximately 8.2 (rounded up).
- The first digit of this answer (8) tells you that the first number of your two-digit RGB value will fall within the eighth set of base 16 numbers, or the 80s.
- The second digit of this answer (.2) tells you that you're 20% of the way through the eighth set; 20% of 16 (remember, you're in base 16) is about 3.
- Add 80 plus 3 to arrive at your approximate RGB value of 83.

See, now how hard is that? Too hard. Well, if you're finding this all a little too much to follow, here is an easier way. Head on over to `www.datastic.com/tools/` and check out the Color Cop product. With this tool, you can simply pick an RGB color, and it provides the correct hexadecimal value.

Table 5-1 Named Colors and Their RGB Values

Named Color	*Percentage*	*RGB Value*	*Hexadecimal*
Black	(0%, 0%, 0%)	(0, 0, 0)	#000000
Green	(0%, 50%, 0%)	(0, 128, 0)	#008000
Silver	(75%, 75%, 75%)	(192, 192, 192)	#C0C0C0
Lime	(0%, 100%, 0%)	(0, 100, 0)	#00FF00
Gray	(50%, 50%, 50%)	(128, 128, 128)	#808080
Olive	(50%, 50%, 0%)	(128, 128, 0)	#808000

(continued)

Table 5-1 *(continued)*

Named Color	***Percentage***	***RGB Value***	***Hexadecimal***
White	(100%, 100%, 100%)	(255, 255, 0)	#FFFFFF
Yellow	(100%, 100%, 0%)	(255, 255, 0)	#FFFF00
Maroon	(50%, 0%, 0%)	(128, 0, 0)	#800000
Navy	(0%, 0%, 50%)	(0, 0, 128)	#000080
Red	(100%, 0%, 0%)	(255, 0, 0)	#FF0000
Blue	(0%, 0%, 100%)	(0, 0, 255)	#0000FF
Purple	(50%, 0%, 50%)	(128, 0, 128)	#800080
Teal	(0%, 50%, 50%)	(0, 128, 128)	#008080
Fuchsia	(100%, 0%, 100%)	(255, 0, 255)	#FF00FF
Aqua	(0%, 100%, 100%)	(0, 255, 255)	#00FFFF

The Long and the Short of It, Absolutely and Relatively

One of the great things about CSS is the freedom that it gives Web developers to develop styles the way they want to, as opposed to the way that some programmers think is best. As the old saying goes, everything comes with a price, and nowhere is that more apparent in the CSS specification than with length units.

Length unit choices abound in CSS. You can use any of the following units of measurement in your style sheets, although some are more widely used than others:

- Inches
- Centimeters
- Millimeters
- Picas
- Points
- Pixels
- Em
- x-height

No doubt, many of those units of measurement will look familiar to you if you've worked in the print world, or just written a document in Microsoft Word. Your challenge is to decide which one should you use for what — some of these units of measurements (such as picas, which are used predominantly for print publishing) just don't make practical sense for use in conjunction with a Web browser.

The CSS specification makes the distinction between absolute and relative lengths. *Absolute lengths*, which include inches, centimeters, millimeters, picas, and points, are fixed unit measurements. Relative lengths, such as pixels, em, and x-height, specify a unit length in relation to another length property.

Keep in mind these overarching rules when using length units. All these units support real numbers; that is, numbers that can include decimal points. Additionally, unit values can be either positive (+) or negative (–). And as far as syntax construction goes, unit designations should directly follow the number value, as in the following example:

```
Margin-right: 1.5in
```

Absolute units, practically speaking

Up to bat first is the easy and rarely used grouping of unit measurements.

Inches, centimeters, and millimeters are the old standbys for measurement. A *point* is described, at least by the CSS specification, as $\frac{1}{72}$ of an inch. And a *pica* is equal to 12 points, or $\frac{12}{72}$ of an inch, if you prefer.

Now comes the inevitable argument about which of these units is the best for measurement. Designers love to argue points versus picas, and residents of the United States will argue inches and feet versus the metric system any day of the week. The truth is that in the world of computer displays, your choice of measurement doesn't really matter one way or another because all these units of measurement aren't all that useful for items rendered to the screen. If, for example, you were designing HTML documents to be printed, then using these units of measurements might be valuable. Most Web designers, however, make pages for the screen; unfortunately, most browsers don't know enough about an individual's monitor settings to be able to render .5 inch accurately.

Even the CSS specification itself downplays the usefulness of these measurements: "Absolute length units are only useful when the physical properties of the output medium are known." Not exactly an endorsement, when you get right down to it.

If you cannot quench your unstoppable thirst to use these unit measurements, all the syntax that you'll need to know is in Table 5-2.

Table 5-2 Absolute Length Unit Syntax

Unit	Style Representation	Example
inches	in	margin-left: 1.0in
centimeters	cm	margin-top: 3cm
millimeters	mm	line-height: 7mm
points	pt	font-size: 12pt
picas	pc	font-size: 2pc

Relatively easy units

The more useful kin of the unit kinds are the three relative units. These units are defined in relationship to some other length property. A *pixel,* which is defined in relationship to the monitor, is the one most often used in Web authoring, and by far the easiest to understand. The other two, *em* and *x-height*, are defined in relationship to elements in the document.

The ever-changing pixel

Look really closely at a computer monitor (like one day when you're at work trying not to fall asleep from boredom), and you'll see that it's made up of a bunch of tiny little dots, nested within a bunch of little boxes. Each one of those boxes is a pixel. When you set your monitor to a resolution of 1024 x 768, or 800 x 600, you're specifying the number of boxes from one end of the screen to the other, both horizontally and vertically.

Think about this for a moment, and you can see how this can be a bit of a conundrum. When my monitor is set to 800 pixels wide, the relative length of a pixel is larger than when my monitor is set at 1024 pixels wide. Knowing that, how can I accurately expect to measure distance? Similarly, if I have two monitors side by side, one 15 inches wide and the other 21 inches wide, I have the same kind of problem — only now the variable isn't the screen resolution but the actual screen itself.

Despite all this angst, pixels are ironically enough the preferred unit of measure for displays. Almost by accident, the pixel became the default unit of measure when Web designers started using graphics in Web development.

Pixels are a great way to measure a graphic's size. For those of you who have ever built a table in HTML, you know that the best way to create a table that will never move, no matter what browser you're viewing it in, is to use graphics of fixed sizes to lock the table into place.

Because of these reasons, the pixel almost always wins. In Chapter 4, I use pixels to describe the font sizes of a newspaper article. The following bit of code shows some common ways in which pixels can be used in styles, such as to call position, font size, and margins. See the results in Figure 5-1.

```
.pixel_usage {
      position: absolute;
      top: 100px;
      left: 100px;
      width: 300px;
      font-family : Arial, Helvetica, sans-serif;
      font-size : 11px;
      margin-left: 1px;
margin-right: 1px;
margin-top: 2px;
margin-bottom: 2px;
}
```

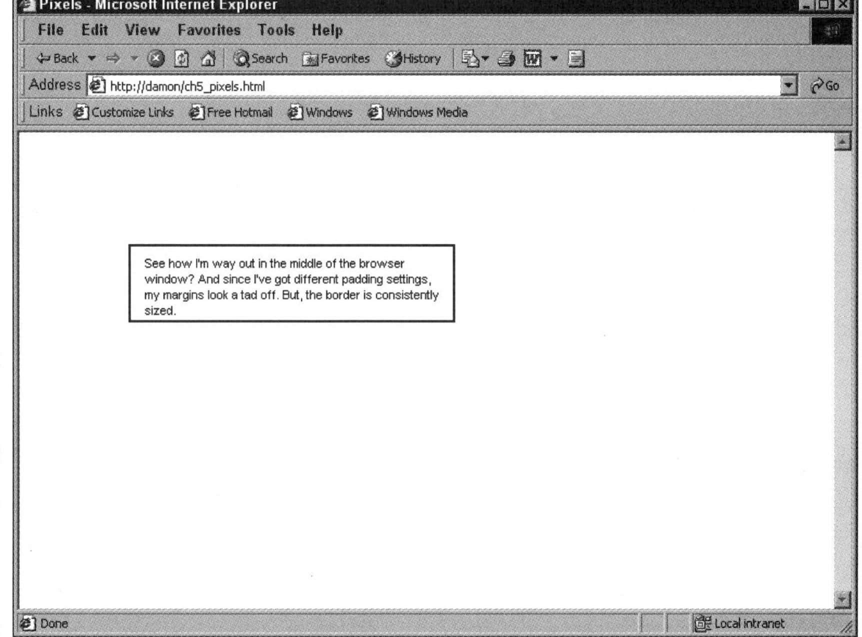

Figure 5-1: Pixels are the most common form of measurement in Web development.

The em connection to other elements

I'm here to tell you how incredibly smart you are and don't even know it. You already know what an em is. (C'mon . . . work with me, here.) Um, the amount of space a lowercase letter *m* takes up? Correct! Thank you for playing along, Contestant Number 1!

In CSS terms, em is dictated by the default size of an element using a different measurement unit. Here's an example. Say I set the following rule for all `<P>` elements:

```
P { font-family: Arial;
   font-size: 12px;
   }
```

This rule dictates that all text contained within a `P` element will be 12 pixels high. Now, say I've got the following bit of text within a `P` element:

```
<p>Now, tell me again why I'd ever want to use the em
        length?</p>
```

This would display as 12-pixel-high Arial text, as shown in Figure 5-2.

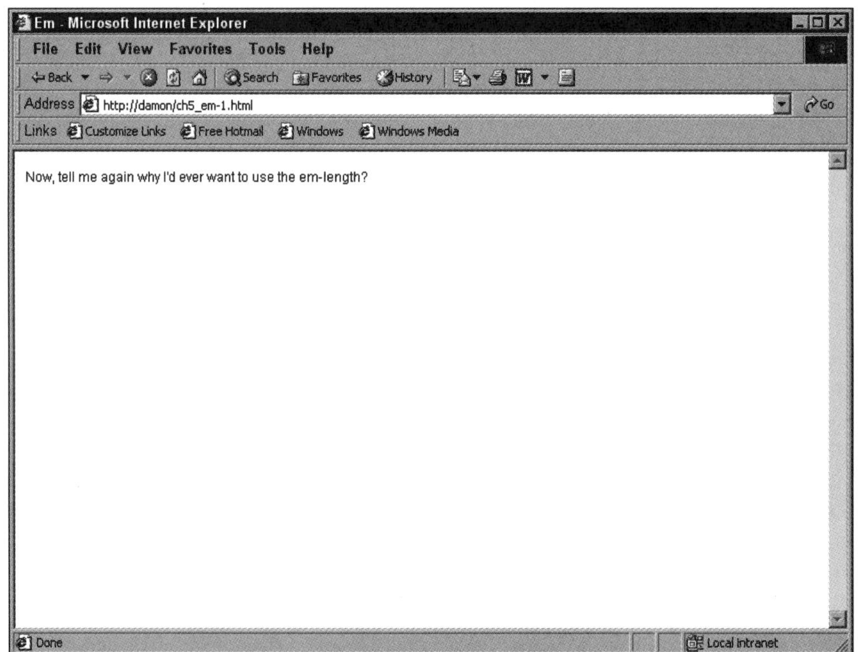

Figure 5-2: Here's some text without an em.

So far, everything's working according to plan. Here I'll added another rule to my style sheet as follows:

```
SPAN {
font-family: Arial;
font-size: 2em;
    }
```

To my original text in the P element, I'm instead going to make the following change:

```
<p>Now, tell me again why <span>I'd ever want to use</span>
        the em length?</p>
```

The net result is that the text *I'd ever want to use* becomes twice as large — in this case, 24px — as the rest of the text in the P element, as shown in Figure 5-3. What happened in this example is that the SPAN rule dictates that whatever it encompasses becomes twice as large as the specified font.

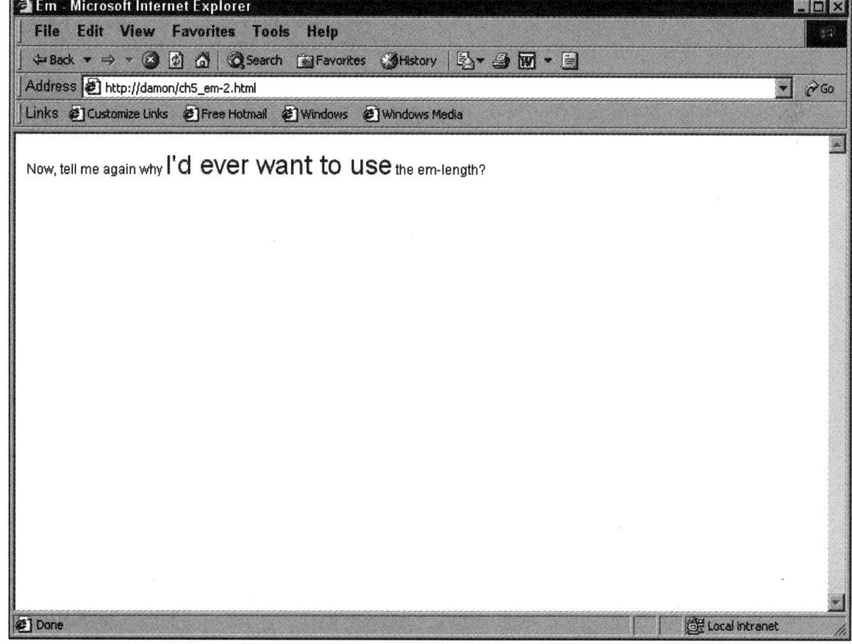

Figure 5-3: The SPAN element calls a rule that sets the text to twice the size of the default P element.

The x-height factor

The term x-height dates back to the invention of the printing press. *x-height* is the height from top to bottom of the lowercase *x* in a given typeface. Consequently, x-height depends on the font being used. This wouldn't be a problem if everyone in the known universe used Times New Roman, but then you wouldn't need Cascading Style Sheets at all.

Admittedly, x-height has very limited uses. In fact, after more than four years using style sheets, I'm hard pressed to think of an instance when using x-height was a grand idea, but what the heck! — maybe you'll be the first to think of a really cool application for this device. Here's how it works.

Suppose that I've got the very simple following rule in my style sheet:

```
<STYLE>
.xheight {
   font-size: 2ex;
       }
</STYLE>
```

and in the body of my HTML document, I've created the following ultra simple example:

```
<p class="xheight"><font face="arial">Default Arial at
           2x</font></p>
<p class="xheight"><font face="Times New Roman">Default Times
           New Roman at 2x</font></p>
<p class="xheight"><font face="Courier">Default Courier at
           2x</font></p>
<p class="xheight"><font face="Verdana">Default Verdana at
           2x</font></p>
<p class="xheight"><font face="Helvetica">Default Helvetica
           2x</font></p>
```

What x-height does in this example is take the default size of the font and multiply it by twice the x-height for that font. The results, shown in Figure 5-4, are varying sizes for each of the font faces.

Many fonts don't embed a default value for x-height in the font itself, which means that the browser has to calculate the value on its own. Both Internet Explorer (IE) and Netscape currently assume that they can calculate the default value for x-height by using one half of the value for em. This estimate isn't entirely accurate, but in most cases, it's a reasonable approximation.

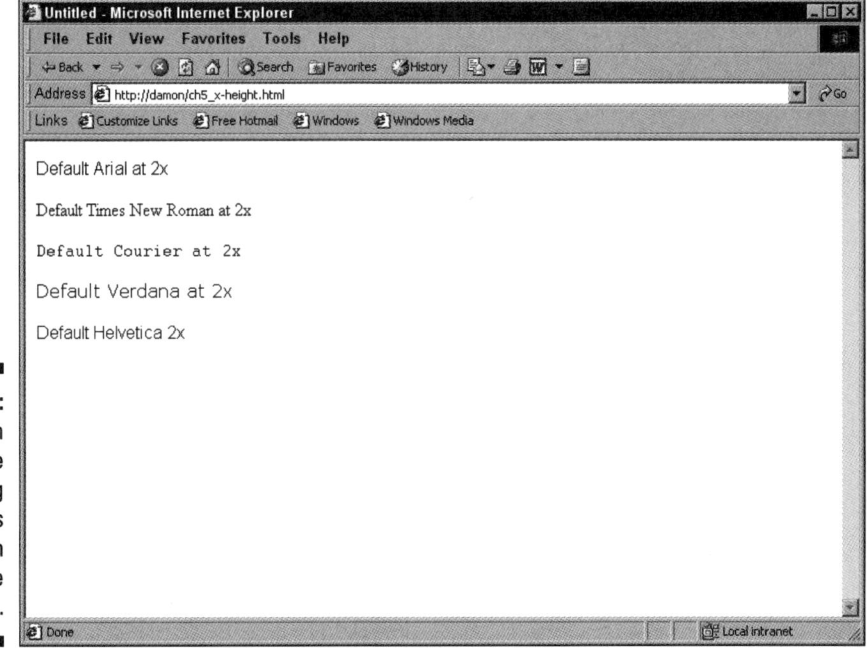

Figure 5-4: x-height can produce varying results based on the type of font.

Discovering More Units

Everyone uses the obvious and common color and length units in CSS. You also have some others at your disposal, however, including:

- **Percentage units:** These are used mostly for color.
- **URLs:** This is just a standard definition of a URL.
- **Angle units and values:** These are used for aural style sheets to determine location of sound.
- **Time value:** Also used for aural style sheets, these values are used to indicate time.
- **Frequency value:** These are used mainly to determine pitch.

Unless you're going to be dealing with some of the more obscure elements of CSS, such as developing aural style sheets, then some of these may not be of much value to you. Get it, *value*?! (Ah, sometimes I kill myself . . . okay, maybe not.) Regardless, read through the following sections to discover which of these more rare units may be of use to you.

Using percentages for more than color

In the CSS specification, percentage units are primarily used to call color values. (Skip back to the earlier section "Seeing red . . . and green and blue" for more on color values.) The basic rules are as follows:

- Percentages can be a real number; thus, they support decimal places.
- Percentages can be either positive or negative.
- Percentages must be followed directly by a % sign.

Here's a simple example to describe how percentages work in other contexts. Suppose that I have all my <P> tags set up as follows:

```
P {
   font-family: arial;
   font-size: 12px;
   text-indent: 10%;
   }
```

In the body of my HTML document, I include the following text:

```
<P> Hey, why am I so far away from the left side of the
            browser window. </P>
```

As you can see in Figure 5-5, the resulting text will be indented 10 percent from the left side of the screen.

URL: A unit or a value?

In CSS, you can specify a URL to use for applications like the background image of a page. If you want to argue semantics, a URL technically isn't really a unit. The CSS specification, however, refers to a `url` unit that includes a URL even though the syntax shows it in the value location.

The syntax to add a URL unit is pretty straightforward, and looks like this:

```
background:
            url("http://www.mysite.com/images/background.gif")
```

The rules for the URL value are also pretty straightforward:

- The rule must include `url`, followed directly by an opening parenthesis: (
- The URL itself can be standalone, or bracketed either by double quotes: " " ; or by single quotes: ' '

- The URL must be followed by a closing parenthesis:)
- Single spaces are allowed in the rule except as noted by the first bullet in this list

With all properties that call for a URL, you can use either an absolute or a relative URL. Here's an example of an absolute URL

```
(http://www.mysite.com/images/background.gif)
```

and an example of a relative URL

```
/images/background.gif)
```

In general, using the relative URL is better because if the folders move or the name of the site changes, then the URL usually remains unaffected.

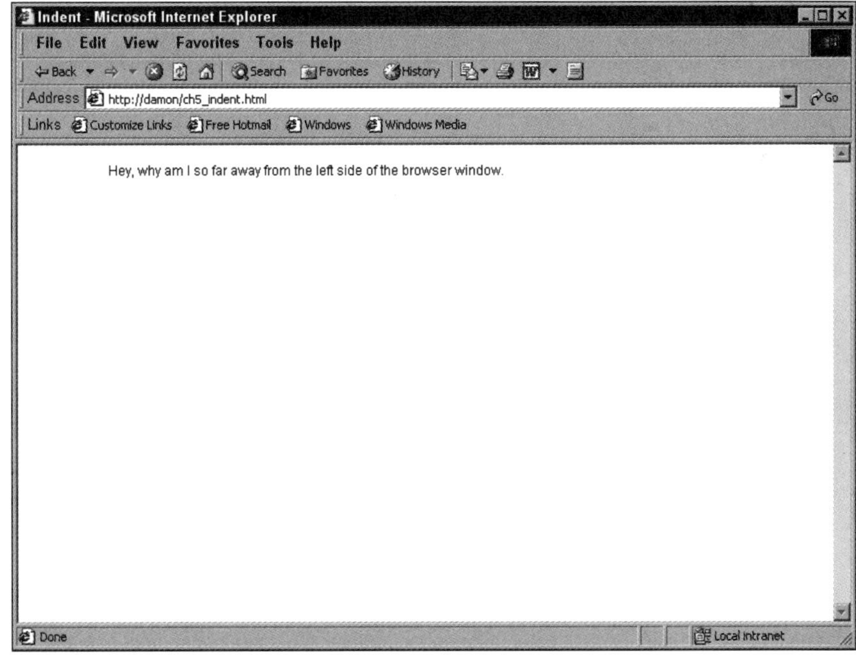

Figure 5-5: Use percentages to indent text.

The aural units: Angle, time, and frequency

Three different units (angle, time, and frequency) that apply specifically to these styles are worth mentioning here. Aural style sheets, which are geared for people who are visually impaired, provide an auditory representation of the HTML content. (I discuss aural style sheets in more detail in Chapter 15.) Specifically, the various aural style sheet units do the following:

- **Angle:** You use the angle unit to produce special sounds in a 3-dimensional sound environment. Mind you, this is all theoretical, because aural style sheets aren't yet fully supported by any browser. The units for angle are either in degrees (`deg`), grads (`grad`), or radians (`rad`), and follow the same rules as the length units I describe in the earlier section "The Long and the Short of It, Absolutely and Relatively."
- **Time:** With aural style sheets, you can stop, pause, and play sounds. Because you've got to have some sort of idea about how long a sound should play, and when it should pause or stop, time values in CSS are represented in two fashions: milliseconds (`ms`) and seconds (`s`).
- **Frequencies:** Frequency is a common unit of measurement. In this case, the units are hertz (Hz) and kilohertz (kHz).

Chapter 6

CSS Font and Text Properties

In This Chapter

- Formatting text with font properties
- Getting creative with text decoration
- Specifying text properties
- Lining up with text alignment
- Adding emphasis with indents
- Creating visual breaks with text spacing

If you just want to dabble with Cascading Style Sheets (CSS), font and text properties are a great place to start because they're all well supported, easy to understand (unless of course, something goes terribly wrong), and easy to incorporate into your existing site. Especially if you plan to overhaul your site completely, text properties are a good place to start because they provide an easy way to set some initials rules and structure for your site.

Making good use of font and text properties really kicks your work with CSS into overdrive. In this chapter, I show you how choosing fonts and formatting text produce a lot of look-here, try-this, isn't-this-a-cool-look ways to present information on your Web pages.

A Font of Fonts

The CSS specification, as well as a number of books, devotes an incredible amount of page space to getting up and running on the font properties. Here, I'll give you the basics so you can learn how to hit the ground running with the font properties in no time flat! (Unless, of course, you'd rather that I bore you with a ton of details, charts, diagrams, and blueprints. . . .)

Different platforms (PC, Macintosh, and Unix) render fonts and font families differently. Simply put, this means that fonts look different on different platforms. Although text in 8-point Times may look fine on a PC, it's too tiny on the Mac to be viewable. This is more proof that you should always test everything you build on as many platforms as you can when you're creating Web sites.

Font-family values

One of the many great things about CSS is that you don't really have to worry about individual fonts anymore. If you're familiar with fontography at all, you know how much of a pain remembering the names of individual fonts can be. With the `font-family` property, you no longer have to worry about names such as *Arial Black Condensed Extended Oblique Italic Gothic.* You can specify an entire family of fonts (instead of specifying an individual font) and let the browser worry about choosing the right font. CSS enables you to be a little more general in your approach to setting fonts in your pages, and therefore, reach a broader group of people.

With the `font-family` property, you can specify both font family names as well as generic fonts (which leave the picking of the actual font up to the browser). In either case, the syntax is exactly the same, and follows this basic rule:

```
H1 {font-family: Arial;}
```

With `font-family`, you also have the ability to specify more than one font together. The advantage in this is that you can account for a multitude of platforms within a single rule. Building on the preceding example, I could extend it to include support for both the Mac and Unix platforms, like this:

```
H1 {font-family: Arial, Helvetica, sans-serif;}
```

As you probably noticed, a comma and a space separate the fonts. When you list multiple fonts, the browser reads through the list and takes the first one available on the user's machine.

Note the term *sans-serif* at the end of the previous example. That indicates a generic font — I go into more detail about this (as well to define specific fonts) in upcoming sections.

Why should I care about installed fonts?

One thing to be keenly aware of when selecting non-standard fonts (which is to say anything besides Arial, Helvetica, Geneva, Verdana, and Times) is that some users may not have those fonts you choose on their computers. What happens then? Glad you asked! Suppose that you create a rule to use the Copperplate font, which you don't have on your computer, for all your `H1` elements, like this:

```
H1 {font-family: copperplate;}
```

Check out the resulting display in Figure 6-1. The `H1` element ignored the font you called because it couldn't find it — instead, the page's default (yawn) font (Times) was applied.

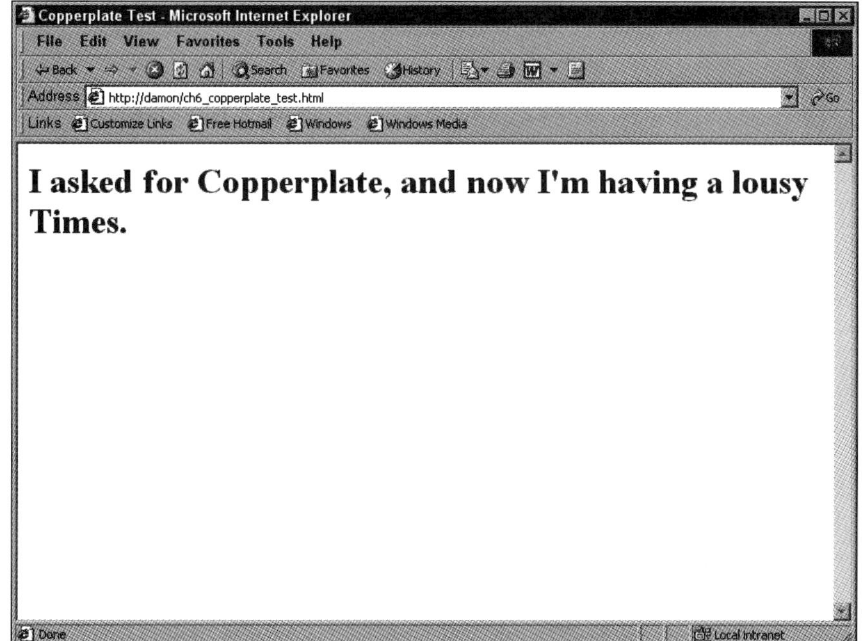

Figure 6-1: Hey! That's not Copperplate!

Beware of spaces and symbols!

Be wary of some rules when creating declarations with `font-family`. If the `font-family` name has a space in it, then it has to be enclosed in single quotes. If I want all my `P` elements to be Times New Roman, my rule must include single quotation marks as shown in the following code snippet — otherwise the browser might get confused about what the font really is:

```
P {font-family: 'Times New Roman';}
```

Similarly, if the font name includes symbols (for example #, &, $, @), then the entire font name also needs to be included in quotes.

Single, not double quotes, are used to maintain integrity when using inline styles, which are styles that are called directly from an HTML element.

Here's how to specify Times New Roman for a specific `P` element:

```
<P style="font-family: 'Times New Roman';">...</P>
```

This inline style wouldn't work if CSS allowed the double quote because the close quote would be read before the word Times, creating an invalid `<P>` tag. Although it would render the element, it wouldn't give you the style you were looking for.

The most common fonts used in Web development are Arial (PC), Times (Mac and PC), Verdana (PC), Helvetica (Mac), and Courier (PC). A good place to check out font information on the Web is the typography section of the CNET builder.com site, which you find at `builder.cnet.com/webbuilding/0-7277.html`.

Generic font families are not so generic

Using the term *generic* to describe fonts is a bit of a misnomer. CSS specifies some common categorizations of fonts (such as serif and sans-serif), and then leaves it up to the browser to pick the closest one based on what's available on the user's computer.

In effect, this categorization of fonts serves mostly as a safety net for the Web designer because chances are pretty good that the user's computer will have a compatible font available to use. If I specify a number of obscure fonts that I know people won't have — or if I'm just lazy and don't care what specific fonts users have on their machines — I can use the generic font families to ensure that the page still looks good.

In Table 6-1, I describe these generic fonts, all of which can be called from the `font-family` property. Look at Figure 6-2 to see each of the generic fonts in action.

Table 6-1 Generic Fonts in CSS

Name	*CSS Value*	*Description*	*Examples*
Serif	serif	A typical typographic font, usually seen in newspapers	Times, Bodoni, Garamond
Sans-serif	sans-serif	Traditionally lacks the angled points and hooks of serif fonts	Arial, Helvetica, Verdana, Universe
Cursive	cursive	Tends to have joining strokes, making them noticeably different than an italic font	Zapf-Chancery
Fantasy	fantasy	A decorative font	Cottonwood
Monospace	monospace	A very simple and evenly spaced font, much like a typewriter	Courier

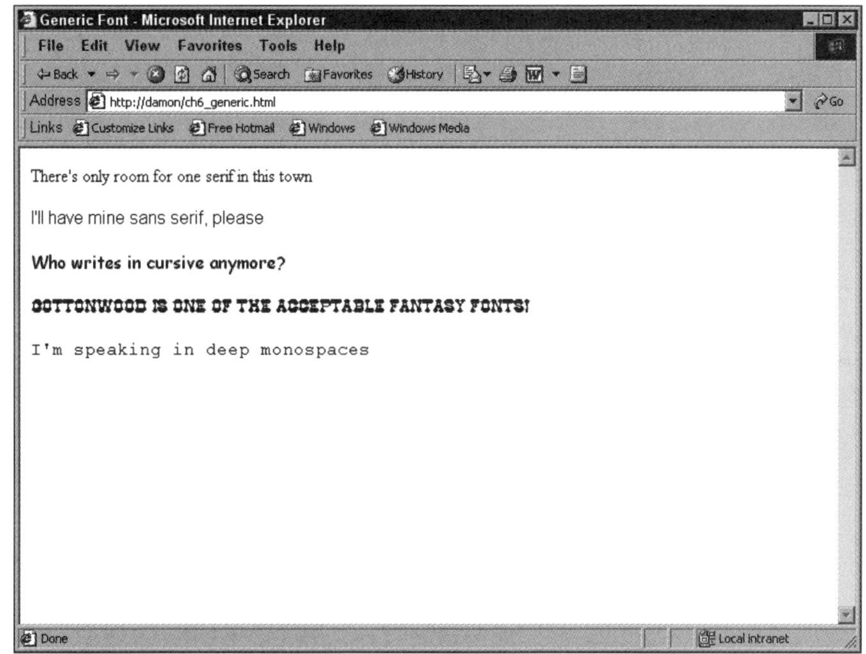

Figure 6-2: The generic fonts, here to serve you!

Add fonts to the `font-family` property to ensure that your users get the proper font delivered regardless of which platform they have. Get in the habit of adding a generic font at the end of every font property declaration so that your users at least get a font in the same category that you intended for them to get.

Dressing Up Your Fonts!

Selecting a font is only half the fun. You can also prescribe a number of other attributes, such as size and style, as well as other more obscure stylistic elements such as width and boldness. These attributes give you the control you need to create compelling text styles on the screen; as you spread your creative wings, refer back to these sections for examples on the proper syntax to use.

Font-size, with your hosts Absolute and Relative

Font-size dictates the size of the font, as you may have guessed. The `font-size` property can accept two different kinds of values, absolute values and relative values. Absolute and relative mean something different in this context than they did when you saw them back in Chapter 5. Here, absolute means a fixed sized based on a length value. Relative simply means that the size of a font will be in relation to another font size specified someplace else in the document. Here are all four different value types you can specify for `font-size`:

- **Absolute size:** This is a series of pre-set values that the CSS specification includes for font sizing. The list of absolute sizes includes the following values:
  - xx-small
  - x-small
  - small
  - medium
  - large
  - x-large
  - xx-large

  These values assume that medium is the default size for the page, and then scale the values for the other sizes up or down accordingly, using a suggested scaling factor of 1.2 for each value. Why use a scaling factor of 1.2? Who knows, but they swear in the CSS specifications that a scaling factor of 1.5 was too big. What's that translate to, roughly? Check out what text looks like (Figure 6-3) when you set its value from really, really small to really, really large.

- **Relative size:** I love this value set because it's so, well, blunt. Relative size has only two values: `larger` and `smaller`. Clever, eh? Here's how they work. Suppose I have the following rule set up in my style sheet:

  ```
      P {
  font-family: Arial, Helvetica, sans-serif;
  font-size: 14px;
            }
  ```

  Then, in the body of my document, I include the following HTML and CSS combo platter:

```
<P>Did I mention I love the relative values for font-
        size? With it, I can make the text <span
        style="font-size: larger;">larger</span> or <span
        style="font-size: smaller;">smaller</span></P>
```

The resulting output to the screen, as shown in Figure 6-4, is that the word *larger* is larger than the other words in the sentence, and the word *smaller* is smaller than other words in the sentence!

Relative size employs *inheritance*, which is a fancy way of saying that one element got its place in the document hierarchy from another element in the document. I take a much closer look at inheritance in Chapter 9.

- **Length:** Length is another type of absolute value, using a numeric value and unit expression that is assigned to the `font-size` property. In fact, this is the most common way of expressing font size. In Chapter 5, I discuss that you can use any number of different units to express the size of the font, including centimeters, millimeters, inches, pixels, points, picas, em, and x-height units. (Notice that in the previous example, I use a pixel size — abbreviated *px* — for the font size.)

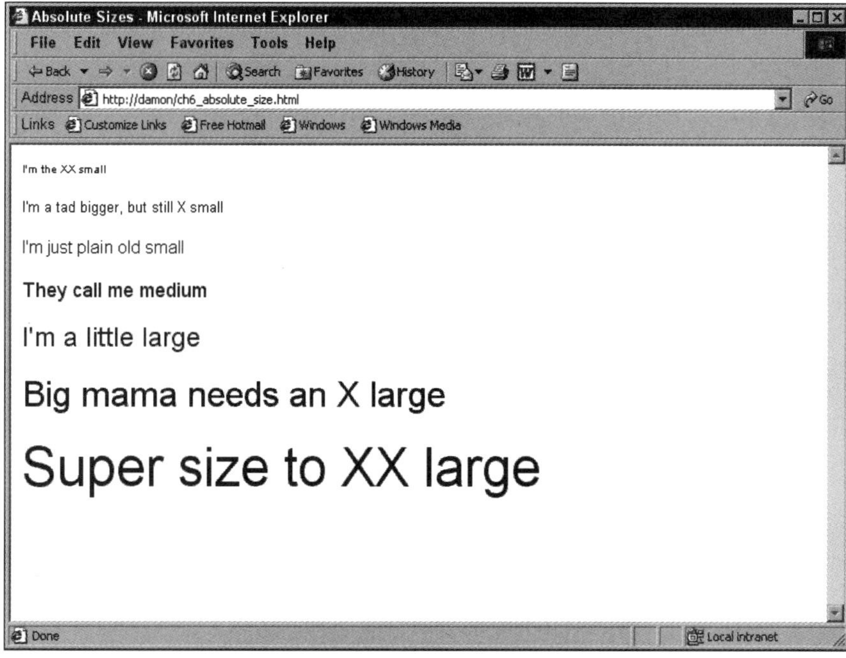

Figure 6-3: Use absolute size to determine font size.

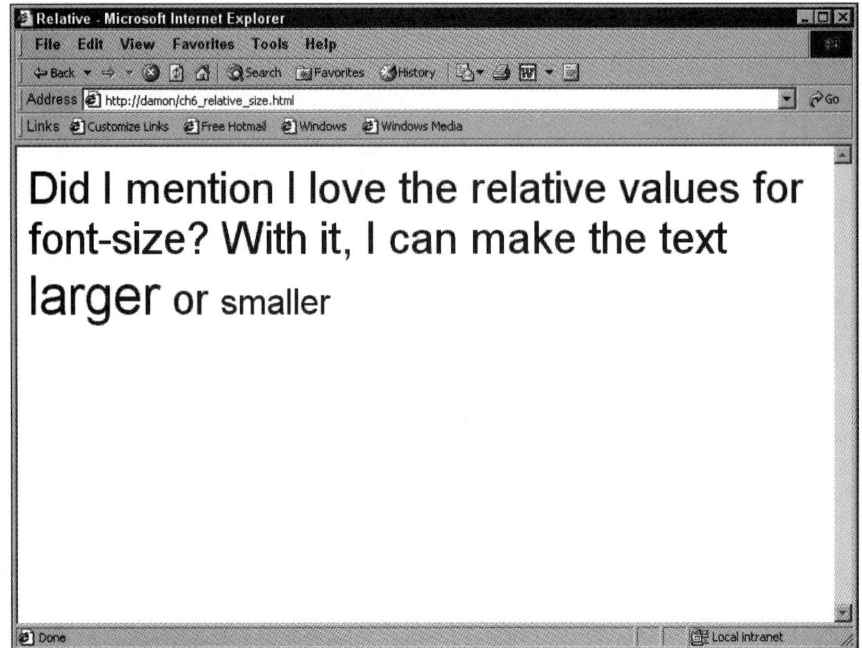

Figure 6-4: Me larger, you smaller. Oh, the simplicity!

If I use the following P elements in my document

```
<P style="font-size: 20px">Look, I'm 20 Pixels high!</P>
<P style="font-size: .5in">Look, I'm .5 Inch high!</P>
<P style="font-size: 1cm">Look, I'm 1 Centimeter
        high!</P>
<P style="font-size: 10mm">Look, I'm 10 Millimeters
        high!</P>
<P style="font-size: 12pt">Look, I'm 12 Points high!</P>
<P style="font-size: 2pc">Look, I'm 2 Picas high!</P>
<P style="font-size: 2em">Look, I'm 2 EMs high!</P>
<P style="font-size: 2ex">Look, I'm 2 EXs high!</P>
```

and I set the default typestyle to Arial, it would generate a page that looks remarkably like Figure 6-5.

- **Percentages:** Percentages are also quite clever, and they work pretty much like relative size that I describe earlier. The only difference is that instead of using those rather clumsy larger and smaller values, you can set a percentage (in the form of a real number) followed directly (no space) by a % sign.

```
<P>Did I mention I like using a percentage for font-size
        as well? With it, I can make the text <span
        style="font-size: 200%;">200% larger</span> or
        <span style="font-size: 75%;">75% smaller</span>
        with a couple of handy keystrokes! </P>
```

See the resulting page in Figure 6-6. Using a percentage as a relative value gives the Web designer a tremendous amount of flexibility when specifying font sizes.

These fonts are stylin'

After you set your font family and font size, add a little spice to your creation from four different style properties, which include:

- `font-style`: For creating italic and oblique (tilted to the right) text
- `font-weight`: For controlling the boldness of the font
- `font-stretch`: For specifying how wide or narrow the font should be
- `font-variant`: For setting fonts to display in different forms, such as small caps

Collectively, these properties give you almost as much control over the display of text as you'd expect from a word-processing application such as Microsoft Word, as shown in Figure 6-7.

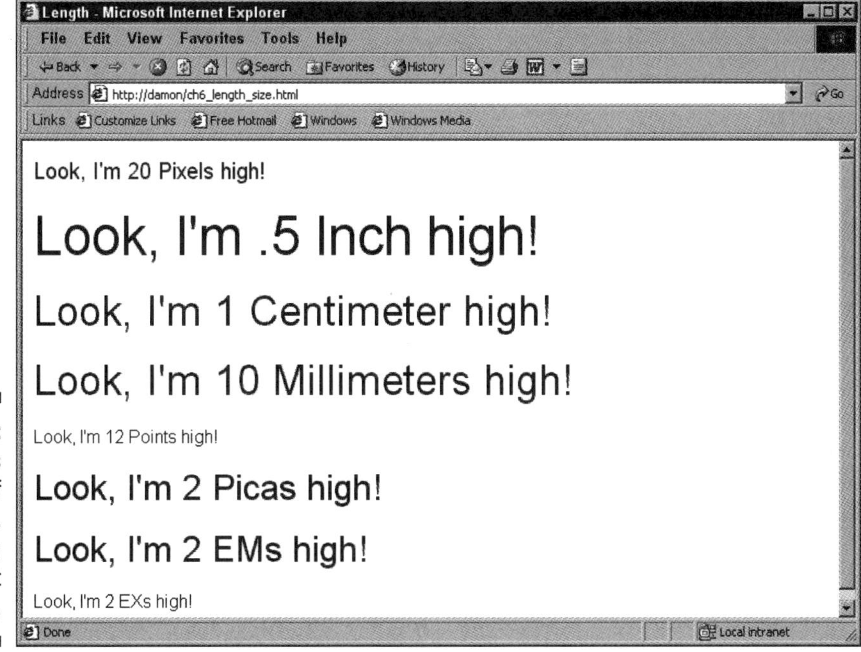

Figure 6-5: Wow, that's a lot of heights . . . getting downright dizzy.

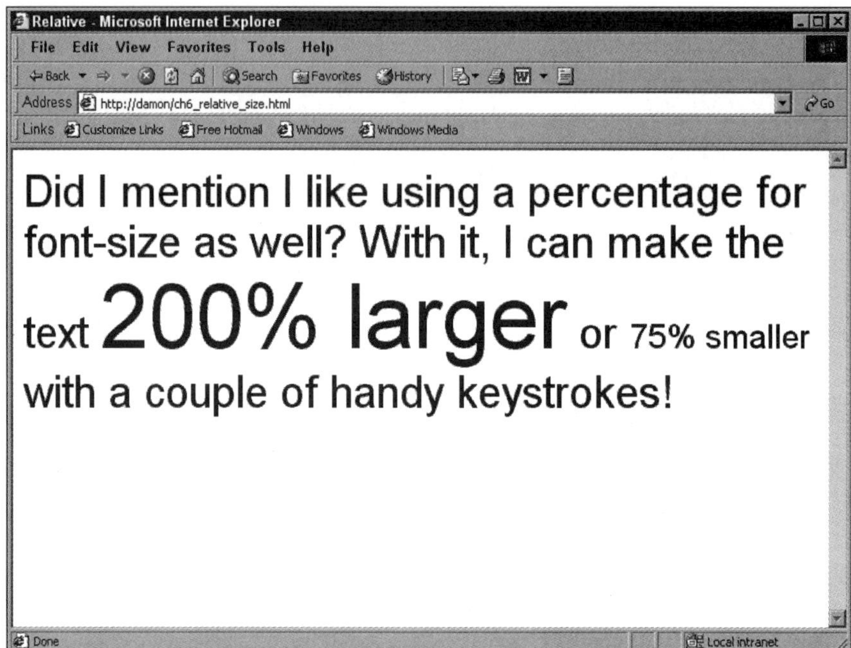

Figure 6-6: Percentages work well for changing font size.

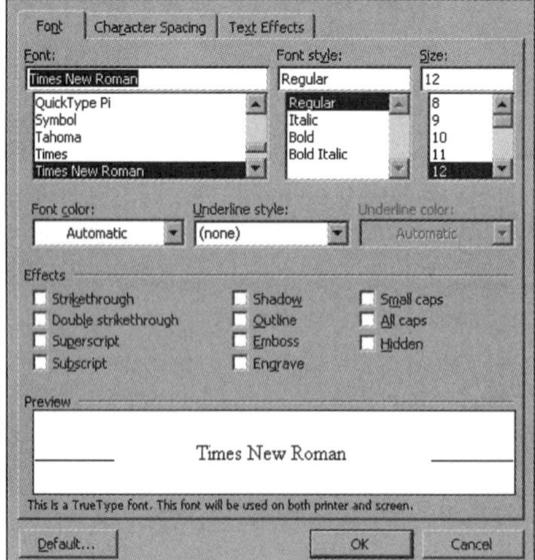

Figure 6-7: Style your fonts bold, slanted, fat, skinny . . . with CSS, you are the master.

These text-formatting properties are all easy to use, and are also universally accepted by the browsers. However, keep in mind that although these properties are fairly common, they still may not look identical on different browsers or platforms. (All these properties can also have their values inherited from other styles. I discuss inheritance in Chapter 9.)

Of all these properties, `font-stretch` is the one that's the most likely to give you the greatest degree of variability in the results from browser to browser. I recommend steering clear of it if you're really concerned about having your font styles look identical on more than just one platform.

In Table 6-2, I list the available values for each of these four style properties, along with what those values mean.

Table 6-2 Style Properties and Their Values

Property	*Values*	*Description*
font-style	normal, italic, oblique	Use normal when inheriting some other font-style and you want to reset the font to having no style settings at all; use italic to make text italic; use oblique to make text tilt to the right.
font-weight	normal, bold, bolder, lighter, 100, 200, 300, 400, 500, 600, 700, 800, 900	The numbers represent different font weights (100 is the lightest). *Normal* is equal to 400. *Bold* is equal to 700. *Bolder* and *lighter* represent the next level either up or down from the inherited style. No value can go over 900 or below 100.
font-stretch	ultra-condensed, extra-condensed, condensed, semi-condensed, normal, semi-expanded, expanded, extra-expanded, ultra-expanded, wider, narrower	These values are in sequential order from narrowest to widest, except for *wider* and *narrower*, which represent the next wider or narrower level from the inherited style.
font-variant	normal, small-caps	At present, this is the simplest of the lot. The only variant is *small-caps. Normal* resets the inherited value back to no variant at all.

Enough Fonts: Gimme Some Text

Don't assume that font and text are synonymous. A *font* is defined by how its characters look in general — plain, fancy, leggy, squatty, flowing, blocky —

which you can further refine (modify) by applying styles to, such as bold or italics. *Text* comprises the blocks of words or headlines that you create in a certain font. You can apply different styles to text, also, but the font that you choose is the fundamental building block. The text properties in CSS tend to deal more strictly with issues of formatting of text rather than individual fonts.

In the remainder of this chapter, I discuss text formatting, but see Chapter 7 for visual formatting, which covers margins, borders, line height, and padding.

Hanging text decorations on the tree

If you were around for the first days of HTML, you'll recall the tag called `<BLINK>...</BLINK>`. As you can probably figure out from its name, text inside the `<BLINK>` tag would blink like it was 1977 all over again, and *Saturday Night Fever* was the number one movie in America.

Well, the `<BLINK>` tag may be gone, but the idea lives on in the `text-decoration` property. You can use this property to make content stand out or just look cool. Specifically, here's what you can do with the `text-decoration` property:

- Underline your text.
- Overline your text, which puts a line above the text.
- ~~Strikethrough~~ your text, which puts a line straight though the text; CSS calls this *line-through*.
- Blink . . . blink . . . blink your text.
- Do nothing with your text, which resets text to plain when you've inherited a different `text-decoration` value.

Don't fall too deeply in love or go too overboard with the `blink` value because browsers aren't required to support this feature. In fact, Internet Explorer has chosen not to support it, which is just a darn shame. Boo!

The following code snippet includes all possible values for the `text-decoration` property:

```
.underline {
   text-decoration: underline;
   }
.overline {
   text-decoration: overline;
   }
.line-through {
```

```
        text-decoration: line-through;
        }
    .blink   {
        text-decoration: blink;
        }
    .boring   {
        text-decoration: none;
        }
```

In Figure 6-8, see the results of what these values will generate onscreen, assuming that the default font used is Arial 12px. And, no, you can't see the blinking, but you get the idea . . . idea . . . idea.

Only the shadow knows

CSS2 introduced a new property: `text-shadow`. To be brutally honest, this property just doesn't get a lot of play in the Web design world. Maybe it's because it's too much of a designer property, and integrators don't like to use it. Or maybe — just maybe — it's widely ignored because none of the major browsers have implemented it yet. My money's on the latter.

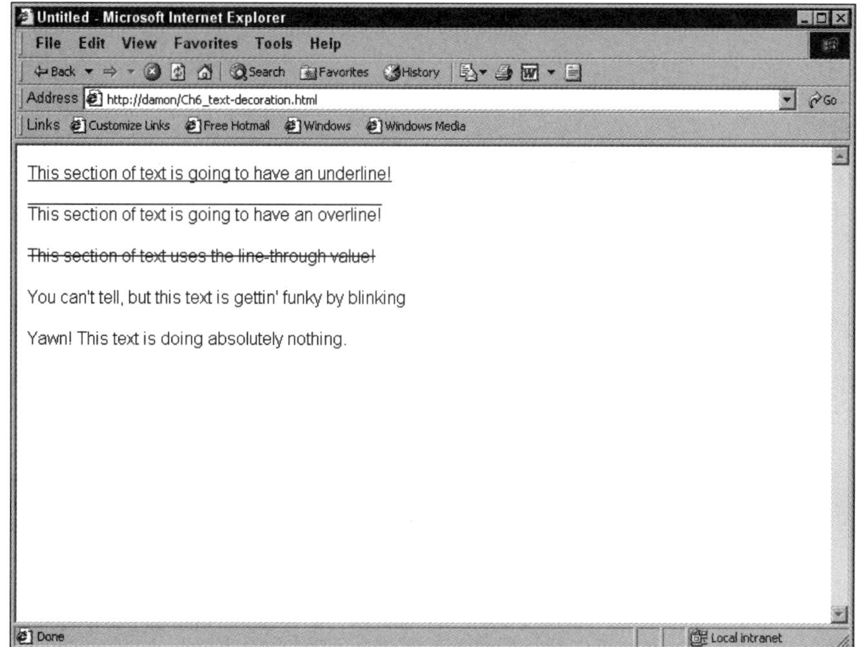

Figure 6-8: The various styles of text-decoration.

When you use this property, however, you can effectively simulate what the shadowing tools can do in Photoshop (cool!), and to a lesser degree, what Word and PowerPoint can do. Use `text-shadow` to specify:

- The horizontal and vertical distance of the shadow
- The direction of the shadow (right or left)
- The blur radius of the shadow (how blurry should the shadow be)
- The number of shadows (layers of shadows on top of one another)

This puppy is just flat-out cool. Here are some style rules to give you an idea of how it works. I chose pixels as my units, but you could substitute any of the units that CSS allows:

```
.shadow_left_blurry   {
      text-shadow: -3px 3px 3px red;
      }
.shadow_right_notblurry{
      text-shadow: 3px 3px 0px red;
      }
.shadow_center_blurry    {
      text-shadow: red 0px 0px 3px;
      }
```

The top rule offsets the shadow by using negative values for the horizontal shift and then a positive value for the vertical shift down. The third value is the blur, and the fourth is the color. Similarly, the second rule shifts to the right, then down, but has no blur and is still red. The third rule would create an eclipse effect by having no horizontal or vertical shift, but allowing for a blur. Note that the color is at the beginning this time. With `text-shadow`, the color specification can be at the beginning or the end of the value declaration.

Here's how to make two shadows appear on top of one another.

```
.shadow_left_blurry    {
      text-shadow: -3px 3px 3px red, 3px 3px 0px yellow;
      }
```

Line it up!

Aligning text is another way you can make text stand out — or *not* stand out, depending on your intent. You can horizontally align text in any of these four ways:

Flush (all the way to the) left; also called rag-right

Flush (all the way to the) right; also called rag-left

Centered

Justified (a fancy way to describe text that has even right and left margins, like this block of text does as it goes on and on touching both sides of the page in all its inherent rambling-ness)

Use the `text-align` property in CSS to set horizontal alignment of text. Here's how they look in a style sheet:

```
<style>
   H1 {text-align: left;}
   P {text-align: right;}
   BODY {text-align: center;}
   DIV {text-align: justified;}
</style>
```

Using these basic alignment rules above, Figure 6-9 shows how the content is displayed when rendered through the screen to the browser.

`text-align left` is the default value for alignment in both HTML and CSS, so the only reason you'd ever need to use this value is to reset the alignment of an element from some other alignment back to being the default left.

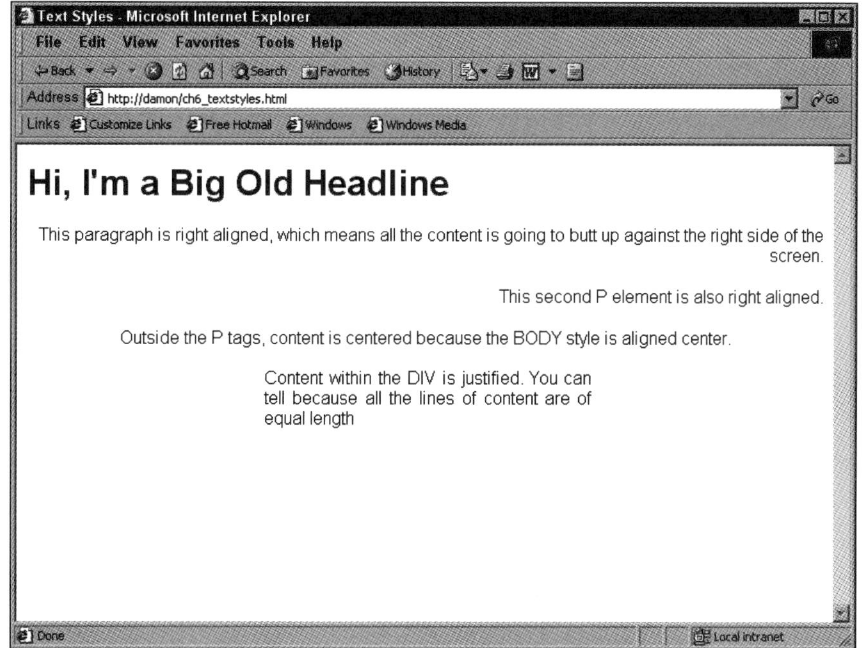

Figure 6-9: This DIV element is justified.

Text alignment values are inherited, so unless you specify a different alignment for sub-elements to a BODY element, all elements on that same page retain its value. For more on inheritance, see Chapter 9.

With justification, CSS does have some limitations. Most word processors can incorporate hyphens to make justified text look less space-y and more natural. CSS has no such algorithm for including hyphens, so your text is likely to look a little less elegant if you justify text.

Excuse me, Doctor, I've got an indentation on my line

Another way to make text stand out is to indent it, like for lists or bullets. (For more on indenting, thumb through Chapter 5 where I discuss units.) The `text-indent` property enables you to indent the first line of an HTML element using one of two value schemes, namely:

- **Length:** Specify the length of the indent by using one of the several unit types available, such as pixels or centimeters.
- **Percentage:** Specify the percentage of the width of the element that the first line should be indented.

To find out more about available unit types, especially lengths and percentages, check out Chapter 5.

The following example shows you how the property can be displayed in styles:

```
<style>
.pixels {text-indent: 30px; }

.negative_pixels {text-indent: -30px;}

.percent {
      position: absolute;
      top: 150px;
      left: 100px;
      width: 300px;
      font-family: arial;
      font-size: 12px;
      text-indent: 50%;
   }
   </style>
```

To give you some idea of how it could be used in the context of a page, I've thrown in some basic HTML to show how the styles can be applied to different elements. Here's the code; you can see the results for both browsers in Figure 6-10.

```
<P class="pixels">This is an indentation of 30 pixels on a P
           element. </P>
<P class="negative_pixels">What happens if you use a negative
           value? The text bleeds off the screen, so be
           careful! </P>
<P>What if I try to indent a <span class="pixels">SPAN
           element inside a P element? In Internet Explorer,
           nothing. In Netscape 6, nothing. But, in older
           versions of Netscape, it indents!</span></P>

<DIV class="percent"> This DIV element has a 50% indent, but
           the element is only 300 pixels wide, so the indent
           is half that, or 150 pixels, on Internet Explorer.
           Netscape will still try to center it on the entire
           page </DIV>
```

Unfortunately, as you can see in Figure 6-10, Internet Explorer (IE) and Navigator are notably different in their implementations of the `text-indent` property. Because of this discrepancy, you're likely to get varying results unless you keep the indents limited to HTML elements that are left- or right-aligned on the screen and don't involve absolute or relative positions.

I need my space!

Another method of adding some variety into text formatting is to introduce space to text elements at the word level or at the character level. Get a little crazy and go in the other direction — reduce the white space altogether. Both options are accepted and available, and here's how.

Although these spacing features aren't used all that often, they have a high novelty factor. In terms of sheer usefulness, these properties tend to make pages functionally less user friendly than simply letting the text flow as it will.

Excuse me while I spread out

CSS comes equipped with two different properties to handle text expansion: `letter-spacing` and `word-spacing`. The former adds space in between each letter in each word, and the latter adds space in between words. These properties are especially handy when you're working with text that needs some kind of special emphasis. Like `text-indent`, `letter-spacing` and `word-spacing` both can take values of any of the supported unit types in CSS, such as pixels or centimeters. Unlike `text-indent`, though, these two properties will not accept percentages as valid values. You can even give negative values to the two properties, just in case you feel like cramming your words or letters together.

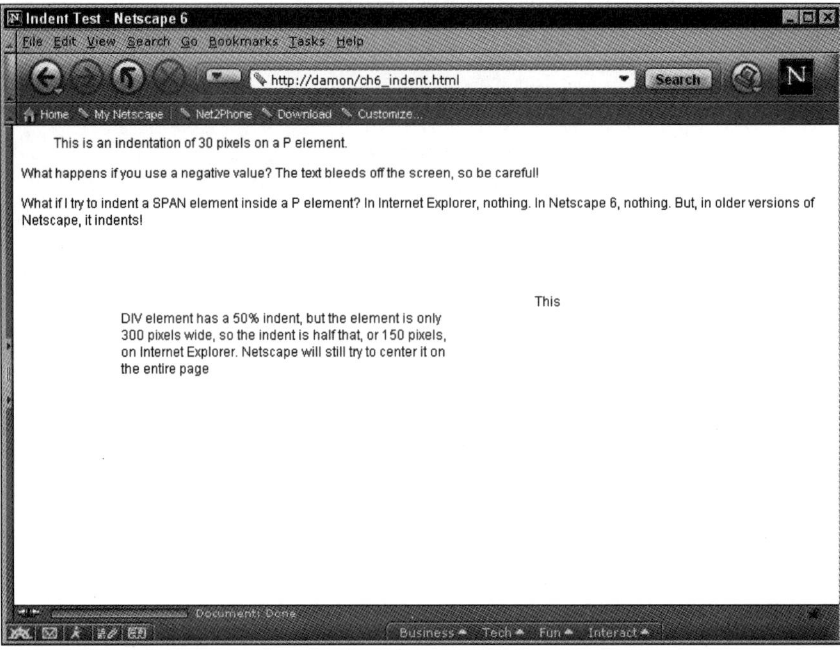

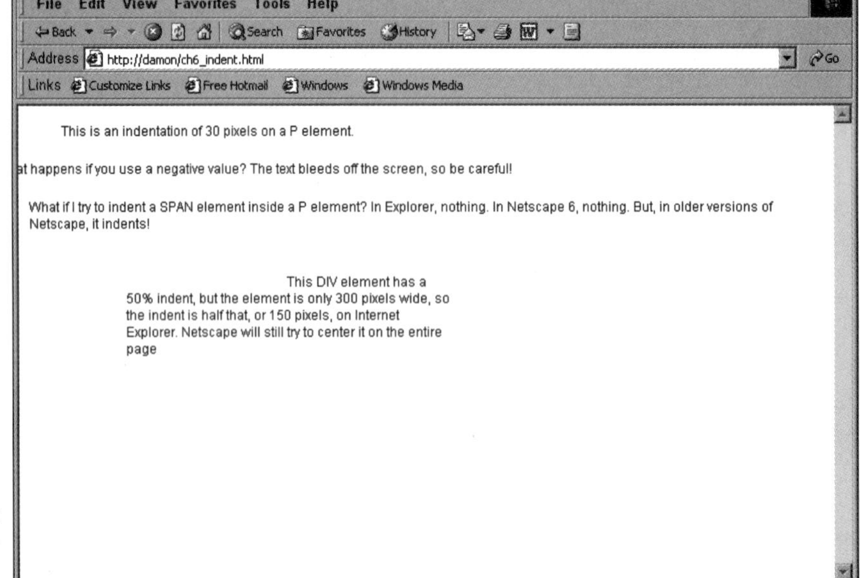

Figure 6-10: The indented HTML, on both Navigator (top) and Internet Explorer (bottom).

Until recently, `word-spacing` has not really been adopted by any of the browsers. Explorer 4 and 5 (on the Mac) have support for it, but strangely, not on the PC; Netscape 6 includes support for it on both the PC and the Mac.

The top line in Figure 6-11 shows the results of using `letter-spacing`, and the bottom line shows the results of using `word-spacing`, according to the two rules I created in my HTML document:

```
.letterspace {
      letter-spacing: 10px;
         }

.wordspace {
      word-spacing: 30px;
      }
```

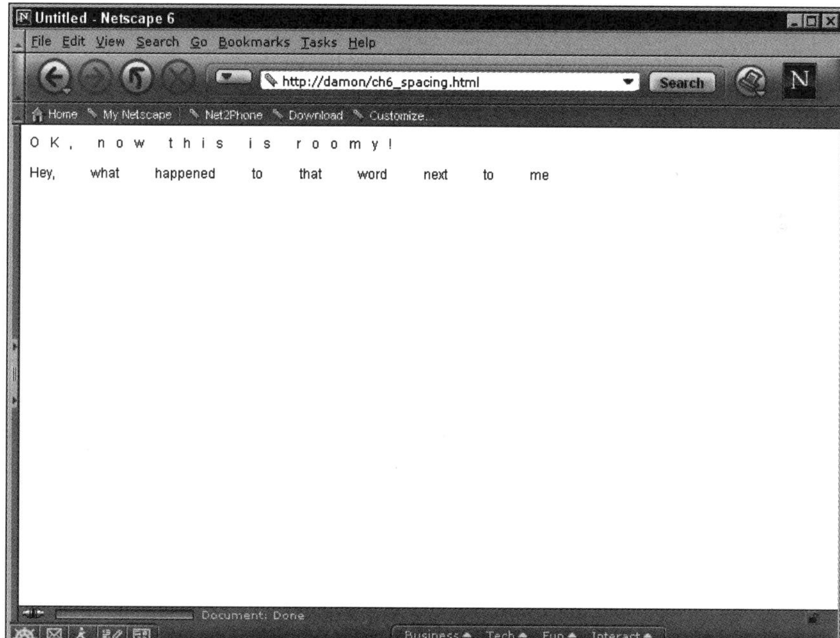

Figure 6-11: The roomy confines of letter and word spacing.

Wrapping with white space

If you want to eliminate text wrapping (when text automatically continues to the next line) in your site — scroll and scroll and scroll to the right to keep reading text — use `white-space` property in CSS. You might use this property if, say, you were creating a timeline that needed to just keep on scrolling to the right. The three values you can set for this property are:

- `pre`: This value prevents the browser from doing things such as making line breaks, and it limits line breaks only to hard breaks in the HTML code when you use certain elements, such as `BR`.
- `nowrap`: This value goes one step further, negating even `BR` elements in HTML. If you really don't want any breaks, then use this value!
- `normal`: Because this property allows inheritance, this value sets the property back to normal.

This property isn't well supported, at least not in Internet Explorer. IE 5.5 (for the PC) now supports the `nowrap` and `normal` values, and IE 5 (for the Mac) now supports it fully. Previous versions of IE, though, don't really support this property at all. As for Navigator, it supports all three values in Version 6, and it supports `normal` and `pre` in previous versions.

Capitalizing on capitalization

The judicious use of capital letters (or lack thereof) can be an effective way to style text for attention. The `text-transform` property of CSS enables you to set all your words to uppercase, lowercase, or initial capitalization. So, why, you may be asking, didn't the CSS specification just throw in small caps with this one, instead of relegating it to some obscure `font-variant` property? These are the mysteries that we'll all go to our graves wondering about . . . or not.

Use these values to set a `text-transform` property.

- `uppercase`: Hello, Rocket Science Department? Yup, IT'S ALL CAPITAL LETTERS.
- `lowercase`: you guessed it — all lowercase letters, à la ee cummings.
- `capitalize`: Also Called I-Caps, This Value Capitalizes The First Letter Of Each Word.
- `none`: This puppy reverts your text back to normal.

Check 'em out in Figure 6-12.

Guess what? This property is actually well supported by IE and Netscape. Woo hoo!

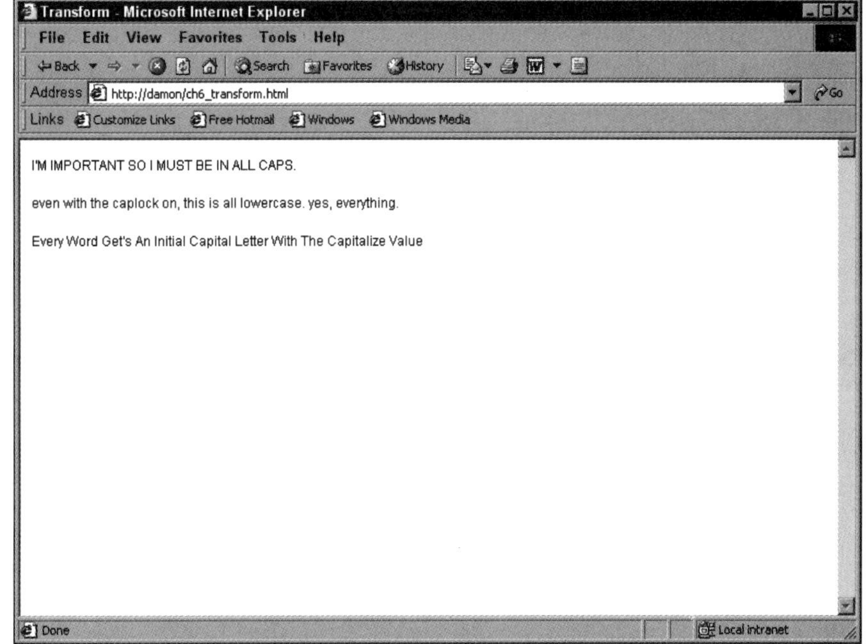

Figure 6-12: All caps, no caps, or I-caps.

Chapter 7

Styles and Visual Design

In This Chapter

- Understanding the Cascading Style Sheet box model
- Spacing out with padding, borders, and margins
- Discovering the nitty-gritty of the visual formatting model
- Working with visibility properties and layers
- Adding colors to the foreground or background
- Using the CSS background properties

This chapter is an interesting one, if I may be so bold, because it covers more properties than any other chapter. These properties aren't exactly the sexiest ones you'll find in the Cascading Style Sheet (CSS) specification (except for the `visibility` and `z-index`). Rather, this chapter is all about the workhorse properties — the ones that do most of the grunt work and never get any of the credit. For the dog lovers out there, I refer to these as the Australian cattle dogs of Cascading Style Sheets. Strangely, these properties often cause people the most difficulty because while mundane, they are somewhat complex in concept. I take extra care here to make sure that the explanation behind each of these properties is clear and concise.

In a nutshell, the properties in this chapter can be broken into a few key categories, including:

- Content display, or how things are displayed using CSS
- Hierarchy and visibility of content
- Content spacing
- Content color

For each of these categories, I first tell you what the category is all about, and then show you what you can do with the properties that make up the category. And then there will be a test at the end of the chapter.

Kidding! Give your Aussies a call-to whistle and wave them to come by hard to drive home these properties to work for you! That'll do. (Dog talk.)

The Box Model Shows on the Big Screen

You can't help but love the term *box model*. Whether it's wafer-thin models lofting boxes above their heads while they strut and pose — or big bulky boxes lumbering down a catwalk (that new corrugated cardboard is all the rage this season!) — this term always brings a smile to my face!

The box model term describes the rectangular boxes that surround every element (`P`, `H1`, `DIV`, `SPAN`, and so forth) in an HTML document. What's a little tricky is that these aren't real boxes, but rather an invisible representation of the dimensions of the document element. Actually, you could see the box by using the `border` property, which I discuss later in this chapter in the section "Setting up the border patrol."

The size of the box is influenced by several items, including:

- The amount and size of text in the element
- Padding
- Borders
- Margins

Together, these items determine the physical size of the element as it's displayed on the screen. If you have the following code in your HTML document:

```
<H1>Hi, I'm an H1 element, otherwise known as a headline</H1>
```

and assuming that you don't have any padding, borders, or margins, then the box for that content element is the area bound by the highest point of a character, the lowest point of a character, the furthest right point of the last character, and the furthest left point of the initial character. In Figure 7-1, you can see the above code, using the default text properties. To help illustrate this point, I use small circles to highlight the top, bottom, left, and right points and I also use a solid black line to show the size of the box.

This box model concept is important because you (the heir-apparent to the CSS-scripting kingdom) can place almost any content element anywhere you like on the screen. And you can do it in a number of different ways. You can place content elements on top of one another, or you can place them in relation to one another — even one after the other. As a reference point, however, you first need to know how the size of the element you're placing, and the box model enables you (and the Web browser) to determine this.

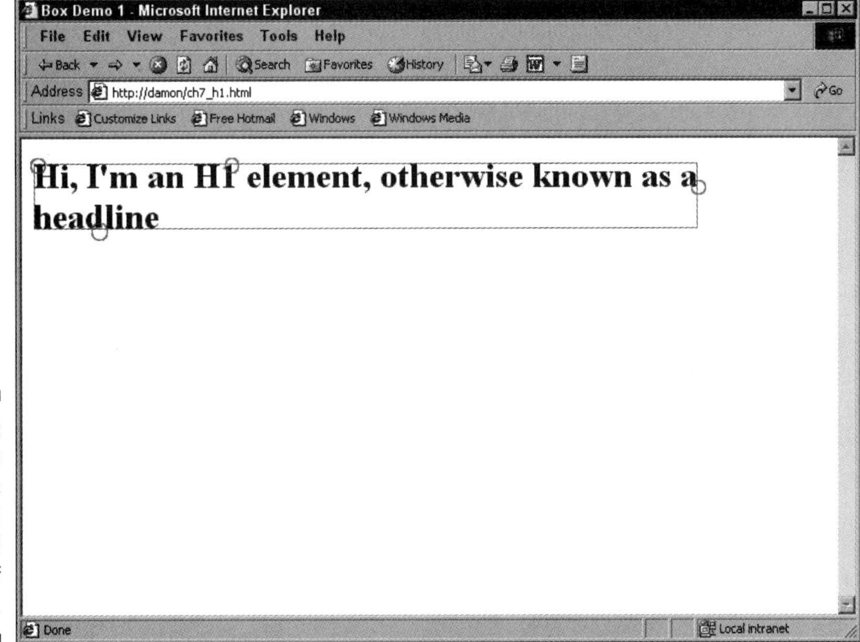

Figure 7-1: Note the four points markers and the overall size of the box.

How Space Affects the Box Model

In the previous section, I mention that text, padding, borders, and margins together help determine the overall size of the box. Check out Figure 7-2, which I recreated from the CSS specification. You can see how padding, borders, and margins all add up to create a larger box than that specified only by the content's bounding box.

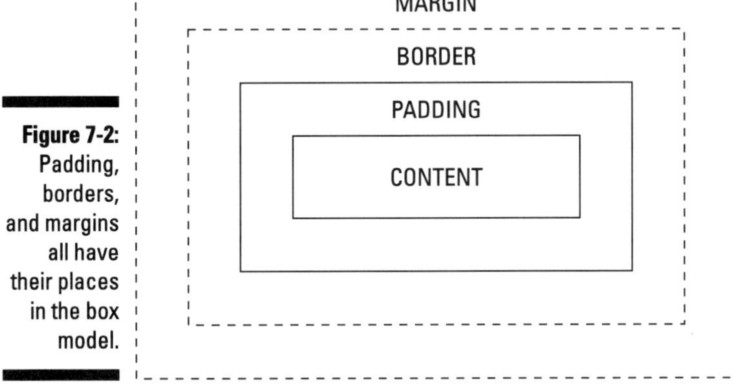

Figure 7-2: Padding, borders, and margins all have their places in the box model.

CSS uses these three different spacing schemes because each one does something critical yet different. Here are their basic definitions.

- **Padding:** Much like shoving a pillow in your pants to cushion the fall when you fall off your bicycle, *padding* simply puts additional space around the content element itself. You typically use this spacing feature to prevent the border from butting against the content directly. The padding properties specify the width of the padding area of a box.
- **Border:** *Border* is kind of a strange property because most borders involve a line surrounding some content. With CSS, you don't have to specify a line to go with the border width — in effect, border can be both a border and more padding. The border properties specify the width, color, and style of the border area of a box.
- **Margin:** Refer to Figure 7-2, and you can see that the content side of the box visually ends with the border. Adjust the *margin* to offset the content, padding, and border against other elements on the screen, just like the margin in a Microsoft Word document. Margin properties specify the width of the margin area of a box.

The CSS specification doesn't dictate that you have to use any of these spacing features. Just be aware that they exist and that they're interrelated — but not required.

All three spacing tools include properties for adding space to the top, bottom, left, and right parts of the box. You can also specify different values for each, as I explain in the upcoming sections.

Don't expect a warm welcome from browsers for the spacing schemes. Expect to spend a lot of time fiddling with these settings to achieve the look you want.

Putting on your padding

To give Web developers maximum flexibility when adding space around content elements, CSS provides support for five padding properties:

- `padding-top`: Use this property to add space *above* the content element.
- `padding-bottom`: Use this property to add space *below* the content element.
- `padding-left`: Use this property to add space to the *left* of the content element.
- `padding-right`: Use this property to add space to the *right* of the content element.
- `padding`: Use this property to specify values for the above four properties within a single property.

The padding properties can accept any of the units specified for length measurements (as I detail in Chapter 5), but the most commonly used measurement for all the space properties is pixels. The most common application of padding is to put some distance between the content and the border surrounding it.

Check out the following style rule:

```
.padding {
   padding-right: 0px;
   padding-left: 10px;
   padding-top: 30px;
   padding-bottom: 50px;
   border: solid 1px;
   }
```

This rule contains padding for all the sides of an element. Note that I also include a `border` property — which I discuss in the following section — to show a single-pixel border around the content element. This will make it possible to see the padding in action.

For this example, I include the following HTML in my document, which just includes plain old text and the call to the padding rule:

```
<DIV class="padding">Check out the differences in the
            distance between where the content ends and the
            border line begins. </DIV>
```

As you can see in Figure 7-3, the largest distance is from the bottom of the content to the bottom line, as the rule prescribed.

If you want the `padding` value to be zero for a side of an element, just leave the appropriate property out. The browser will automatically interpret that property as having a zero value.

The `padding` property enables you to accomplish precisely the same thing as the individual properties, except that it's wrapped up into one nice tight package. In Table 7-1, note how using between one and four values can change the way that the `padding` property works.

Table 7-1 Padding Property Logic

Number of Values	*How It Gets Applied*	*Example Syntax*
1	Padding is applied to all sides.	padding: 1px
2	Padding is applied to top and bottom.	padding: 1px 1px

(continued)

Table 7-1 *(continued)*

Number of Values	*How It Gets Applied*	*Example Syntax*
3	First value is applied to the top, the second value to the left and right, and the third value to the bottom.	padding: 1px 1px 1px
4	Values area is applied to the top, right, bottom, and left, respectively.	padding: 1px 1px 1px 1px

Given the logic of the `padding` property as I list in Table 7-1, you could summarize the previous example with a single property declaration (instead of four separate ones), as follows

```
padding: 30px 0px 50px 10px
```

and the resulting output would be the same.

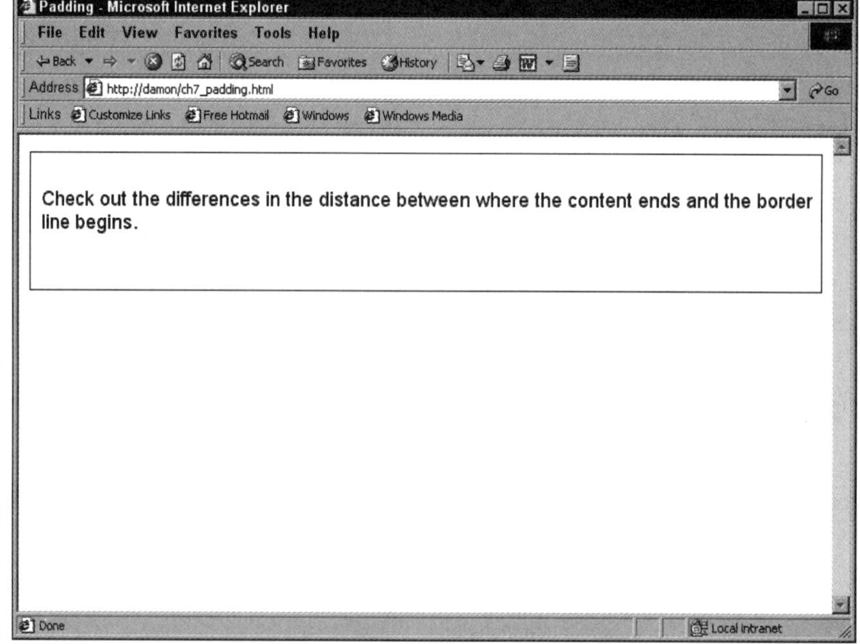

Figure 7-3: Padding, borders, and margins make the content seem small by comparison!

Setting up the border patrol

Conceptually, borders in CSS work identically to the padding, with the added dimensions of width, style, and color. Choices, choices! Like padding, you use borders to specify the width of the border that goes around the outside of the padding and content element. You have a lot of creative options when creating borders: Go a little nuts setting border width, style, and color.

Just how wide is wide enough?

Border width is the first set of properties you can set for a box. Border width sets the size of the border around a given content element, past the content and any padding that's been added.

Determine border width using the following five property options:

- `border-top-width`: Use this to specify the size of the *top* border.
- `border-bottom-width`: Use this to set the size of the *bottom* border.
- `border-left-width`: Use this to set the size of the *left* border.
- `border-right-width`: Use this to set the size of the *right* border.
- `border-width`: Use this to specify values for the other four properties within a single property.

To discover how to further set border width (with values), see the upcoming section "Widening the border widths."

Styling your border

You can also specify the style of border that you want to go around the padding and the content element. Thus, you have five more border properties at your creative disposal, appropriately entitled:

- `border-top-style`: Use this to set the style of the *top* border.
- `border-bottom-style`: Use this to set the style of the *bottom* border.
- `border-left-style`: Use this to set the style of the *left* border.
- `border-right-style`: Use this to set the style of the *right* border.
- `border-style`: Use this to specify values for the above four properties within a single property.

Coloring your border

Finally, in addition to the styles, you can set the color of your border. Like the border width and style properties, you can apply a color to any one side of the border (or each can have different colors), or you can use a summary property to give all sides of your border the same color.

- `border-top-color`: Use this to set the color of the *top* border.
- `border-bottom-color`: Use this to set the color of the *bottom* border.
- `border-left-color`: Use this to set the color of the *left* border.
- `border-right-color`: Use this to set the color of the *right* border.
- `border-color`: Use this to specify values for the other four properties within a single property.

For those of you scoring at home, that's a grand total of 15 properties so far just to handle the borders. Whew! Who knew? Don't be overwhelmed by so many properties to keep track of — after you get the hang of it, it's really a snap. And, the easiest way to get the hang of it is to put these three categories of border properties to good use with some examples. Read through the following section to explore how to set values for the border width, style, and color properties.

Widening the border widths

After you set where you want borders (with a border property), then you can set border width with a value. Imagine for a moment that you want to create a border around all your `H1` elements. The border width properties accept length values, but they also come with three easy-to-remember thickness values. Of course, the CSS specification doesn't specify explicit values for these so the browser must determine the actual values for them.

- `thin`: This value creates a thin line.
- `medium`: Use this value to create a medium line.
- `thick`: This value creates a thick line.

Although the following rules must apply to border width values (`thick`, `medium`, and `thin`), the CSS specification does not require a set size for these values, so these values will vary from browser to browser.

Because these border width values are so general, you're more likely to find yourself using the more precise explicit values. Because of this, I focus my examples there. For example, if you want to add a 1-pixel border around an `H1` element, at first glance you might consider using the following syntax:

```
H1 {
   border-left-width: 1px;
   border-right-width: 1px;
   border-top-width: 1px;
   border-bottom-width: 1px;
   }
```

This syntax is technically accurate, but as I note earlier, border width comes with a summary property (`border-width`). And, really, why use four properties when you can use one? The rules for this property are identical to that of the `padding` summary property I describe earlier — so for all the trouble I went to in the code above, you can get the same effect by using the following syntax in your style rule:

```
H1 { border-width: 1px 1px 1px 1px }
```

In either case, if you apply the rule to some `H1` element text, such as

```
<H1>Look at me! I'm a Headline!</H1>
```

you'd see that the headline doesn't have a border at all. (See Figure 7-4.) Is that possible? Could it be that the browser is, in fact, wrong?

Yes, this is the proper output for the page because — this is the important part! — at this point, no border *style* has been applied. As far as the browser is concerned, there *is* a border, but no one can see it. To make this style visible, you need to add a border style *property* to one or more sides of the border, as in the following example (which adds a solid border to the whole element):

```
H1 {
border-width: 1px 1px 1px 1px;
border-style: solid;
   }
```

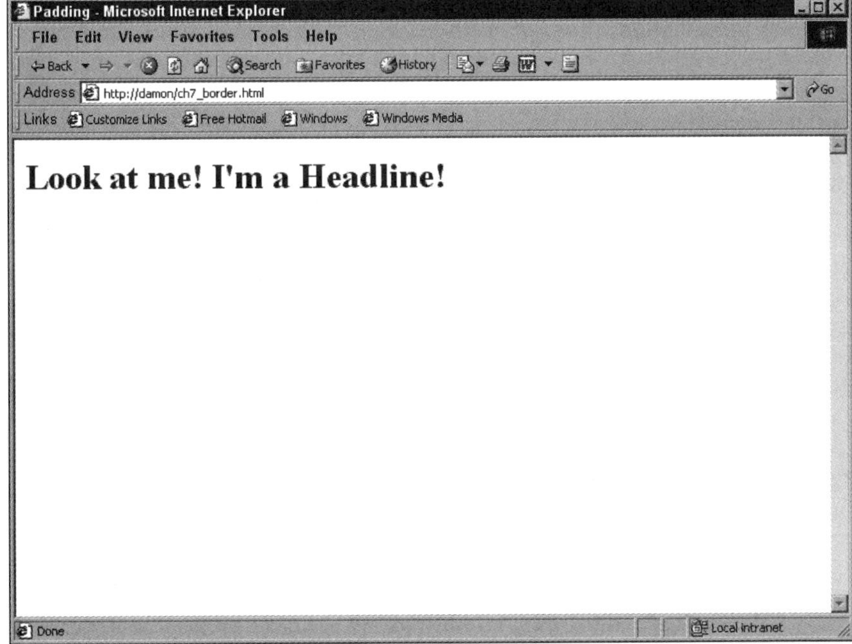

Figure 7-4: Where's the border for my head? Bad browser!

Splash some style on the borders

After you choose your border width and style properties, you can further dress up your border with `border-style` values. (A *style* is just a way of physically representing the border width that is specified in a rule.) CSS supports nine different border style values:

- `solid`: Use this style value to produce a *solid* border.
- `dotted`: Use this style value to produce a *dotted* border.
- `dashed`: Use this style value to produce a *dashed* border.
- `hidden`: Use this style value to produce an *invisible* border.
- `double`: Use this style value to specify *two borders* that together with the white space equal the `border-width` value.
- `groove`: Use this style value to simulate a *furrowed-edge* border.
- `ridge`: Use this style value to simulate a *raised-edge* border.
- `inset`: Use this style value to simulate an *embedded* (impressed) border.
- `outset`: Use this style value to simulate an *embossed* (outdented) border.

You can't really see the double border style unless you use larger values (such as 5px) for your border widths.

You can apply styles in a couple of different ways. Just for the fun of it, imagine that you only wanted to apply a `dashed` border style value to the top of the `H1` element in my continuing example. Modify the style as follows, and see the result in Figure 7-5:

```
H1 {
   border-left-width: 1px;
   border-right-width: 1px;
   border-top-width: 1px;
   border-bottom-width: 1px;
   /*This will add a border style to the top*/
   border-top-style: dashed;
}
```

A single dashed line is nice, but putting a box around the entire element is perhaps more practical. You *could* use each of the individual border styles to make your border rectangle, which would generate a style rule akin to the following block of code. In this example, the style would generate `H1` elements with dashed lines on the top and bottom, and solid lines on the left and right.

```
H1 {
   border-left-width: 1px;
   border-right-width: 1px;
   border-top-width: 1px;
   border-bottom-width: 1px;
```

```
/*This will add a border style to the top*/
border-top-style: dashed;
border-bottom-style: dashed;
border-left-style: solid;
border-right-style: solid;
}
```

But the better, more efficient way to style this is to use the `border-style` summary property to handle all your borders in one quick step. Here's how to recreate the example above with very simple syntax. Check out the results in Figure 7-6.

```
border-style: dashed solid dashed solid
```

The easy way to remember the values' order for the summary properties is to think of a clock. The values always rotate clockwise beginning at the top, then the right side, then the bottom, and finally the left side. In clock talk, you start at 12, and then go to 3, 6, and 9.

Changing border colors

You set the border color value just like the border properties of line width and style. Knowing that, you can refer to the earlier examples of how to style your `H1` element. For simplicity's sake, assume that you've consolidated your style rule down to two properties, as follows:

```
H1 {
border-width: 1px 1px 1px 1px;
    border-style: dashed solid dashed solid;
    }
```

If you want to add some color to the borders of this rule, you could apply the rules individually by using one of the following values:

- `border-top-color`: Set this value to color the *top* border.
- `border-right-color`: This value colors the *right* border.
- `border-bottom-color`: Use this value to color the *bottom* border.
- `border-left-color`: This value colors the *left* border.

Or you could make your job more simple by using the `border-color` summary property. Imagine that you want to make the top and bottom dashed lines blue, and the two border sides red. Use the `border-color` summary property with the following syntax to generate that effect:

```
border-color: blue red blue red;
```

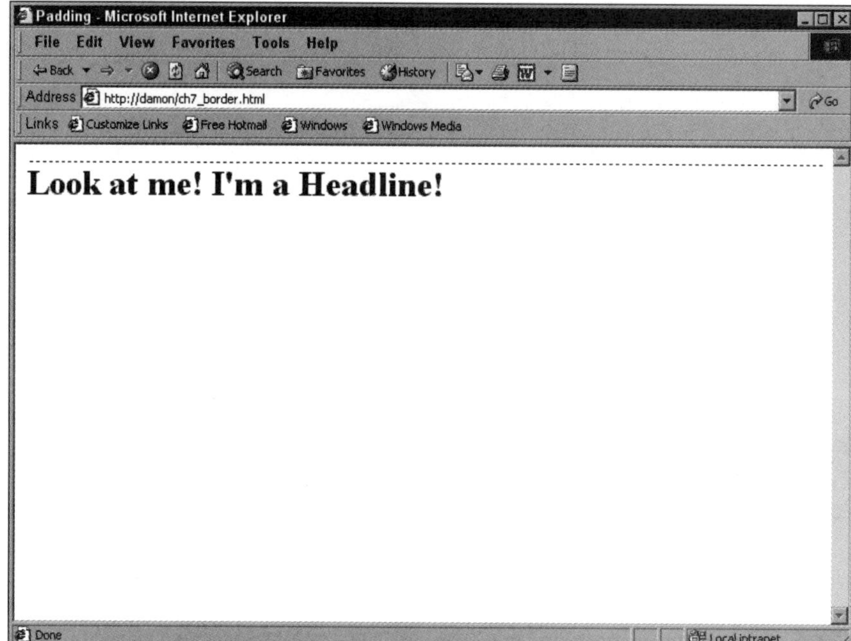

Figure 7-5: Nice dashed line!

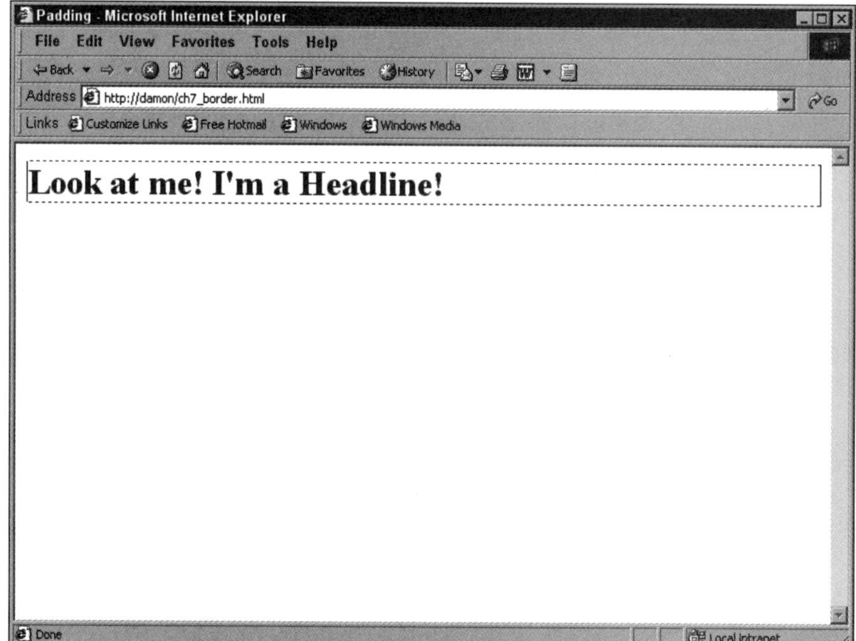

Figure 7-6: Different property, same result!

The rules for how the three values get applied when using the summary properties are the same for all the space summary properties; I list these in Table 7-1.

I want to make you aware of some weird anomalies with border colors. For example, if you came across the following style rule:

```
P    {
   border-width: 1px 1px 1px 1px;
    border-style: dashed solid dashed solid;
   font-family: Arial;
   font-size: 12px;
           color: blue;
}
```

that was applied to the following HTML and inline styles:

```
<P style="border-top-style: dashed;  border-bottom-style:
           dashed; border-left-style: solid; border-right-
           style: solid;"> Hey, what's up with the color?</P>
```

then surprisingly, the regular old `color` property gets applied not only to the text in the `P` element but to the border as well. The reason for this is (according to the CSS specification) that the border properties inherit their color values from the color property *if* no `border-color` value exists.

To counteract this inheritance property, you have to use one or all the `border-color` properties. In this case, if you want to simply reset the border color to the default, you could use a value of `black`. The resulting style rule would look as follows:

```
P    {
   border-width: 1px 1px 1px 1px;
    border-style: dashed solid dashed solid;
   border-color: black;
   font-family: Arial;
   font-size: 12px;
           color: blue;
}
```

The kings of summary properties

More summary properties! Yipes! They're multiplying like Tribbles. In addition to the summary properties for each of the property classes (width, style, and color), CSS also includes summary properties for each side of the box model, as well as the box overall. Hence, the five additional properties:

- `border-top`: Use this property to set the width, style, and color of the *top* border.
- `border-right`: Use this property to set the width, style, and color of the *right* border.

- `border-bottom`: Use this property to set the width, style, and color of the *bottom* border.
- `border-left`: Use this property to set the width, style, and color of the *left* border.
- `border`: Use this property to set the width, style and color of all the borders.

These properties all work according to the same overall structure, with the declaration being followed by `width` value, the `style` value, and then the `color` value, as follows:

```
property: <border-width> <border-style> <border-color>
```

Attention, Houston: The side-specific border properties are for the border you specify, and the `border` property specifies values for the whole box (all four sides).

If you want to create a 10-pixel wide, double-styled, cyan border around your `P` elements (wind it up, now!), you could use the following syntax to create it:

```
P { border: 10px double cyan }
```

and it would generate a double border just like the one in Figure 7-7.

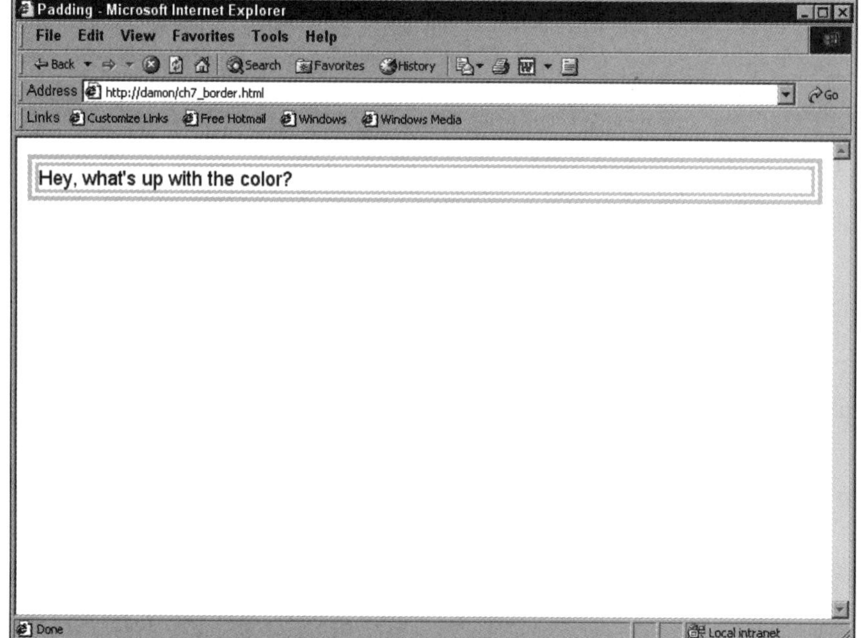

Figure 7-7: Nice border!

Add a little margin on your toast!

The margin properties (surprise, surprise!) work identically to the padding and border properties. The margin properties offset the rest of the content element (content, padding, and border) from other content elements in the document tree. Margins include the following properties:

- `margin-top`: Use this property to set the margin on the *top* of the content element.
- `margin-right`: Use this property to set the margin on the *right* of the content element.
- `margin-bottom`: Use this property to set the margin on the *bottom* of the content element.
- `margin-left`: Use this property to set the margin on the *left* of the content element.
- `border`: Use this property to set the margin on all sides of the content element.

If you want to create a 5-pixel wide margin on the top of your `H1` elements, you could use the following syntax to create it:

```
H1 { margin-top: 5px}
```

Visualizing the Model

The CSS *visualization model* is just a super-fancy term for the properties that involve the display of content to the screen. One could correctly argue — and I have — that nearly every property in the specification involves the display of content to the screen.

In practical terms, what makes these properties any different than the box model properties (that I discuss in the first half of this chapter) is that this class of properties deals specifically with the interaction of content elements in an HTML document when the browser renders them to the screen. The box model properties, conversely, don't really care about the final output but rather just the content elements themselves. For example, the *make-up* of a `P` element (its padding, borders, text formats, and so forth) is considered part of the box model, but the *size* and *position* of that `P` element on the screen are the realm of the visualization model. Check out Figure 7-8 for a visual rendition of this relationship.

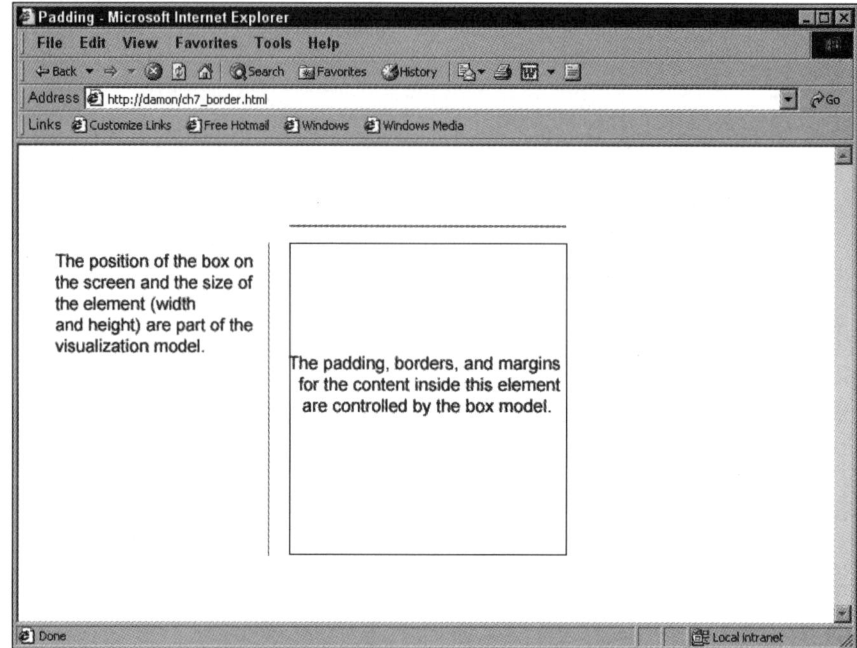

Figure 7-8: The visualization and box models.

The properties in the visualization model can be sorted into five categories:

- **Positioning:** Use these properties to set the position of a content element on the screen.
- **Display type:** These properties are used to set the way you want an element to be displayed.
- **Box size:** These properties set the width of a content element.
- **Visibility:** This property either displays a content element as visible or not.
- **Layering:** The `z-index` property sets the depth on the screen of content elements.

In this chapter, I only cover display types, box size, visibility, and layering. Positioning is the largest of the categories; because it's used so often, I give it its very own chapter (Chapter 8).

I want to introduce the term normal flow, which I also discuss in Chapter 8. *Normal flow* is the logical progression of running through the elements in an HTML document from top to bottom. If you have an HTML document with the following structure:

```
<BODY>
<H1>...<H1/>
<P>...</P>
```

```
<DIV>...</DIV>
</BODY>
```

the normal flow would dictate that the browser renders the elements in this order: H1, P, and DIV.

What's your display type?

The display property tells an HTML element how it should be displayed on the screen. Most HTML elements (P, DIV, H1...H6) are blocks, and apply to the box model rules that I discuss in the first half of this chapter. However, there are some anomalies to this rule (such as the list element), and not all elements are the same. The syntax for the rule is as follows:

```
display: value;
```

All the HTML elements come pre-equipped with their own display properties, so you'll probably never have to change them, except when you're using the visibility property. (I describe this in the upcoming section "Hey, where did everyone go?") CSS allows you to overwrite the default values by using the display property. Because the default HTML style includes display properties for all the elements in an HTML document, the display property doesn't exactly get used all that often when using style sheets on HTML documents.

The display property is exceptionally useful when displaying non-HTML documents (XML, for example) in which the display type has never been specified. The display property, however, does have its uses in HTML. For example, making tables in CSS requires using the display property extensively. (For a complete discussion on making tables with CSS, peruse Chapter 13.) In Table 7-2, I describe the various values that you can apply to the display property.

Other then amending the display property when creating tables in CSS, I recommend that you don't touch the display type for a given content element in HTML.

Table 7-2 display Property Values

Value(s)	*Description*
block	Creates a box as I describe in the section "Visualizing the Model."
inline	Generates a box around a piece of content that is part of a block.

(continued)

Table 7-2 *(continued)*

Value(s)	*Description*
list-item	Creates a list box, which is a block, and then also an inline box for the list bullets.
run-in and compact	Both these properties generate either an inline or block element depending on where the element is located in the document structure.
marker	Generates a dynamic marker element for generated content. (See Chapter 12 for more on generated content.)
table inline-table table-row-group table-header-group table-footer-group table-row table-column-group table-column table-cell table-caption	All these values are used to create tables in CSS (see Chapter 13).

And the pitch is wide and high . . .

One of the really cool properties you can set with style sheets is to specify the size of a content element. This style applies to both the width and height of the content element, and can even supercede properties set at the box level. Your copy of CSS comes equipped standard with two primary content properties, `width` and `height`, plus a host of other ancillary properties that enable you, the Web developer, to play with maximum and minimum heights, as well as line spacing.

Open wide . . . wider . . .

The most commonly used sizing property is `width`, which can accept the `lengths` and `percentages` value types, as well as the `auto` value, which you set to choose the size of the block element based on the other elements in the normal flow.

Every content element in the document tree already has its own pre-determined width, based on the size of the content in the element, plus the padding, borders, and margins. By using the `width` property, you can extend and collapse that size.

Here's an example to illustrate how you can apply this property. Suppose that you're creating a typical headline and body copy; you might set up a couple of style rules like this:

```
H1 {
   font-family: Arial;
   font-size: 24px;
   padding: 1px;
   border: 1px solid;
   }
P {
   font-family: Verdana;
   font-size: 12px;
   padding: 5px;
   border-top: 1px dashed;
   }
```

With no constraints put on the P or H1 elements, they will naturally have a width that's based on the size of the browser window. The larger the window, the wider the element becomes. In Figure 7-9 is an 800-pixel-wide window with some placeholder HTML thrown in to show the line breaks.

If you want to make all your P elements 200 pixels wide instead of whatever the browser window is set to, add the following declaration to the P rule:

```
width: 200px;
```

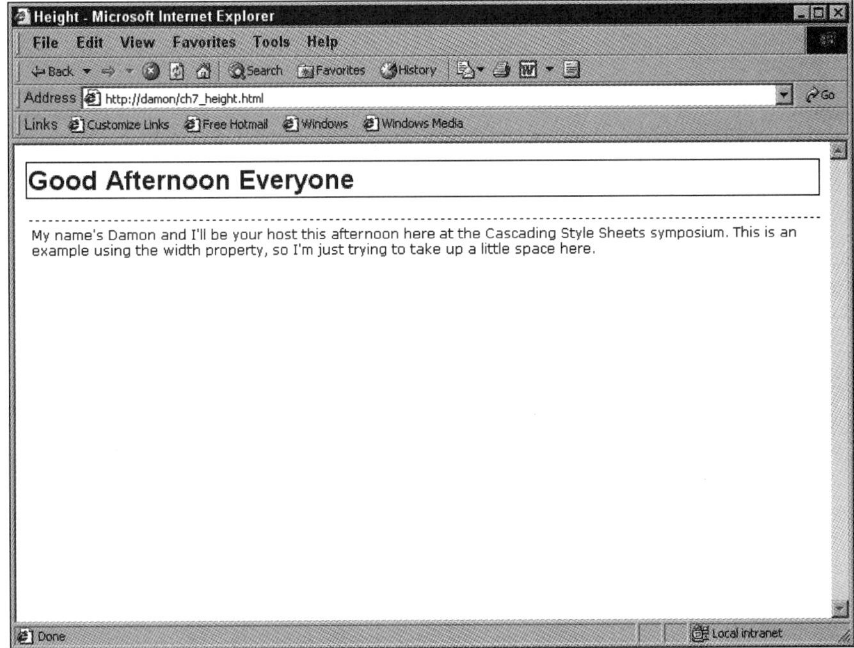

Figure 7-9: A CSS symposium . . . yeah, right.

The change in the rule generates a completely different output to the screen, as shown in Figure 7-10. Now the text appears in a block and doesn't run the span of the page.

Even though you decreased the width of the `P` element, the widths of the padding and borders are kept intact.

In addition to the `width` property, CSS also includes two other width rules: `min-width` and `max-width`. These two properties set minimum and maximum boundaries for content elements, and leave the actual determined size up to the browser, within the boundary constraints. You can use the properties separately, or in conjunction with one another. They accept the same values as `width`, with the exception of the `auto` value.

Ain't no height high enough

The `height` property in CSS works nearly identically to the `width` property, accepting the same three value types. The one noticeable difference between the two is that you can't give a `height` value that's less than the computed `height` value of the element. (Well, technically you can give a value for less than the computed value, but the browsers will just ignore that value.)

For example, if I add

```
height: 15px;
```

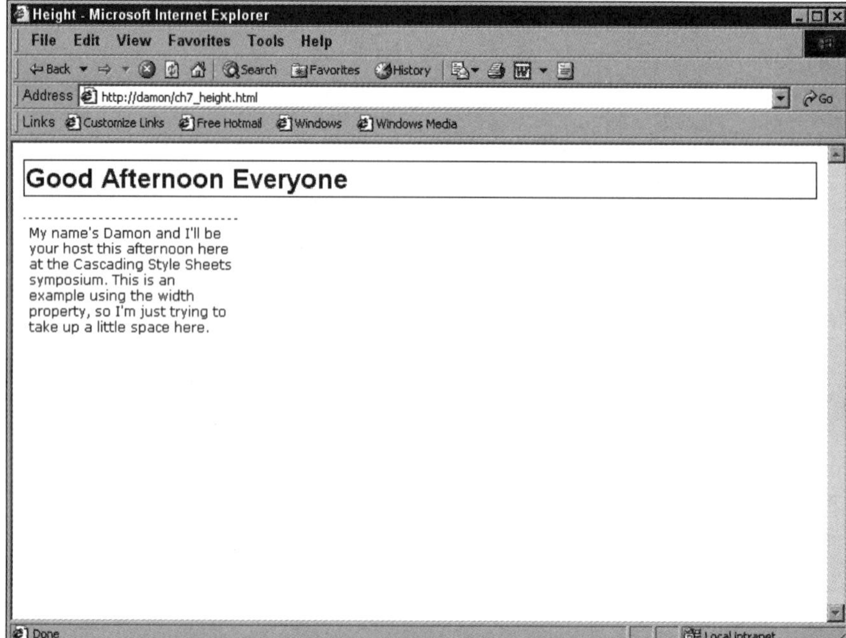

Figure 7-10: The P elements are now only 200 pixels wide.

to the `H1` rule from the previous example, I create the following rule:

```
H1 {
   font-family: Arial;
   font-size: 24px;
   padding: 1px;
   border: 1px solid;
   height: 15px;
   }
```

However, I already know that the headline is going to remain 24 pixels high, based on the `font-size` attribute. The browser just ignores the height value and instead uses the calculated value for the element.

The distance between two lines

Here's another one of those sets of properties that seems a little out of place in the visualization model: line spacing. I think it belongs with the text properties, but it lives here. Who am I to argue?

The two properties in this category, `line-height` and `vertical-align`, enable you to change the spacing between lines and to change the position each line has against that spacing according to a percentage or numeric value, or one of the following values:

- **`baseline`:** Set this value to align the element with the base of the parent element.
- **`sub`:** This value creates a subscript.
- **`super`:** This value creates a superscript.
- **`top`:** Use this value to align the top of the box with the top of the line box.
- **`text-top`:** This value aligns the top of the box with the top of the parent element's font.
- **`middle`:** This value puts the text in the middle between the lines.
- **`bottom`:** Use this value to align the bottom of the box with the bottom of the line box.
- **`text-bottom`:** Set this value to align the bottom of the box with the bottom of the parent element's font.

Here's a brief example of how to amend line spacing in CSS. From my earlier example using the `P` rule:

```
P {
   font-family: verdana;
   font-size: 12px;
   padding: 5px;
   border-top: 1px dashed;
   width: 400px;
   }
```

If I add the following two declarations:

```
line-height: 30px;
vertical-align: top;
```

together, they add 30 pixels to the distance between each line of text in the P element, and each of those lines is vertically aligned to the top (meaning that the inserted space is completely below the bottom of each text line). See the result of applying these two declarations in Figure 7-11.

Hey, where did everyone go?

The visibility property is perhaps the easiest property in the entire specification to use. It also happens to be one of the most fun properties to use too, so that's always an added bonus! Like you probably figured out from its name, use this tool to play Houdini with your elements. The property comes with three values:

- visible: The element is shown.
- hidden: The element is not shown.
- collapse: When used with CSS table elements, the element is hidden and removed so that other elements can move up to take its place. If used on other elements, it works the same as hidden.

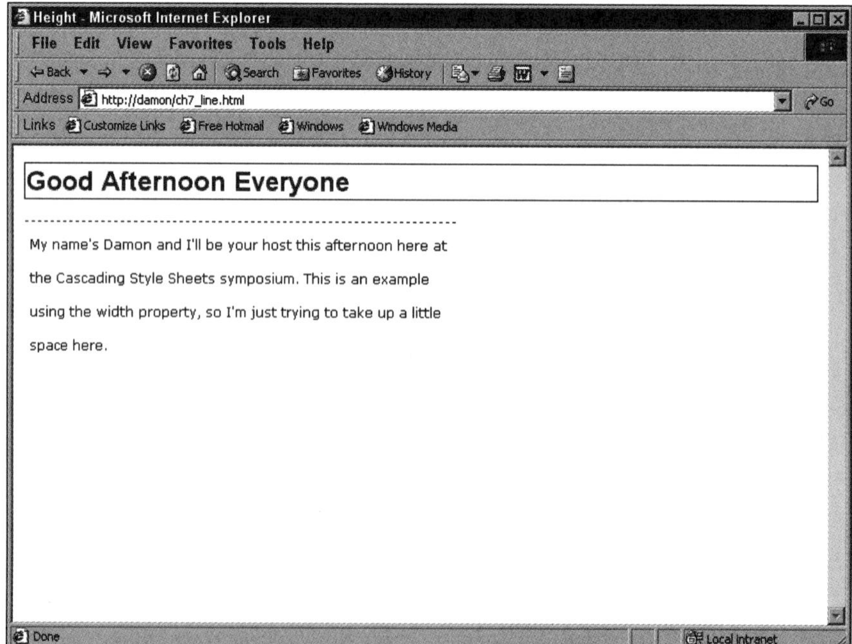

Figure 7-11: Ahhh . . . leg room!

If you have the following rules set up in your style sheet:

```
H1 {
   font-family: Arial;
   font-size: 24px;
   padding: 1px;
   border: 1px solid;
   }
P {
   font-family: Verdana;
font-size: 12px;
   padding: 5px;
   border-top: 1px dashed;
   width: 200px;
   }
```

and you apply `visibility: hidden;` to the `H1` rule, all headlines in the document — located no matter where — become invisible. (Refer to Figure 7-11 to see the headline, and then see how it disappears in Figure 7-12.)

Note that the space is still there where the headline was. That's because the element is still there — it's just not rendered. To remove the element completely, you also have to remove it from the normal flow. You'd have to change the `display` property to `display: none;` in the `H1` element.

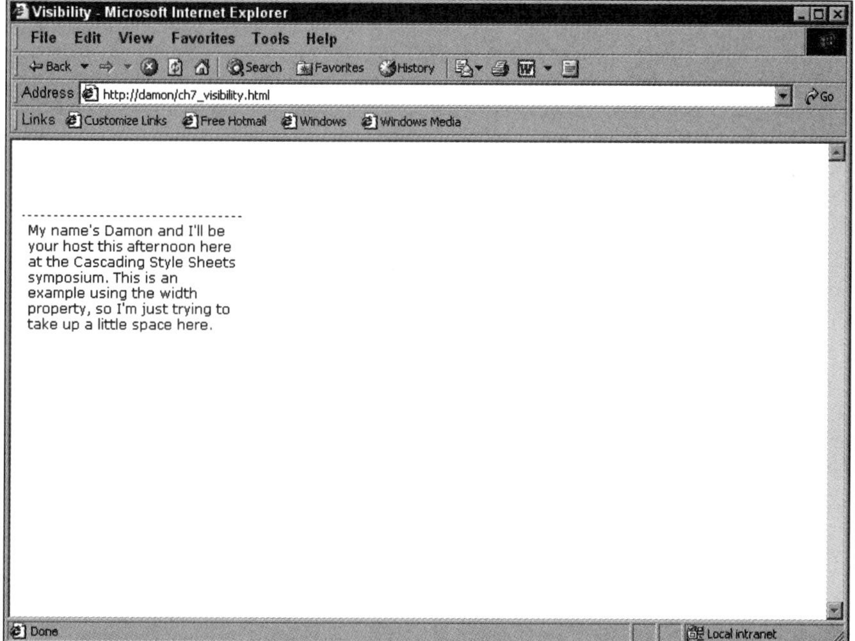

Figure 7-12: Ostrich City: Hiding your head.

Layering it on thick

Layering — stacking images — is yet another tool that breaks the traditional clunky HTML design paradigm. And, even better, the layering magic you can make with `z-index` property is simple! (You know, I just like saying that out loud: "*zeee*-index." Kinda sporty, eh?)

This wacky name comes from the z-axis coordinate of a 3-dimensional plane, like the one in Figure 7-13. Dust off your algebra-nightmare memory bank to recall the basic 2-dimensional place with an x-axis (horizontal) and a y-axis (vertical). Now think 3-D, and you add on the z-axis, which represents depth. Check it out in Figure 7-13.

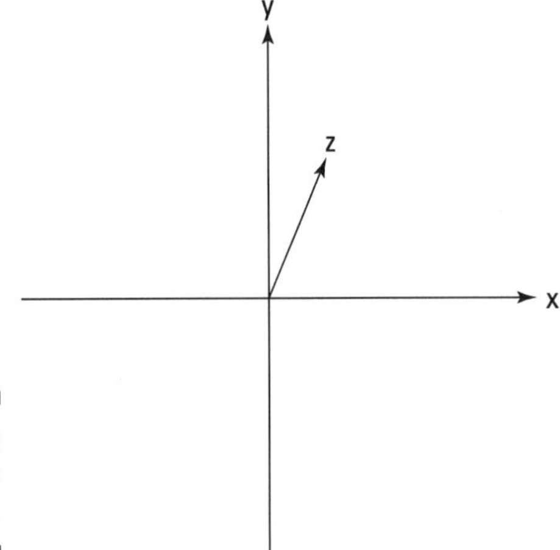

Figure 7-13: z equals depth.

Upon first inspection, you might question the value of this property. If all the HTML document elements are just moving top to bottom in the normal flow, what's the use in having a depth value for an element? That's where positioning properties come into play. As you can read in Chapter 8, with CSS you can position elements anywhere on the screen, including on top of one another. That's when the z-index becomes of supreme importance. In this discussion, however, I only address its syntax.

The `z-index` property for an element takes an integer value. The default value for a box element on the screen is 0. Both positive and negative values can be given to the `z-index`, and the overall syntax for the rule looks as follows:

```
z-index: 1
```

The rules of interaction for `z-index` are not complicated, but they do largely depend on what styles are being applied. So, for example, if you have a `P` element with a `z-index` of `1`, that `z-index` of `1` is for the `P` element itself in relation to other elements in the document at the same level as that `P` element. Child elements contained within the `P` element will have `z-index` values in relationship to one another, but not to other child elements of the `P` element siblings. (For a detailed discussion on parents, children, and siblings, I recommend reruns of *The Waltons*. When you get bored with that, you could always read through Chapter 9 of this book. You might even find the juicy parts where they squabble over their inheritance.)

Adding a Splash of Color

I discuss the `color` property throughout this book, but I want to reinforce that you can set color properties for anything that's willing to take a tint, such as text, characters, lines, borders, and whatever else that can be drawn to the screen using CSS. The `color` property can accept a host of different values, including red-green-blue (RGB) colors, hexadecimal values, and standard HTML colors, all of which I describe in detail in Chapter 5. The syntax is as simple as it is compelling:

```
color: red
```

In Chapter 5, I include a handy table that lists the common colors and their named, percentage, hexadecimal, and RGB values.

In addition to the basic `color` property, CSS also supports a specific background color property, appropriately called `background-color`. It accepts precisely the same values as the `color` property (such as `red`), and it also supports a `transparent` value that generates no background at all.

Check out the following rule:

```
P {
    font-family: Arial;
    font-size: 12px;
    padding: 5px;
    border: 3px solid;
    width: 200px;
    background-color: red;
    }
```

When you apply this rule to a `P` element, this rule generates a red box in the background, as shown in Figure 7-14.

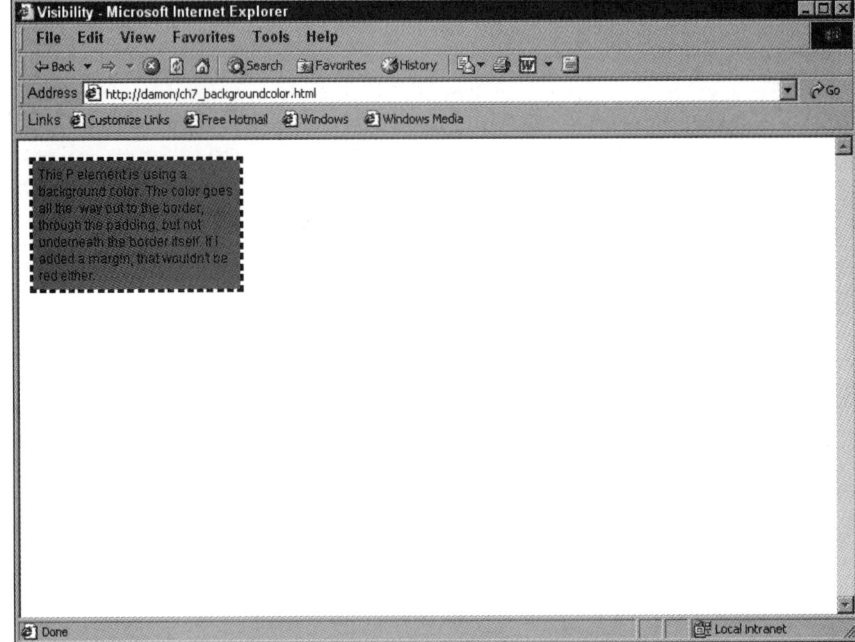

Figure 7-14: The background-color property in action.

Use `background-color` to apply the set color to the padding of an element, but not underneath the border or to the margin.

What's Going On in the Background?

The final stop in the CSS visual design world tour is the background properties. This is a pretty handy little set of properties I hope you use after you really get into your style sheet rhythm. As a bonus, they're pretty well supported by the browsers, too! One of the properties in this family is `background-color`, which I discuss in the previous section. The others include:

- `background-image`: Use this property to *place* an image in the background.
- `background-repeat`: Use this property to *repeat* the image in the background.
- `background-attachment`: Use this property to specify *whether the background image moves.*
- `background-position`: Use this property to *set the image's position* against the element.
- `background`: Use this summary property for all the background properties mentioned above.

The `background-image` property is a welcome sight for anyone who's had to endure the pains of putting background images in HTML tables. Using this property alone will probably save you hours on your development time. For a value, `background-image` takes a URL that should point to an image file. Often times, the property is used in conjunction with `background-repeat` to determine how many times the image should be repeated, and in which fashion it should be repeated.

You can give `background-image` a value of `none` to remove an inherited image.

The `background-repeat` property can take the following values:

- **`repeat`:** Use this value to repeat the image in *both directions*.
- **`repeat-x`:** Use this value to repeat the image *horizontally*.
- **`repeat-y`:** Use this value to repeat the image *vertically*.
- **`no-repeat`:** When you use this value, the image is rendered only once (that is, not repeated after that).

For example, if I want to take a simple image and repeat it across and down the entire background of my site, I might create the following rule:

```
BODY {
   background-image: url("images/happy.gif");
   background-repeat: repeat;
   }
```

Without even putting one line of code in your HTML `BODY` element, you've already got one of the happiest home pages on the Internet (see Figure 7-15). If you only wanted to repeat the `.gif` image across the top, use `background-repeat: repeat-x;` instead; see the results of that in Figure 7-16.

The two values for the `background-attachment` property are also very straightforward. When you assign a `scroll` value, the background image moves with the page while the user scrolls up and down the page. In contrast, assigning a `fixed` value keeps the image in place when the user scrolls the page.

The last of the main background properties, `background-position`, is perhaps the toughest to get your head around. This property can take three different value types:

- Percentage pairs
- Length pairs
- A pair of preset values
    - Top, center, bottom
    - Left, center, right

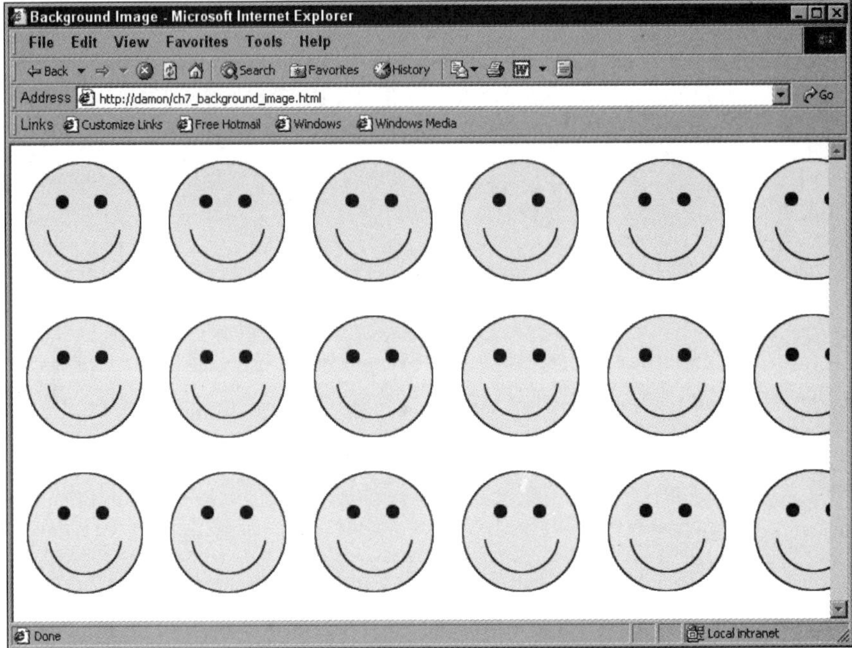

Figure 7-15: A sea of smiling faces.

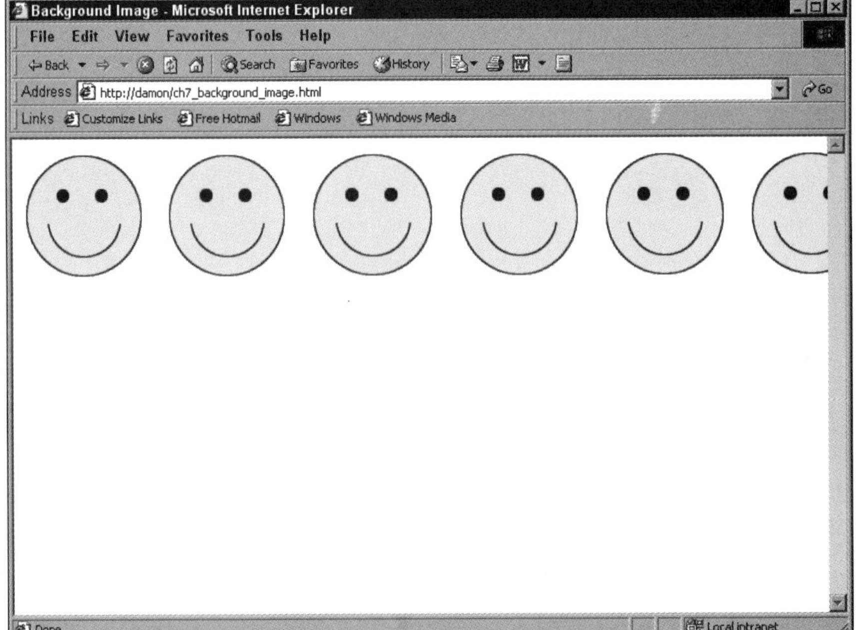

Figure 7-16: A row of smiling faces.

The first two are in pairs because the percentages and lengths specify the offset from the top left corner of the element. For example, the following rule

```
BODY {
    background-image: url("images/happy.gif");
    background-repeat: no-repeat;
    background-position: 50px 50px;
    }
```

places the smiley face `.gif` image 50 pixels to the left and 50 pixels down from the top of the browser window, as you can see in Figure 7-17.

Although this rule uses pixels, you could also use percentages.

For all the pair combinations, the first value is the left offset value, and the second value is the top offset value.

In addition to the lengths and percentages, the `background-position` property comes with pre-set values that offset background images. In Table 7-3, I describe those values that provide a reasonable (if somewhat unnecessary) alternative to using the length and percentage values.

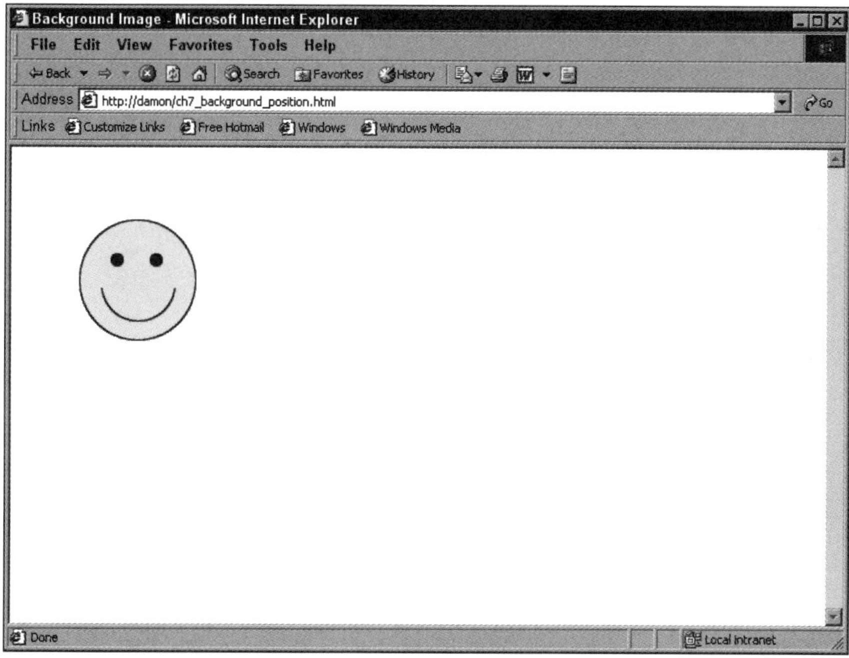

Figure 7-17: Place an image with the background-position property.

Table 7-3 background-position Pre-set Values

Value Pair	*Percentage Equivalents*
top left and left top	0% 0%
top, top center, and center top	50% 0%
right top and top right	100% 0%
left, left center, and center left	0% 50%
center and center center	50% 50%
right, right center, and center right	100% 50%
bottom left and left bottom	0% 100%
bottom, bottom center, and center bottom	50% 100%
bottom right and right bottom	100% 100%

Finally, you could use the `summary` background property. This background property enables you to apply all the background properties, including `background-color`, using one single rule. The syntax is as follows:

```
background: background-color background-image background-
          repeat background-attachment background position;
```

Tie it all together and be brave. To this rule (from earlier in this section):

```
BODY {
   background-image: url("images/happy.gif");
   background-repeat: no-repeat;
   background-position: 50px 50px;
   }
```

add a background color and make the image scroll. Your rule would look like this:

```
BODY {
   Background: blue url("images/happy.gif") no-repeat scroll
           50px 50px;
   }
```

You don't have to have all the values set for this property to work correctly. The browser will still read the property even if you only have one value in there. And that's the suggested order, but you can place them in any order you like.

Chapter 8

Positions Everyone!

In This Chapter

- Using HTML tables for development
- Absolute positioning puts you in your place
- Relative positioning puts you next to someone
- Fixed positioning . . . maybe
- Playing newspaper editor with floats

Positioning is, in my most humble opinion, the most fun attribute of CSS. If you've ever spent any amount of time building tables in HTML in order to get a graphic or a menu in precisely the right place on the screen, then you know that this process is boring, tedious, and frustrating. Mon Dieu! Isn't there an easier way?

Cascading Style Sheets to the rescue! Ironically, although CSS can make positioning content on the screen a snap, the number of sites that take advantage of these CSS properties is actually quite small. The first barrier to adoption, I believe, is the institutional mindset of many of today's Web developers. Admittedly, redeveloping an entire site is no easy task, especially those that are complex in their underlying HTML design. Understandably, the thought of ripping apart a bunch of tables and replacing them with CSS positioned elements is both daunting and in some ways impractical. The second barrier is the lack of cross-platform compatibility. That's just a fancy way of saying that it's hard to get positioning to work the same on both Internet Explorer (IE) and Netscape Navigator.

Regardless, I can't think why you shouldn't use the CSS positioning properties to give yourself more control over the visual style of your site. The future of mainstream Web development depends on wide-scale adoption of these kinds of properties, or Web developers will remain tied to inherent limitations of HTML.

If you're already comfortable with how the TABLE element works in HTML, then feel free to skip right past this next section.

So, Just How Bad Is HTML Anyway?

Before I jump into using style sheets for positioning, I want to review how elements are positioned on the screen using HTML.

This is a primer on HTML tables only, and doesn't include all the things you can do with tables in HTML. From our shameless cross-referencing plug department, if you'd like more information on HTML, please check out *HTML 4 For Dummies*, 3rd Edition, by Ed Tittle, Natanya Pitts, and Chelsea Valentine, published by Hungry Minds, Inc.

Tables in HTML are defined by the TABLE element, simply outlined with the following syntax:

```
<TABLE>...</TABLE>
```

Like those found in word-processing programs such as Microsoft Word, tables are made up of rows (side to side) and columns (up and down). In HTML, a row is defined by a <TR></TR> tag, and individual column cells in the row are defined by a <TD></TD> tag. For example, if I have a table of two rows and two cells in each row, the syntax looks like this:

```
<!--- this starts the table -->
<TABLE>
<!-- This begins the first row -->
<TR>
<TD> This is Row 1, Cell 1 </TD>
<TD> This is Row 1, Cell 2 </TD>
<!-- This ends the first row -->
</TR>
<!-- This begins the second row -->
<TR>
<TD> This is Row 2, Cell 1 </TD>
<TD> This is Row 2, Cell 2 </TD>
<!-- This ends the second row -->
</TR>
<!-- This ends the table -->
</TABLE>
```

In Figure 8-1, see how this basic relationship between the tags works.

In addition to these basic structuring elements, over the years HTML has developed a number of custom properties to associate with a table and its elements. I include a number of those properties in Table 8-1.

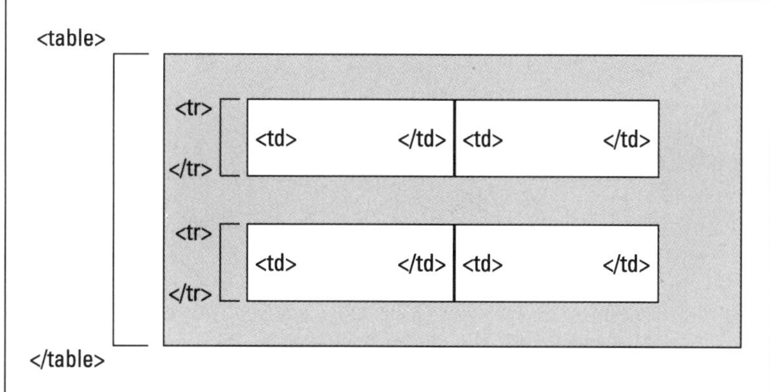

Figure 8-1: The basic structure of a table.

Table 8-1 Some Table Properties in HTML

Property	***Values***	***What It Does***
colspan	integer	Combines individual cells in a table row
rowspan	integer	Combines individual cells across rows
align	right, left, center	Horizontally aligns the content of a table cell
valign	top, bottom, center	Vertically aligns the content of a table cell
width	integer	Specifies the width of a table cell

In addition to some of this basic information, you'll notice some other commonly accepted rules of table design in most sites. These de facto rules are born from years of frustration trying to get both Explorer and Navigator to play nicely with one another. The three big ones are:

- **Embed tables:** Time for bed? Not quite. Embedding tables simply means you put one table inside the cell of another table. Didn't know you can do that one, eh? Ah! I can see the light going on. So *that's* how you can get different rows and column types to work together on the screen. . . . Building on my earlier example, here's how a table embedded with a table looks:

```
<!--- this starts the first table -->
<TABLE>
<!-- This begins the first row -->
<TR>
<TD> This is Row 1, Cell 1 </TD>
<TD> This is Row 1, Cell 2 </TD>
<!-- This ends the first row -->
</TR>
<!-- This begins the second row -->
<TR>
<TD> This is Row 2, Cell 1 </TD>
<TD>
<!-- This is the beginning of the embedded table -->
   <TABLE>
   <!-- This is Row 1 of the embedded table -->
      <TR>
   <!-- This row has three columns instead of of two -->
<TD> This is Row 1, Cell 1 </TD>
<TD> This is Row 1, Cell 2 </TD>
      <TD> This is Row 1, Cell 3 </TD>
      </TR>
   </TABLE>
</TD>
<!-- This ends the second row -->
</TR>
<!-- This ends the table -->
</TABLE>
```

Check out the results in Figure 8-2 to see how this looks in a Web browser.

- **Lock your first row with invisible `.gifs`:** An invisible `.gif`? What tha . . . ? Think of a transparent `.gif` (image) that's 1 pixel wide by 1 pixel high, and you can stretch it to any height or width using an `IMG` element. This is a nifty trick because although Explorer and Navigator browsers both support setting widths at both the `<TABLE>` and `<TD>` level, if you start using `colspans` and `rowspans`, browsers will interpret and then render those width values differently. The only way to have a table exactly the size you want with cells precisely the width you want is to use images to lock them down.

  Here's how to construct a table precisely 500 pixels wide, with the cells 200 and 300 pixels wide, using an invisible `.gif` (called `hidden.gif`) and the following syntax:

```
<TABLE>
<TR>
<TD> <IMG src="images/hidden.gif" width="200"
        border="0"></TD>
<TD> <IMG src="images/hidden.gif" width="300"
        border="0"></TD>
</TR>
<TR>
```

```
<TD> This is Row 2, Cell 1 and it's 200 pixels wide</TD>
<TD> This is Row 2, Cell 2 and it's 300 pixels wide</TD>
</TR>
</TABLE>
```

- **Always include widths:** The clever readers will notice that I didn't follow my own advice (to always include widths), but that was intentional so that I can explain this here. (Tricky, eh!) Wherever possible, you should always include widths in your table cells. Sometimes it really just doesn't matter, like when you've got empty table cells. But if you want to ensure that you're getting precisely the width you want, then setting widths is a good habit to get into, especially because browsers render HTML to the screen in different ways. By including both the images and the values, you ensure that no matter what browser you're using, the tables are being rendered consistently. So, to be more precise in the previous example, I really should have the following bit of code:

```
<TABLE width="500">
<TR>
<TD width="200"> <IMG src="images/hidden.gif" width="200"
        border="0"></TD>
<TD width="300"> <IMG src="images/hidden.gif" width="300"
        border="0"></TD>
</TR>
<TR>
<TD width="200"> This is Row 2, Cell 1 and it's 200
        pixels wide</TD>
<TD width="300"> This is Row 2, Cell 2 and it's 300
        pixels wide</TD>
</TR>
</TABLE>
```

I realize I gave you a lot to digest, but stick with me. What if you want to create a layout like that in Figure 8-3? Can you see the solution to the problem? Creating a layout this complex requires at least three embedded tables — and perhaps more, depending upon the complexity of some of the items in the various sections. This design, although somewhat complex, is pretty much the industry standard for news sites such as CNN, ABC, ESPN, and ZDNet, as well as pretty much any site that uses the traditional upside-down-L navigation model (the *upside-down L* refers to the primary navigation along the top, and the secondary navigation along the left-hand column).

The reality behind this design is that it's a pain to maintain, and to make it work on all browsers, you've got to use nearly every single one of the elements I mention. Moreover, if the site is at all dynamic (has changing content), then you're probably only altering a small snippet of a table to create a template that can be applied generically to a number of different pages on the site.

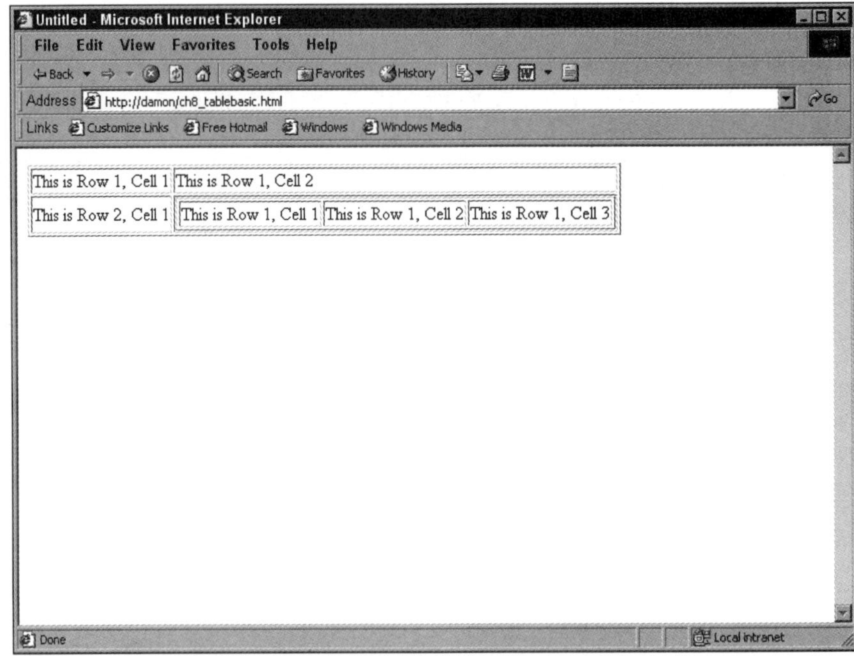

Figure 8-2: When your tables are tired, embed them!

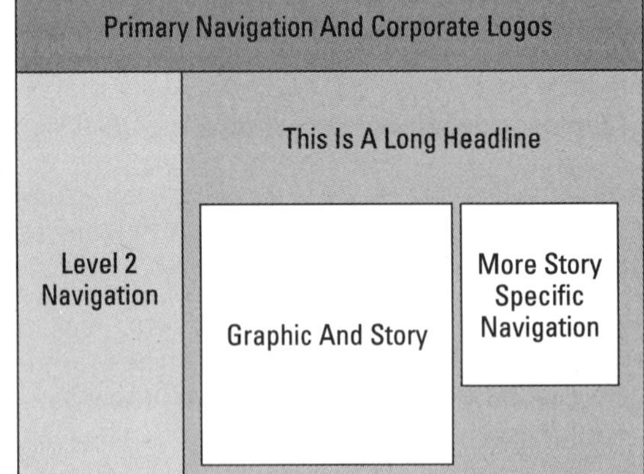

Figure 8-3: Complex, yes. Doable? Absolutely!

Old habits die hard, even though the CSS positioning properties are perfectly suited to make this part of Web development a lot easier.

I've included the HTML for the embedded table design on the CD-ROM that accompanies this book.

The Basics of Positioning

Before you turn yourself into a modern-day Jackson Pollock and start throwing content up on the screen with a vengeance, take a brief moment to review some of the basics of positioning in CSS. You have more than one way to position content using style sheets; the three basic types of positioning (plus a close cousin) are

- **Absolute positioning:** My personal fave, absolute positioning enables you to take content and place it at a specifically defined location on the screen. This is also the most common form of positioning used.
- **Relative positioning:** Use relative positioning to place content relative to other elements in the document. A simple example of this is offsetting a snippet of text 12 pixels to the left of a graphic, regardless of where that graphic lives on the screen.
- **Fixed positioning:** This big fella uses the same algorithm for placement on the screen as does absolute positioning. The main difference between the two is that fixed positioned elements generally don't move, even when you scroll the browser.
- **Floats:** Floats are kissing cousins of the wrap features in products such as QuarkXPress and PageMaker. Essentially, a float sits on top of a content element — whether positioned absolutely or relatively — and wraps the content underneath it around the object in the float.

The other big thing to keep in mind when doing positioning is the box model. (I cover the box model in detail in Chapter 7.) Remember that all content elements — no matter how they're positioned — are all part of the document tree, and, therefore, are all related to one another.

Different positioning types interpret the box model properties differently. For example, elements using absolute positioning don't give a darn about other elements in the document tree. They're just put up on the screen — if you decide to put two elements on top of each other, so be it! With relative positioning, however, you need to know where other elements are in the document structure — above, below, horizontal — to know how to correctly render them to the screen.

Up, Down, Right, Left!

Before I dive into the various positioning schemes, I first want to discuss a bit about the syntax that CSS use for determining position. To be able to place any content on the screen, you need at least two points to determine where the content will begin. Remember your high school math classes . . . ew, math, gross: To place a point on a line, you need both a vertical (y) and a horizontal (x) coordinate.

Use CSS to basically do the same thing; that is, use CSS to determine how high (or low) to place an element and also to set how far left or right the element sits. Being the magnanimous scripting language that it is, however, CSS provide you with four different positioning properties that will enable you to place your content on the screen. Called *box offsets*, the default value for all these properties is zero. Thus, if you didn't assign any values at all to them, your content would always end up in the top-left corner. These positioning properties are

- `top`: This property specifies how far the top line of content will be offset from the top. The *top* is defined by which positioning scheme you use. If, for example, you use absolute or fixed positioning, the top is the top of the browser window. If it were relative positioning, it would be the offset of the previous element.
- `bottom`: This property specifies how far from the bottom that the bottom line of the content will be placed.
- `left`: Using this property offsets your content from the left. This positioning also depends on the scheme that you choose.
- `right`: Using this property offsets your content from the right, according to the positioning scheme you choose.

With these positioning properties, you can use any of the CSS-supported unit types. However, for convenience and standardization with other elements on your Web page, your best bet is to use pixels.

Look at Figure 8-4 to see how this works. By using just a generic box, note how the various properties interact with one another to create a position on the screen. Remember though, in most cases, that you won't need to use all these properties because position can be determined by only using two of them. For example, if you use top, you don't need bottom; and if you use right, you don't use left.

Use these properties in conjunction with a positioning scheme because each of the position properties (left, right, top, and bottom) only works in conjunction with a positioning scheme (absolute, relative, fixed) page.

Put Your Content Right . . . There! Absolutely!

Absolute positioning (see the earlier section "The Basics of Positioning") is my favorite positioning scheme because it's the no-fuss, no-muss workhorse of element positioning. Just tell the browser where you want to put something, and your wish happens in the blink of an eye! (Okay, maybe it's not quite that simple, but it's darn close.)

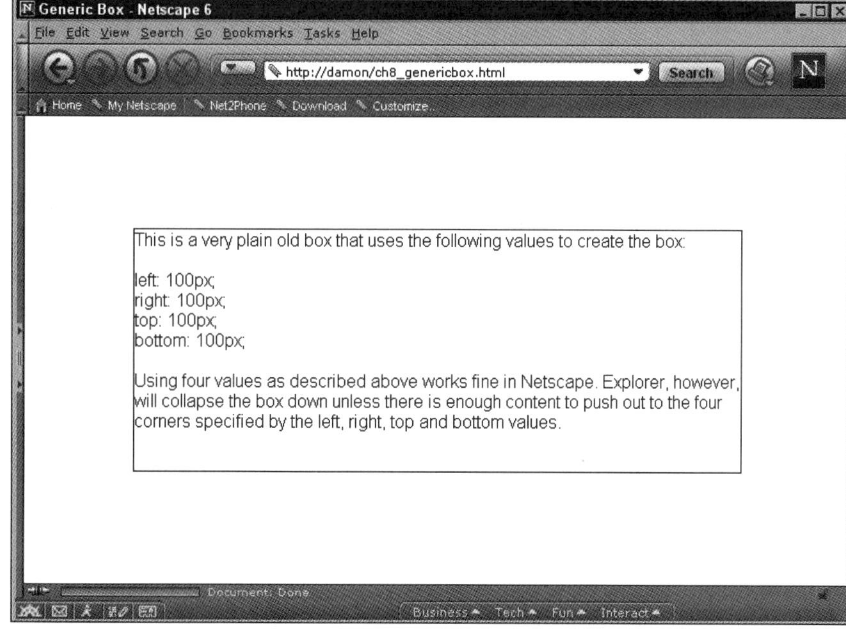

Figure 8-4: Each of the four properties can be used to place a box on the screen.

Basic properties of absolute positioning

Use the `position` property to set absolute positioning (and also relative positioning and fixed positioning). To set absolute positioning as this property's value, check out the following code snippet:

```
.style { position: absolute;}
```

(For more on relative and fixed positioning, see the upcoming sections "Positioning the Relatives" and "Somebody Fix This Positioning," respectively.)

After you choose a positioning scheme, you need to determine the screen location for your content. (You don't just use the position property by itself; you need to set its value, also.) Absolute positioning works outside the normal flow of the elements of an HTML page, giving you the freedom to put your content anywhere you want on the screen. Think of the browser window as one big Etch A Sketch with which you can position elements using the box offsets, as shown in Figure 8-5.

Here's a relatively simple example to illustrate how this works. Suppose you have a 300-pixel-wide column that you want to position in the middle of an 800 x 600-pixel browser window, and you also want this column to be offset from the top of the browser by 100 pixels.

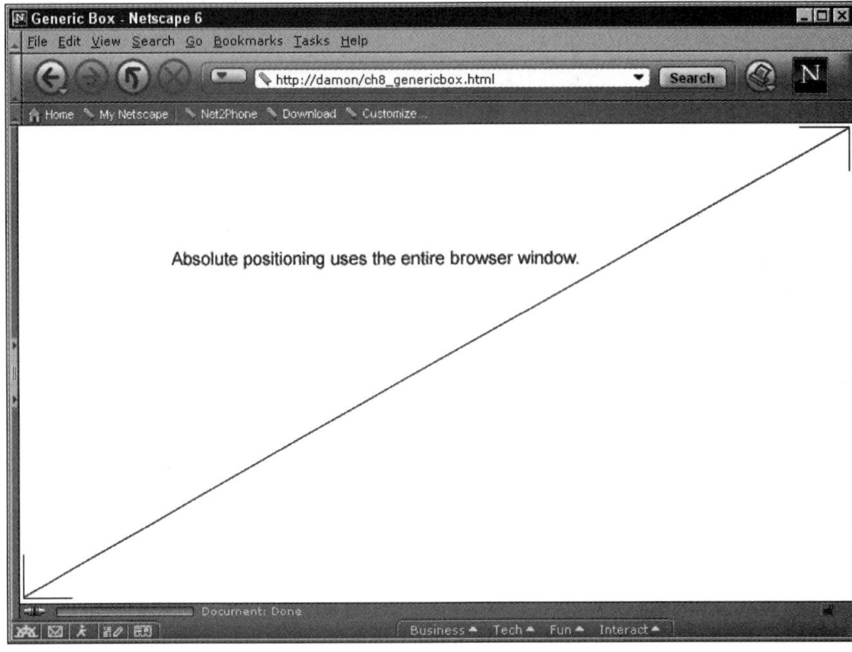

Figure 8-5: The screen is your playground with absolute positioning.

To create that style, follow these steps:

1. **In your style sheet, create a rule for the column.**

   For simplicity, name this rule `middle`.

2. **Set the size of the column using the `width` property.**

   Because the column is 300 pixels wide, the syntax would be

   ```
   width: 300px;
   ```

3. **Choose a positioning scheme.**

   Because you want to use absolute positioning, the syntax is

   ```
   position: absolute;
   ```

4. **Calculate the center position for the column.**

   Although this calculation is the trickiest part, it's really not that complicated. If you want the column to be centered on the page, first subtract 300 (its width) from 800 (the page width), and then divide that result by 2. Your answer (250) tells you how far from the left or right of the screen that the left or right column edge needs to be placed. In this case, because you're placing it right in the middle of the page, it's 250 pixels from either side of the screen.

5. **Position the element horizontally.**

   Because you know that your element needs a 250-pixel offset, use the `left` or `right` properties to set the position. I recommend that you set from the left because that's the more standard convention. The syntax is

   ```
   left: 250px;
   ```

6. **Position the element vertically.**

   To offset the element 100 pixels from the top of the browser window, use this syntax:

   ```
   top: 100px;
   ```

The resulting style, in total, would look like this.

```
.middle
   {
      width: 300px;
      position: absolute;
      left: 250px;
      top: 100px;
   }
```

See the result of calling the style from a `DIV` element in HTML in Figure 8-6.

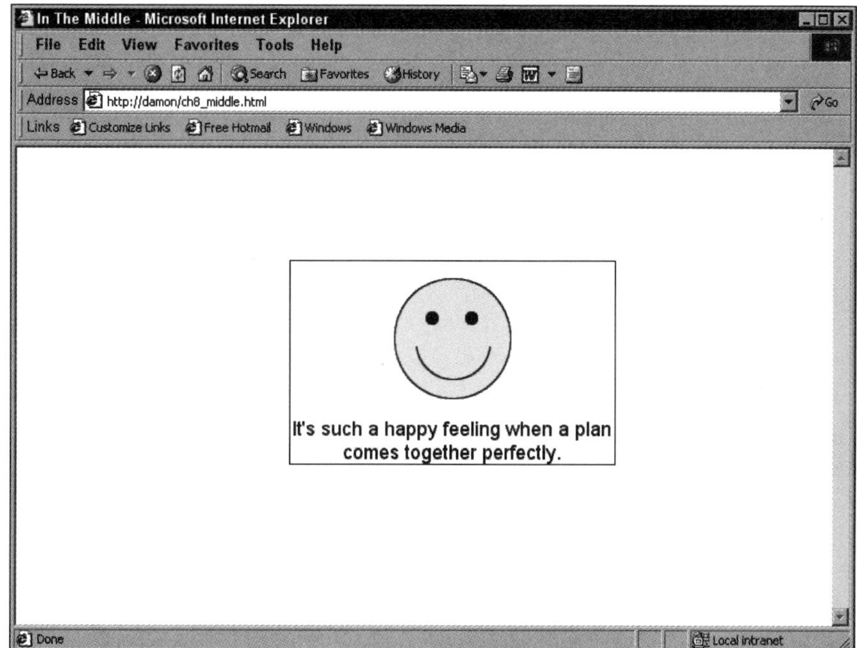

Figure 8-6: A little content happiness in the center of the screen.

Overlapping positioned elements

One of the first questions that I always hear when I'm working with developers on style sheets is whether two elements can be placed on top of one another with absolute positioning. My stock answer (I just wait for the groans) is, "Absolutely!" However, when you overlap absolute positioned elements, you then have to be cognizant of which element overlaps which. That's where the `z-index` property comes into play. (For more on the `z-index` property, read through Chapter 7.)

I've created two images, Happy and Unhappy, to illustrate this principle. Happy is a happy fellow because it's a warm gorgeous weekend in San Francisco, which is a rarity. Unhappy . . . well, he's bummed out because he couldn't go out and play in the sun this weekend because he had a book to write. (Figure out which of these fun-loving characters is the author of this book.) Because nobody likes to be around an unhappy person, I want to ensure that Unhappy is in the background (behind Happy) when I put pictures of the two of them on the Web.

To start, I create two rules in my style sheet, `happy` and `unhappy`, as follows:

```
.happy
   {
      width: 150px;
      position: absolute;
      left: 100px;
      top: 100px;
      z-index: 1;
   }

.unhappy
   {
      width: 150px;
      position: absolute;
      left: 175px;
      top: 150px;
      z-index: 0;
   }
```

I've got two rules that, when implemented, will overlap one another. Happy is offset from the left by 100 pixels, and Unhappy is offset from the left by 175 pixels. But, because the width of both elements is 150 pixels, there's a 75-pixel overlap of the two horizontally.

The Happy and Unhappy images will overlap vertically, also. Both images are about 140 pixels high. But Happy has a vertical offset of 100 pixels, and Unhappy has a vertical offset of 150 pixels vertically (do the math and you'll find 90 pixels of overlap). What will tell the tale, in this case, is the use of the z-index property. Happy has a z-index value of 1, and Unhappy has a z-index value of 0. This difference tells a browser to render Happy on top of Unhappy, and not to render the overlapping part of the image on the bottom.

Within my HTML document, I create some very simple HTML that calls both of these rules and applies to the happy.gif and unhappy.gif images. Check out the HTML here, and the results in Explorer and Netscape in Figure 8-7:

```
<body>
<div class="happy" align="center">
<img src="images/happy2.gif" width="134" height="139"
         border="0">
</div>
<div class="unhappy" align="center">
<img src="images/unhappy.gif" width="134" height="139"
         border="0">
</div>
</body>
```

Hey, kids, look! Explorer and Navigator are playing nicely together! I wish it were always that easy. For example, if I put text right after the image in the above Happy/Unhappy example, the two browsers would have rendered this to the screen differently. You can use a <BR> tag to fix this problem, but be on the lookout for such pitfalls.

Making complex page layout simple with absolute positioning

You can also use absolute positioning to simplify layout by eliminating initial table nesting. Nope, not all the table nesting goes away, but you can cut down on it significantly.

Refer back to Figure 8-3 for one of those nasty upside-down-L-shaped designs so common in many Web sites (requiring more nested tables than an antique shop owned by a pigeon). Imagine trying to build this monster in HTML. You could create a two-column table, lock the top row of that table, then use the colspan property and nest the navigation in the second row of the table. Then, in cell one of the third row of the table, you would nest another table for the secondary navigation. In cell two of row three, you'd nest another table to work on the headlines and graphics.

Doesn't that just sound ugly? That's three separate nestings before you've even put something on the page. By using absolute positioning, however, I can achieve the exact same result with three simple rules and no initial table nesting. To illustrate this, take a look at Figure 8-8. I took Figure 8-3, color-coded it, and cut it into three different pieces.

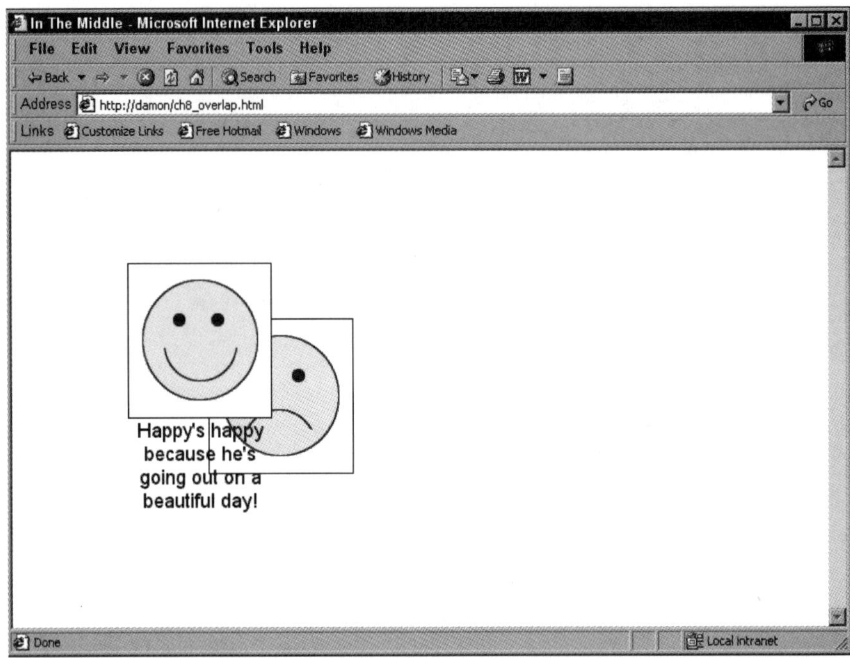

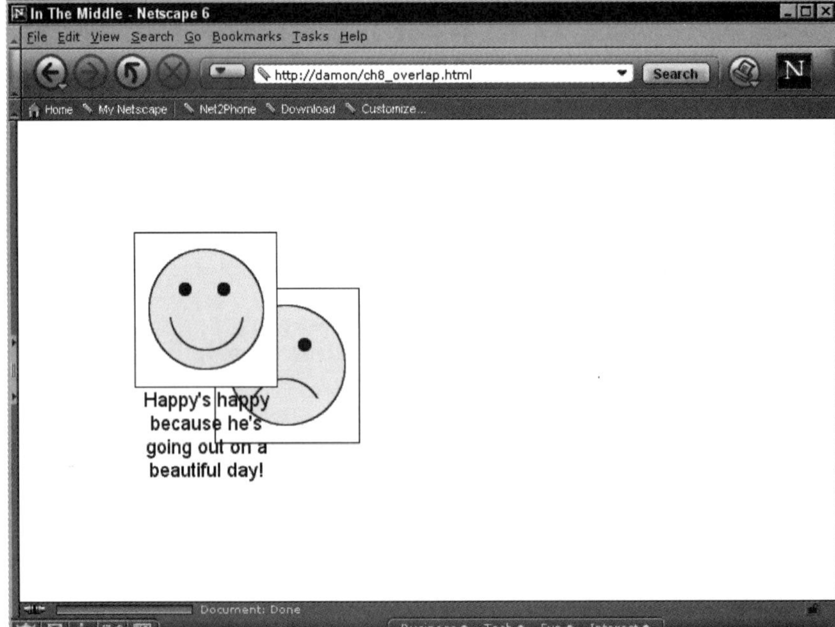

Figure 8-7: Happy's on top in both Explorer (top) and Navigator (bottom).

Primary Navigation And Corporate Logos

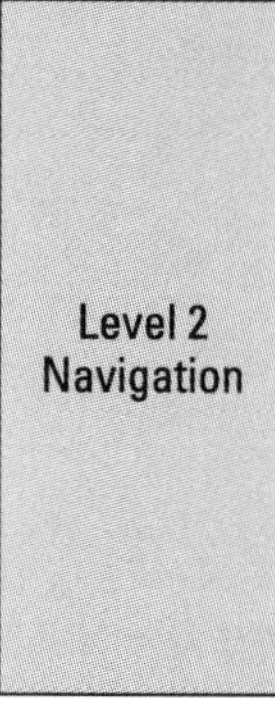

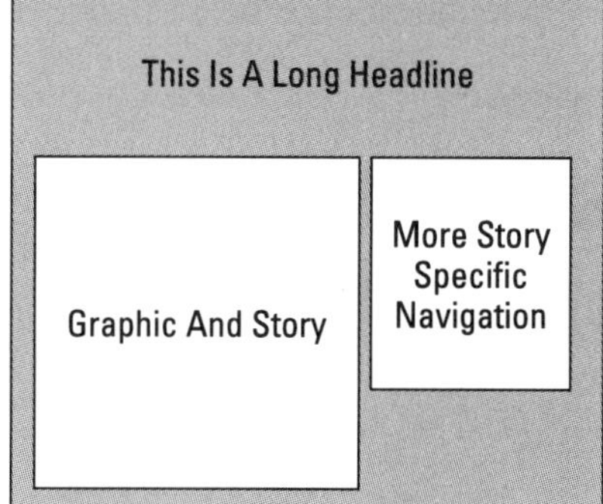

Figure 8-8: Figure 8-3, all chopped up.

Before I dive into the details, remember that this is an example using graphics. If this were really a site, you'd probably be putting content (HTML, images, and text) into these various content blocks, not big old `.gif` placeholders!

To accomplish this, follow these easy steps:

1. **Create a rule for the top navigation area.**

   We know that this piece is going to be flush with the top of the screen, as well as flush left. The image is 506 pixels wide. The rule for the top navigation area looks as follows:

   ```
   .nav
      {
         width: 506px;
         position: absolute;
         left: 0px;
         top: 0px;
      }
   ```

2. **Create a rule for the side secondary navigation area.**

   The left navigation will also be flush left, and it needs to sit right under the top navigation area. Because the top navigation graphic is 83 pixels high, you want the left navigation area to be offset by 83 pixels from the top of the browser window. The left navigation area is 121 pixels wide, too. The resulting rule, which I call `nav2`, would look as follows:

   ```
   .nav2
      {
          width: 121px;
          position: absolute;
          left: 0px;
          top: 83px;
      }
   ```

3. **Create a rule for the body to include the headline, content, and other navigation elements.**

   The body area will be offset 83 pixels from the top. Additionally, it'll be offset 121 pixels from the left side of the screen because it's sitting next to the left navigation. Incidentally, the body image is 385 pixels wide. The resulting rule, which I call `body`, looks as follows:

   ```
   .body
      {
          width: 385px;
          position: absolute;
          left: 121px;
          top: 83px;
      }
   ```

4. **Call the rules from the HTML.**

   Again, because this is just an example with graphics as placeholders, all I'm doing in the actual HTML is calling the three rules using `DIV` elements and slapping the images in those `DIV` elements. Here's the HTML to do this:

   ```
   <div class="nav"><img src="images/page_nav.gif"
          width="506" height="83" border="0"></div>
   <div class="nav2"><img src="images/page_nav2.gif"
          width="121" height="315" border="0"></div>
   <div class="body"><img src="images/page_body.gif"
          width="385" height="314" border="0"></div>
   ```

Tah dah! Together, these rules and styles recompose the image to its original form in the browser, as shown in Figure 8-9.

The one downside to this model is that it simply will not work on older browsers. If you plan on supporting IE 3.0 or anything below Netscape 4.0, then you'll have to stick to tables. No CSS elements will work in those browsers, not just the positioning properties.

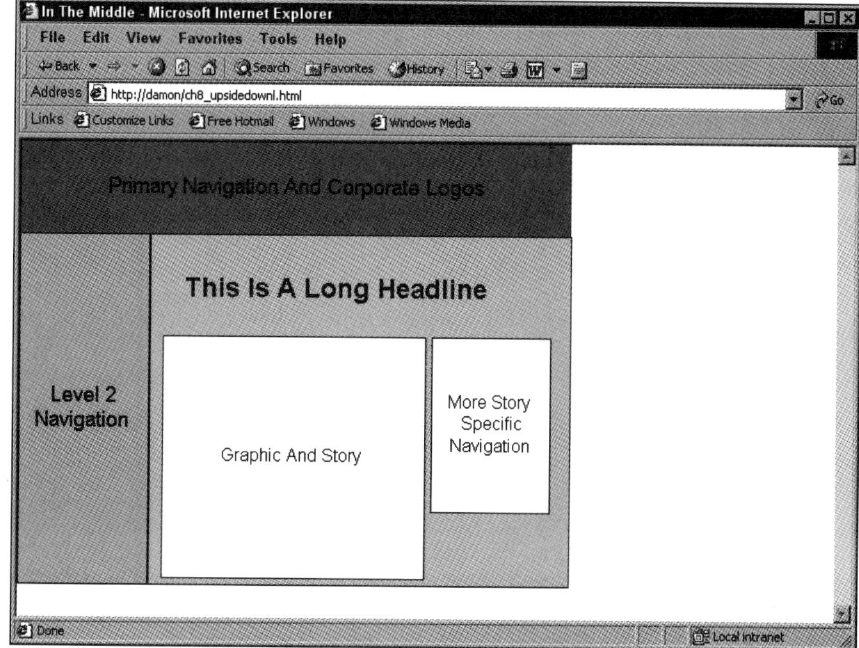

Figure 8-9: Figure 8-3, recomposed in a browser window.

Positioning the Relatives

After absolute positioning, relative positioning is the most common form of positioning in CSS. Of course, that's not saying much. Although relative positioning is well supported by browsers, even fewer folks are taking advantage of the relative positioning property.

Relative positioning is straightforward and pretty darn simple to use. The first thing to know about relative positioning is that it works, in principle, precisely like absolute positioning in that it uses the `position` property and some combination of values — `top`, `bottom`, `left`, and `right` to determine a location. The syntax for setting relative positioning is as follows:

```
position: relative;
```

And, as with absolute positioning, the box offset properties determine the distance from the top, bottom, left, and right. The difference between relative and absolute is this: For absolute positioning, the box offsets are used to determine the position of the content against the browser window; for relative positioning, the box offsets determine the location of a content element against:

- The normal flow of the page

  or

- An absolutely positioned element

Watch out below, or above, or right, or left!

Here's a hypothetical case where relative positioning makes sense. Suppose I'm working a *For Dummies* promotion, and I've put the following text in my HTML document as follows:

```
<body>
<P>The great thing about a For Dummies book is that you don't
            have to be a technical geek to understand them.
            You can laugh, sing, dance, and otherwise goof off
            with your audience. And really, how many other
            publishing companies will give you that
            opportunity? Plus, we're all a little dumb
            sometimes, aren't we?
</P>
</body>
```

With no style rules at all in my complete HTML document — save one to get rid of Times because I'm not a big fan of that font — the output looks like what you see in Figure 8-10.

Now, just for fun, add the following rule to the style sheet:

```
#Offset
   {
   position: relative;
   top: 25px;
   left: 25px;
   }
```

and then call it in the HTML directly after the last line using the following SPAN element:

```
<span id="Offset">Hey I'm not DUMB!!!.</span>
```

When the page is rendered to the screen, the *Hey I'm not DUMB!!!* element is rendered 25 pixels below and to the right (yes, offsetting using the left property pushes your text to the right) of the last character in the flow (in this case, a *?*). Calling the offset rule will offset an element 25 pixels below and to the left relative to the previous element in the flow. You can see this phenomenon in Figure 8-11.

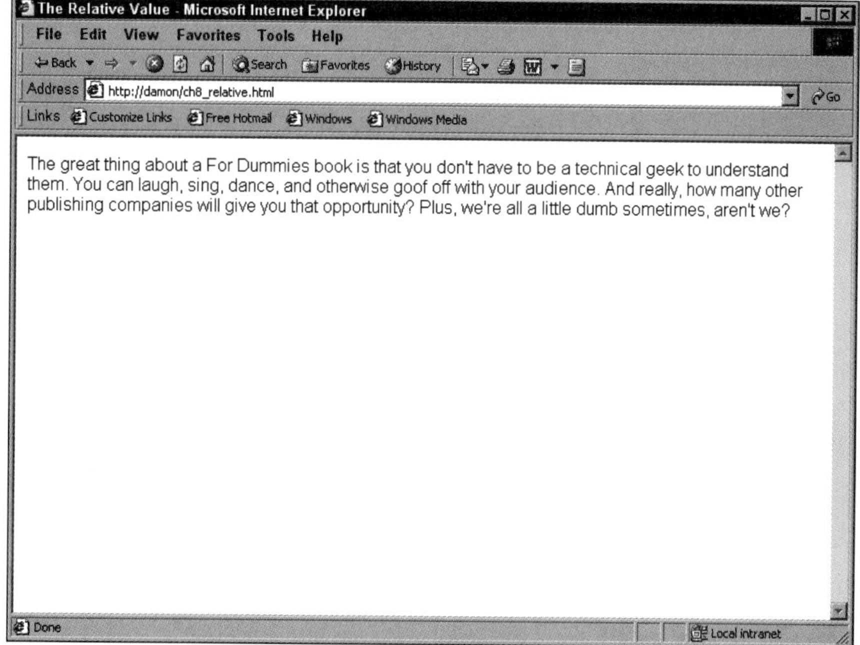

Figure 8-10: I love being a *For Dummies* author!

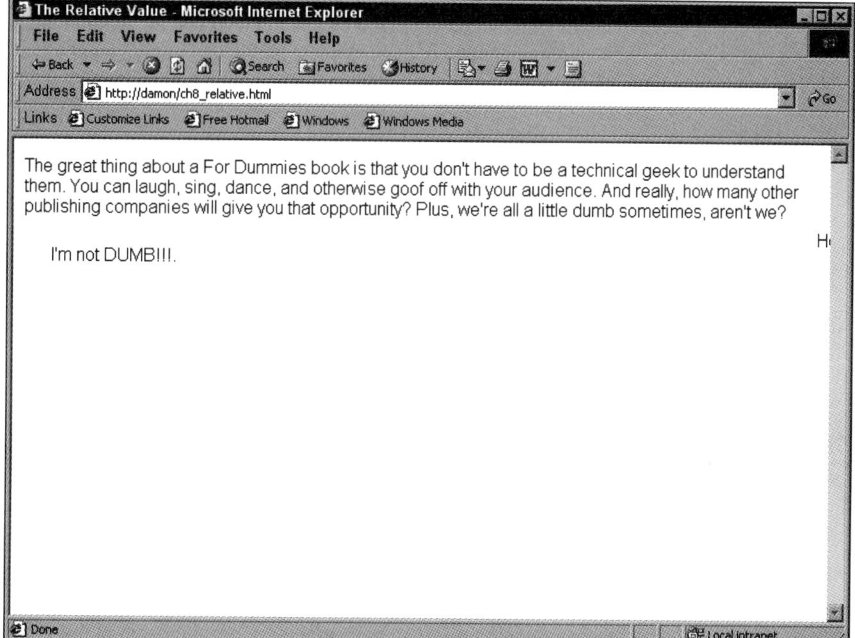

Figure 8-11: Not being DUMB is relative.

What happens if you call that rule some other place in that paragraph? Well, that's where things can get a little ugly. Suppose that you call the `offset` rule on the second sentence that begins with, *You can laugh* . . . . This sentence would be rendered 25 pixels down and to the left of the last character. However, the following (third) sentence would be precisely where it would have been if you had not offset that second sentence. Check out the resulting train wreck in Figure 8-12.

Remember that the positioning properties take an element out of the normal flow of the page, rendering them separately. So even if you ended that `P` element and then slapped a `TABLE` after it in your HTML, that *Hey I'm not DUMB!!!* line will be rendered right over the top of whatever is in that table. Similarly, if you call the rule from within a table cell, the element will be rendered right over the top of other content in the table.

Now, here's an area where Explorer and Navigator diverge. They work similarly when elements are rendered using relative positioning. However, when those same elements start bumping into other elements (images, tables, and so forth), they do act differently because the specification doesn't really specify how they should act. So, be careful when rendering objects on top of one another!

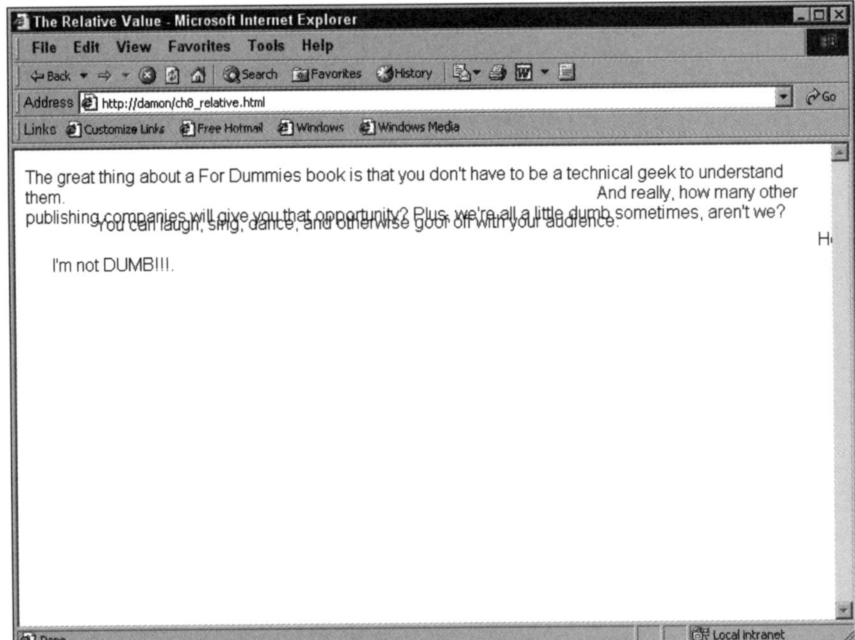

Figure 8-12: Yikes, I'm overwriting other lines!

Relative to the absolutes

What if I'm using absolute positioning and then want to use relative positioning to my absolute elements? Is such a thing possible? Of course! When you have objects outside the normal flow of the page, notably absolutely positioned elements, relative positioning works exactly the same way. Going back to our previous example, say that I've got that same first set of HTML text contained within my BODY element:

```
<P>The great thing about a For Dummies book is that you don't
           have to be a technical geek to understand them.
           You can laugh, sing, dance, and otherwise goof off
           with your audience. And really, how many other
           publishing companies will give you that
           opportunity? Plus, we're all a little dumb
           sometimes, aren't we?
</P>
```

This bit of content is considered in the normal flow. Now I want to add an absolutely positioned element to the mix, and then position an object relative to that absolutely positioned element? Ooooh, tricky!

To accomplish this, just follow these steps:

1. **Add the appropriate rules to your style sheet.**

   In this case, I've got two rules I need to add to the style sheet. I create a default DIV rule that makes the DIV absolutely positioned at 100 pixels from the top and the left, and draw a border around it so that I can see it when it renders to the screen. Also, I need to create my relatively positioned element, which is my Happy image. This style will position the Happy image 50 pixels to the left and below of the starting point of the DIV element. The two rules look as follows:

   ```
        DIV {
        width: 150px;
        position: absolute;
        left: 100px;
        top: 100px;
        border: 1px solid;
     }

   .happy
     {
        width: 150px;
        position: relative;
        left: 50px;
        top: 50px;
     }
   ```

2. **Insert the** DIV **element in the HTML.**

   For this particular example, the syntax for this is especially simple:

   ```
   <div align="center"></div>
   ```

3. **Insert the** SPAN **element into the** <DIV> **tag, call the** happy **style, and include the Happy image.**

   The resulting code looks as follows:

   ```
   <span class="happy"><img src="images/happy2.gif"
           width="134" height="139" border="0"></span>
   ```

To highlight the effect, I made the font size on the initial P element 24 pixels. See the final rendered image in Figure 8-13. From the figure, you can see the normal flow (which includes the text, rendered right down the screen) the way you'd expect. The absolutely positioned element, which is the box outline, is precisely where it should be: 100 pixels from the top of the window and 100 pixels from the left side of the window. And finally, the Happy image is offset 50 pixels from the top of the outline, 50 pixels from the left of the outline.

Try for yourself

Here's a quick exercise for you to try on your own. In an earlier section of this chapter (see "So, Just How Bad Is HTML Anyway?"), I position three images to show how to eliminate the need for nested tables. (Refer to Figure 8-3.) The body content includes a headline, a story, and graphic and story-specific navigation. Using relative positioning makes a whole lot of sense in such an example. Within the body content, you could add three spans, place them in relationship to one another, and then create the content for those elements. Here's how the styles could look:

```
.headline
   {
       font-family: Arial;
       font-size: 24px;
       position: relative;
       top: 15px;
       left: 15px;
   }

.story
   {
       font-family: Arial;
       font-size: 12px;
       width: 300px;
       position: relative;
       top: 50px;
       left: 15px;
   }
```

```
.story_nav
    {
        font-family: Arial;
        font-size: 10px;
        width: 65px;
        position: relative;
        top: 50px;
        left: 325px;
    }
```

Somebody Fix This Positioning

Fixed positioning is intended to work identically to absolute positioning, with one major difference. With fixed positioning, nothing moves, ever. So, even if you scroll the page, the object remains in its initial position when rendered. The syntax for this property would look as follows:

```
position: fixed;
top: 300px;
left: 200px;
```

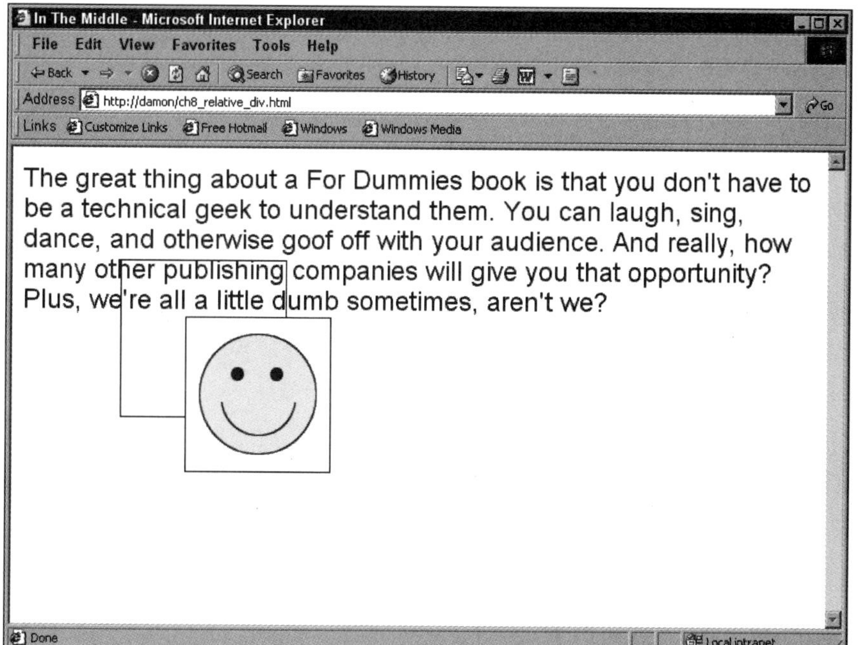

Figure 8-13: Mr. Happy, in relation to the normal flow and the absolute position!

However, although this theory sounds good, no major browser supports it yet. As such, I'm going to dance around this one and simply state that in the world of positioning, you should stick to the absolute and relative positioning models.

Floating Along

The `float` property is an easy concept, one that you don't see used very often in CSS, but if you've ever cracked the pages of a magazine, you'll see this concept used all the time in layouts where an article has a large quote surrounded by the article's text.

Although it generally applies to images, `float` can also be used with a `DIV` or `SPAN` element. Basically, a word-wrapping function built into CSS, you can use one of two properties:

- `float`: Specifies a wrap for a given element in the HTML document
- `clear`: Resets the float in that odd instance that you have two floats lined up against one another

The values for the `float` property are `left`, `right`, and `none`; values for the `clear` property are `left`, `right`, `both`, and `none`.

That's a wrap!

So, imagine for a moment, that you want to wrap your text around an image. Consider the following HTML text, by now quite familiar:

```
<p><img class="happy" src="images/happy2.gif" width="134"
          height="139" border="0">
The great thing about a For Dummies book is that you don't
          have to be a technical geek to understand them.
          You can laugh, sing, dance, and otherwise goof off
          with your audience. And really, how many other
          publishing companies will give you that
          opportunity? Plus, we're all a little dumb
          sometimes, aren't we? </p>
```

You may have noticed that I included a reference to a class called `happy` in the `<IMG>` tag. In my style sheet, I also add a simple little rule called `happy` as follows:

```
.happy   {
   float: left;
   padding: 3px;
   }
```

When this page is rendered to the screen (as shown in Figure 8-14), you can see that the image is floated to the left, and the text wraps around the image. I add padding here because although Explorer automatically puts a little padding around the image, Navigator doesn't (so the padding will serve to offset the image from the text in Navigator). Strangely, though, the `padding` property isn't supported on the `<IMG>` tag in Explorer, so it simply has no effect on it there. Using the `right` value will do precisely the opposite and align the image to the right side of the page.

Clear out!

The `clear` property comes into play when you want to ignore the `float` that's in process. This property basically says, "Aww, forget about this wrap stuff, and put me under the wrapping image." Building on the example in the previous section, if I add the following rule to my style sheet:

```
H1   {
      font-family: Arial;
      clear: left;
   }
```

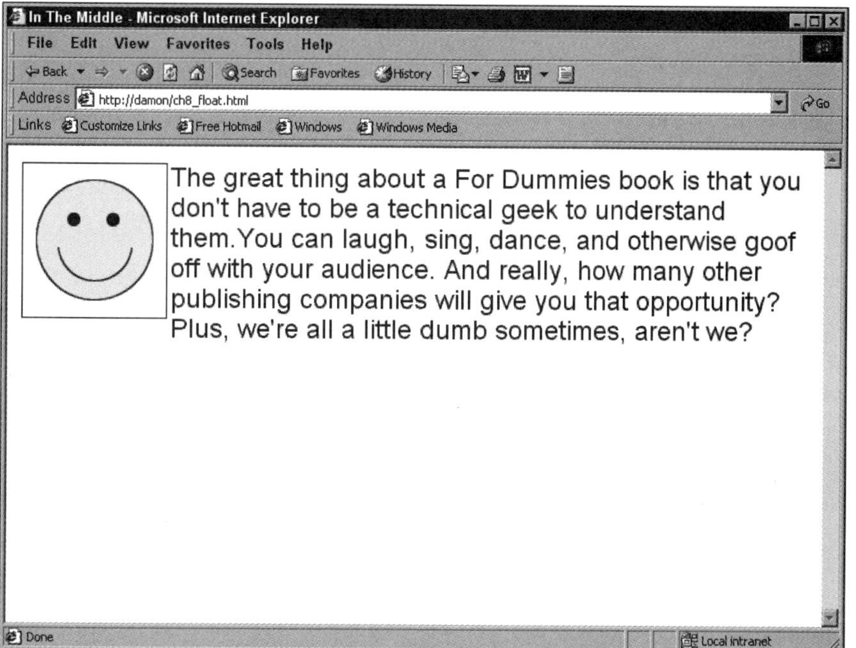

Figure 8-14: Mr. Happy likes his left float!

and then change the HTML code to what follows, you can see how the `float` gets ignored mid-way through, and drops the <H1> element beneath the image, as shown in Figure 8-15.

```
<p><img class="happy" src="images/happy2.gif" width="134"
        height="139" border="0">
The great thing about a For Dummies book is that you don't
        have to be a technical geek to understand them.
        <h1>You can laugh, sing, dance, and otherwise goof
        off with your audience. And really, how many other
        publishing companies will give you that
        opportunity? Plus, we're a all little dumb
        sometimes, aren't we?</h1> </p>
```

If the `float` had been on the right, you would use the `right` value in that case. Similarly, if you're stuck between two images and want to clear both of them, you could use the `both` value.

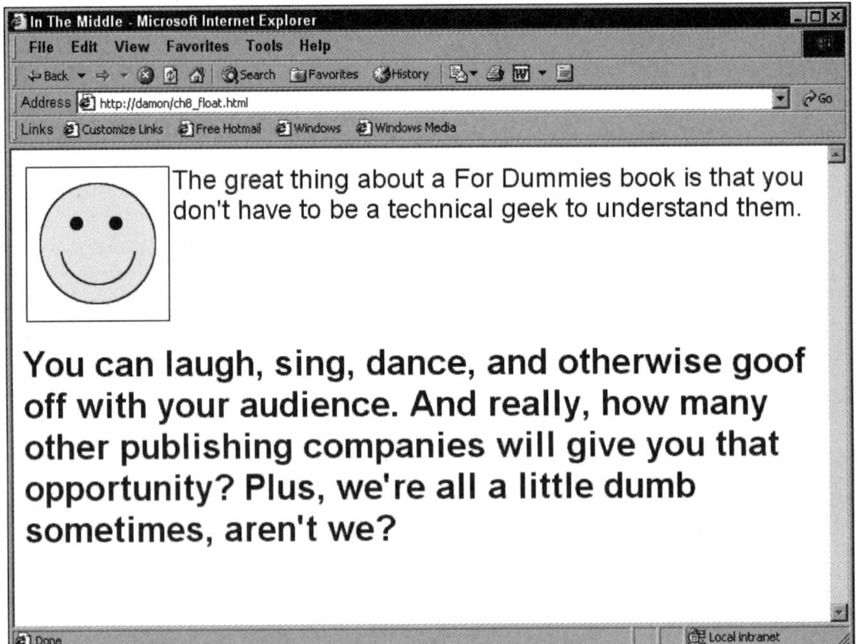

Figure 8-15: Outta my way, float!

Chapter 9

Inheritance under the Hood

In This Chapter

- Understanding how cascading works in style sheets
- Using one style as a basis for another (inheritance)
- Calling the `@import` rule to import styles

In this chapter, I discuss the big *C* (cascading) part of Cascading Style Sheets. In the first eight chapters of this book, I've liberally dropped the cascading part of CSS for the same reason that everyone else just uses the term *style sheets*. Developers simply don't pay that much attention to the word *cascade*. I bet that if you line up ten developers in a row and ask them what the acronym CSS stands for, you'd be lucky if one of them could tell you.

Actually, the concept of cascading isn't that difficult to understand. Any element in an HTML document may have more than one style present. The cascade is the process by which the browser determines which style gets the priority over the others and then gets applied to an element in the document. This is distinctly different than *inheritance*, which is the process of passing a style down from one element to another element in a document. I describe both of these concepts in more detail in the following sections.

I designed this chapter to help you understand how the cascade and inheritance are applied to elements in a document. Here you find these concepts in easy-to-understand terms, but you should really take some time and create your own examples to test the cascade and inheritance on your own work.

How the Cascade in CSS Works

All the cascade really does is to determine which style should be applied to an element in the document. Period. That's it.

Of course, this is made slightly more difficult because in the course of rendering a document, the browser may come up against several style rules that are applied to the same element. When these rules overlap, the browser has to have some way to sort it all out and say, "Aw, heck, just use this one!"

What happens when this virtual train wreck of rules comes crashing into an unsuspecting element? Well, here's what the CSS specification says:

1. **Find all the properties that have been applied to an element.**

   Only those that have been applied count. Toss all the others out.

2. **Apply weight to properties according to where they originated from, in the following order: Author, User, and User Agent.**

   Oh, and you have a wildcard in there, the `!important` declaration, which automatically supercedes the origin of any rule.

3. **Sort by the rule's specificity.**

   I discuss the rules and formulas for specificity in the section "How specific the rule is" later in this chapter.

4. **Then, if the values are still equal after the previous three criteria are met, take the one that is read by the browser last.**

The cascade feature is poorly implemented in the different browsers. Although inheritance (which I discuss in the later sections of this chapter) works reasonably well in the newer browsers, the cascade is still a hornet's nest of problems. Unfortunately, the only sure-fire way to find out whether the cascade is working properly is through trial and error.

Where the style came from

Styles can come from three different sources when the browser renders a page. To know which style to use, browsers have rules (a kind of protocol) for determining what precedence they should assign to selectors coming from each of the sources. The three origins of style sheets, in order of priority, are:

- **Author:** That'd be me, or more accurately, you. *Author style sheets* are those that are contained in a document or linked to it. These are the kinds of style sheets I talk about in this book.
- **User:** *User style sheets* are styles called by your audience, when, for example, you write a feature into a page that enables the user to apply a specific style sheet to a page. Although not very common, I admit, but I have seen this used, and the browser has to know how to interpret these styles in the document hierarchy.

- **User Agent:** The *User Agent* is — in most cases — the browser. The browser has a default set of styles that it loads when no other styles are applied to the page, as shown in Figure 9-1. (These are the same ugly styles you've seen since the early days of HTML.)

To understand how these priorities work, take the case of the H1 element as an example. Suppose that I only have the following rule in my style sheet. ***Note:*** Because this is in my style sheet, it is an Author style:

```
BODY {
font-family: Arial;
font-size: 12px;
}
```

Then, I go ahead and include the following HTML in my document; see the output in Figure 9-2:

```
<BODY>
Hey there everyone. I'm some very nice Arial text, specified
           by the BODY rule.
<H1>And I'm a big old H1. But shouldn't I be 12 pixels high,
           since I'm a child element of the BODY element?
           </H1>
</BODY>
```

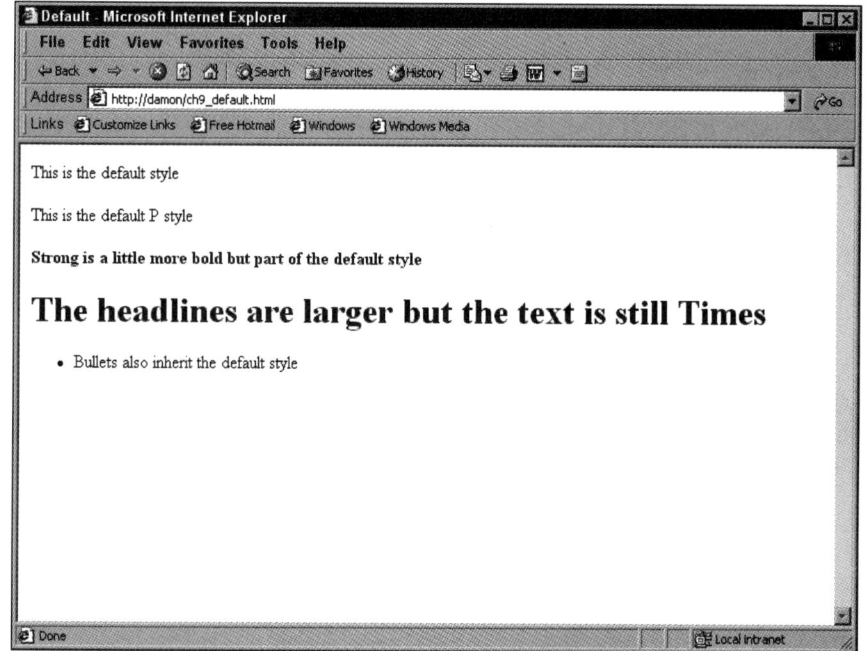

Figure 9-1: The User Agent styles. Oooh, sexy.

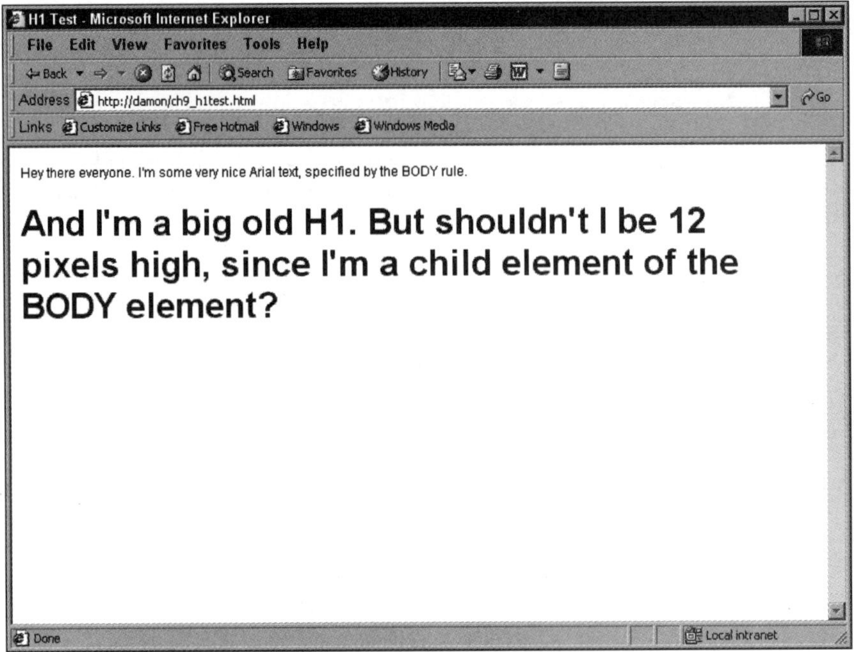

Figure 9-2: Shouldn't that H1 be 12 pixels high? Nope!

As you can see in Figure 9-2, the `H1` element creates a larger font size than the 12 pixels. This is a case where you have two styles, with two different origins, competing for one element, the `H1`. The default style rule for an `H1` element already exists in the document through the User Agent, and that rule states that the `H1` element will be `2em` (this comes from the CSS2 specification) in size. But, the `BODY` element also has a rule from the Author that states that the default text size for the document should be `12px`. The `H1` element *inherits* (I discuss this in more detail in the latter half of this chapter) the `12px` value. In the example, the User Agent style won out because the rules of specificity determine which style rule will be the one the browser eventually uses to render the element. Specificity is described in the following section.

How specific the rule is

Specificity seeks to assign weight to a rule based on just how specific it is. More specific rules generate a higher specificity rating, and thus, a higher priority in the cascade. But, rather than just add up points, the rules of specificity add numbers to columns (a, b, c) which then represent ones, tens, and hundreds to generate a numeric value.

The rules for specificity read like Hoyle's *Rules of Games*. If I didn't know any better, I'd swear that this formula would work wonders at the craps table. Here's how you can calculate specificity of a selector (and yes, this is what the browser does when it renders an element to the screen):

1. **Count the number of `ID` attributes in the selector: that is, any selector that includes a number (#) sign.**

   This will be (a) and represents the hundreds column.

2. **Count the number of other attributes and pseudo-classes in the rule: that is, any selector that includes a period (.), or in the case of a pseudo-class, a colon (:).**

   This will be (b) and represents the tens column.

3. **Count the number of element names in the selector: that is, any selector that includes an element such as `P`, `DIV`, or `BODY`.**

   This will be (c) and represents the ones column.

The value is then presented as `abc`, and the selector with the highest value wins the precedence and a year's supply of Top Ramen. In Table 9-1, I include some possible selectors and their specificity values.

Table 9-1 Selector Specificity Scores

Selector	*a*	*b*	*c*	*Overall Score*
P	0	0	1	1
BODY DIV	0	0	2	2
DIV.cool	0	1	1	11
P.cool.cooler	0	2	1	21
#coolest	1	0	0	100
P#coolest	1	0	1	101

If you want to ensure that a selector gets applied, use an inline style! They have the highest specificity score every time, unless of course, the `!important` value is called, which I discuss in the next section.

Some values are very !important

One counteraction to the natural order of things in the grand Author, User, User Agent, and specificity world is the `!important` value. You can use the `!important` value when you want to ensure that a rule will be applied.

Basically, it gives the selectors within the rule incredibly high cascade values so that they always win. The !important value has one important rule: It must always go at the end of a declaration, right before the semi-colon. Otherwise, it could totally mess up your style sheet.

Here's a quick example that the whole family can try at home!

Combining this important style sheet rule

```
P {
   font-family: Arial !important;
   }
```

with a quick bit of text for the HTML page with an inline style

```
<P style="font-family: Times"> Now, I wonder what font this
          will end up being? The answer: Arial! The reason?
          The !important value</P>
```

and Figure 9-3 tells the tale! The !important value in the P element overrides the inline style.

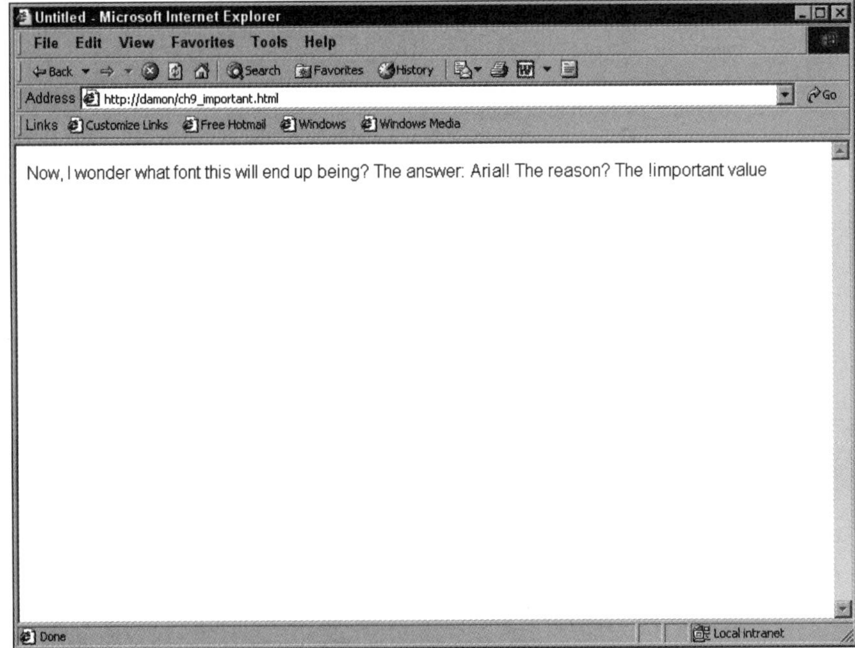

Figure 9-3: So much for the high specificity of that inline style.

The `!important` value only works for elements that match a rule with the `!important` value. If, for example, you're inheriting a rule with an `!important` value, the specificity will still be 0 (zero) on the rule for that element — and thus, will be overwritten if another rule with a higher specificity matches that element.

Note: The `!important` value is not well implemented in the older browsers. Internet Explorer (IE) 5.0 and Netscape Navigator 6.0 both support it, but don't expect it to work consistently across the board in the older group of browsers.

Determining Your Inheritance

Whereas cascade determines the priority, *inheritance* is the practical application of those priorities in a document hierarchy.

A document — any document really — is a collection of elements. A document may just contain text, for example, with no structure at all. Such a document is said to have a completely flat hierarchy. There's no structure to it, except for the structure of the document itself, which carries with it a set of default properties.

Alternatively, a document could be segmented to include any number of categories and sub-categories. So, for example, I may have a book that is segmented into chapters. Within those chapters, I could structure major sections with a series of sub-sections.

Understanding parents, children, and siblings

To understand the parent-child-sibling document hierarchy, take a look at this chapter's structure. Consider the following outline for the chapter:

```
1) Chapter 9: Cascading Your Inheritance
   a. How the Cascade in CSS Works
      i. Where the style came from
      ii. How specific the rule is
      iii. Some values are very !important
   b. Determining Your Inheritance
      i. Understanding parents, children, and siblings
      ii. Inheritance in action
      iii. Using the inherit property
   c. Tasty Imported Rules
```

Item 1), the chapter title, is the highest — or **parent** — level item in the outline. It is the parent of all items beneath it, namely items a, b, and c. Similarly, items a, b, and c are the **children** of Item 1). In relationship to one another, these items are said **siblings** (equal status) of one another. Items i and ii are the children of Item a and only Item a. Items i and ii are also children of Item 1), and are siblings to one another. See this relationship graphically in Figure 9-4.

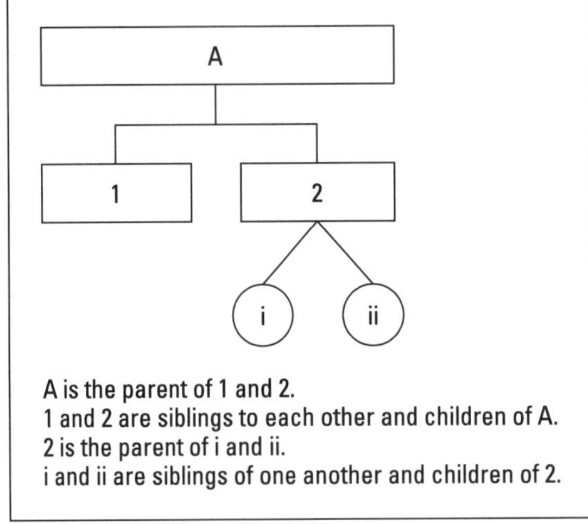

A
1
2
i
ii
A is the parent of 1 and 2.
1 and 2 are siblings to each other and children of A.
2 is the parent of i and ii.
i and ii are siblings of one another and children of 2.

Figure 9-4: The parent-child-sibling relationship.

The same basic logic holds true for an HTML document. In an HTML document, the BODY element is always the highest-level item in the document, making it akin to the chapter title in the above example. From there, though, the hierarchy is determined largely by the interaction of a number of equivalent elements. The major elements include P, DIV, SPAN, A, B, I, and EM.

For example, suppose I have a P element in my HTML document, and within that P element, I have an <A> tag. After I close out the P element, I put a DIV element; within that DIV element, I have two SPAN elements. For this example's sake, imagine the code looked like this:

```
<BODY>
   <P>This is a P. <A>Here's my A tag.</A></P>
   <DIV> Here's the DIV elememt, <SPAN> and it
           contains</SPAN> two <SPAN> SPAN
           elements</SPAN></DIV>
</BODY>
```

In this case, P and DIV are children of BODY, and are siblings of one another. <A> is the child of P, and the two SPAN elements are children of the DIV element, and are also siblings to one another.

If you understand the parent-child-sibling relationship in your HTML document, you can easily figure out how your styles will be applied to various elements in the document.

Inheritance in action

On paper, inheritance looks pretty good. But how does it act when you really start using it? That's the $64,000,000 question! (Nice inheritance, eh?) The rules for inheritance are, in fact, pretty straightforward. Every style element in an HTML document inherits its style from its parent element, unless specified to do something else. So, if you set the following rule for my HTML document:

```
BODY {
   font-family: Arial;
   }
```

you'd find that when you load your page, all the text would be in Arial, regardless of the other elements included in the document, as shown in Figure 9-5. None of the other elements in the document have any styles associated with them, so the page defaults to the Arial font because it was specified for the `BODY` element, the parent element of everything else in the document.

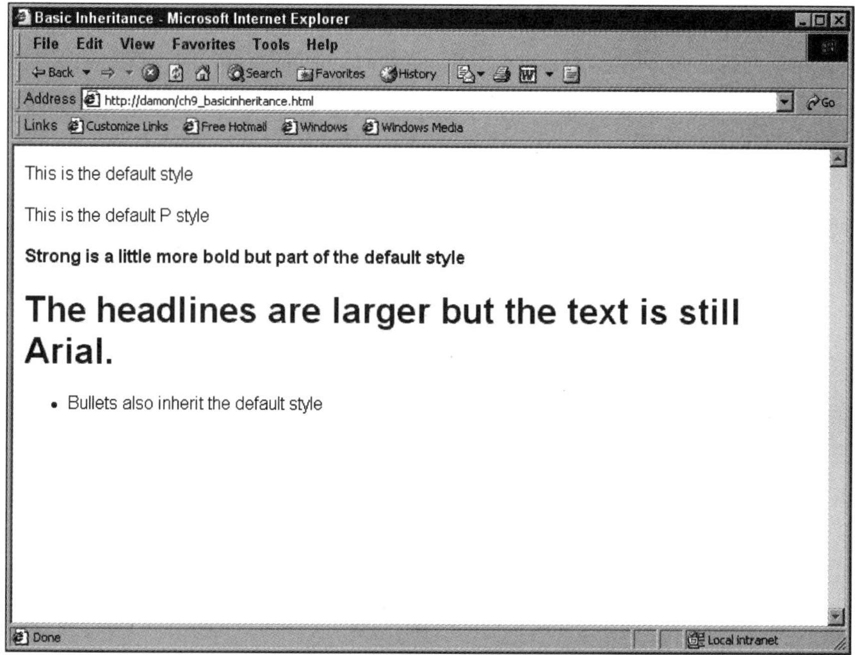

Figure 9-5: No matter what the element, the font remains Arial.

In the following style sheet, a font size is added to the BODY element, and a rule is added for the P elements in the document:

```
<style>
BODY {
    font-family: Arial;
    font-size: 12px;
    }
P {
    font-size: 18px
    }
</style>
```

The first rule of this style sheet dictates that the default font style for the entire HTML document will use a 12-pixel Arial font. Therefore, if a DIV element is created, it will use 12-pixel Arial because no other style except the default style has been specified for DIV elements. If, however, a P element shows up at the party, then the font size for that element should change from 12 pixels to 18 pixels high.

The following code provides an example of when this will happen:

```
<BODY>
This is the default text for the site.
<DIV> This is a DIV element, but since no other style rule
           has been specified for DIVs, then this will
           inherit the font-family and font-size values from
           the BODY element.</DIV>
<P>P elements, however, have a font-size specified for them
           that is different than the default size. The value
           specified for the P element value will overwrite
           the default and it will not inherit the BODY font-
           size value</P>
</BODY>
```

In Figure 9-6, you can see the output of this style rule and HTML combo platter. And yes, indeed, those P elements do look bigger.

Some elements in the document hierarchy — H1 to H6 for example — have font-size specified for them by the browser. I cover this earlier in the chapter in the section "How the Cascade in CSS Works," but I touch on this here in case you try testing the previous example with something else besides a P element.

For one last example of inheritance, see Figure 9-7. From the figure, you can see some similar elements are being applied throughout the document. You can also see some very different things going on with different elements.

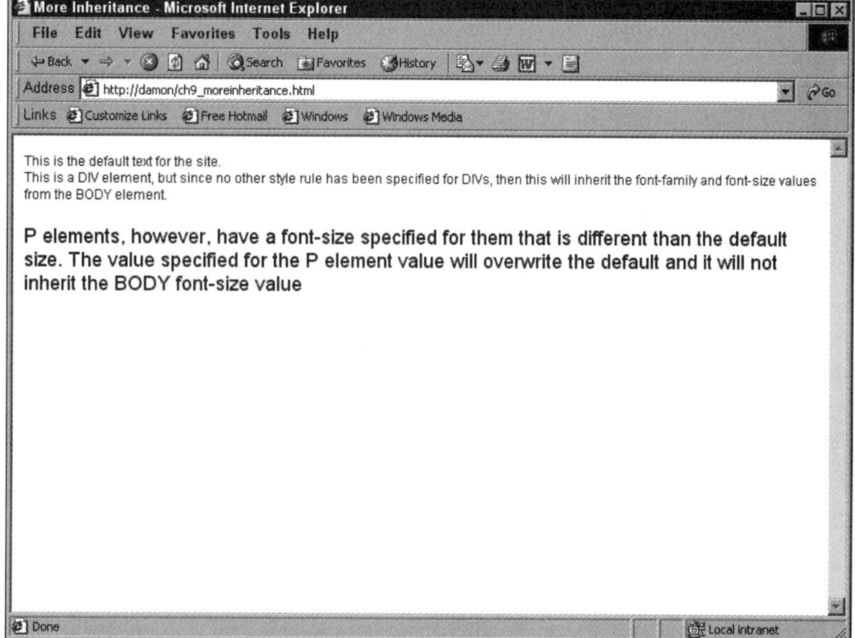

Figure 9-6: Good-sized P elements in this one!

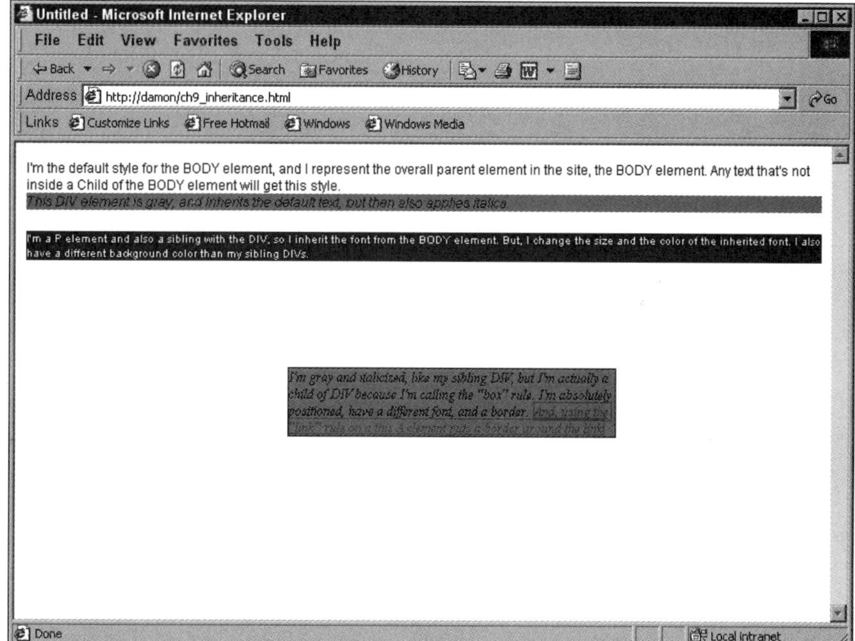

Figure 9-7: There are some similar styles to be found here.

So what's driving this one? The styles that are driving this page are located here:

```
<style>
 BODY {
   font-family: Arial;
   font-size: 12px;
   }

P   {
   font-size: 10px;
   background-color: black;
   color: white;
   }

DIV   {
background-color: gray;
   font-style: italic;
   }
.link {
   border: 1px solid;
   }
.box
   {
      font-family: Times;
      width: 300px;
      position: absolute;
      left: 250px;
      top: 100px;
      border: 1px solid;
   }
</style>
```

Like all the previous examples, the default style for the `BODY` element here is also the 12-pixel Arial font. The other two primary styles, `P` and `DIV`, offer glimpses of how siblings can be both equivalent in the hierarchy but very different in style. The `P` element keeps the font (Arial) but drops the size to 10 pixels and changes the font color. The `DIV` element also uses Arial, but italicizes it. Both the `P` and `DIV` elements also change the background color, overwriting the parent style that has no background color at all. In addition to these primary styles, two additional styles are also available to use.

For this example, here's the HTML that makes up Figure 9-7:

```
<body>
I'm the default style for the BODY element, and I represent
         the overall parent element in the site, the BODY
         element. Any text that's not inside a Child of the
         BODY element will get this style.
```

```
<DIV>This DIV element is gray, and inherits the default text,
          but then also applies italics.</DIV>
<DIV class="box">I'm gray and italicized, like my sibling
          DIV, but I'm actually a child of DIV because I'm
          calling the "box" rule. I'm absolutely positioned,
          have a different font, and a border. <A
          class="link" href="#">And, using the "link" rule
          on a this A element puts a border around the
          link</A></DIV>
<P>I'm a P element and also a sibling with the DIV, so I
          inherit the font from the BODY element. But, I
          change the size and the color of the inherited
          font. I also have a different background color
          than my sibling DIVs. </P>
</body>
```

This HTML provides a great example of how pervasive and far down into the hierarchy inheritance can be applied. The document has the following hierarchy:

```
BODY
   DIV
   DIV
      .box
      .link
P
```

If you go all the way down to the `A` element using the link rule, you can walk all the way back up through the document and follow the inherited attributes, using Figure 9-4 as a guide. The `A` element is inheriting the `font-size` from the `BODY` element. The background color is inherited from the `DIV` element. Finally `font-family` and positioning come as a result of the `box` rule.

Using the inherit property

Although inheritance happens naturally in an HTML document, it's not always consistent, as I discuss earlier in this chapter in the sections covering cascading. With the advent of CSS2, the designers created a new value that enables Web developers to control what gets inherited and how. You can use `inherit` with *any* property in CSS. Yes, that's any property! Suppose I have the following style rules:

```
<style>
BODY {
font-family: Arial;
font-size: 12px;
}
```

```
H1   {font-size: inherit;
   }
</style>
```

With the inherit property, all H1 elements in the document using these rules would be 12 pixels.

inherit is a new property in CSS2 and has really not been implemented well. Most of the older 4.0 browsers don't support this property yet, and quick tests with both IE 5.5 and Navigator 6.0 show that IE does not yet support this property, but Navigator does.

Tasty Imported Rules

Use the @import rule as another way to collect a style and include it in the document, making it a friendly next-door neighbor to the <LINK> feature in HTML.

The @import syntax allows for two variations, as follows:

```
@import "stylesheet_name.css"
@import url {"stylesheet_name.css";}
```

After you use this property, you can then call styles from that style sheet and apply them to the document you're working with. And yes, you can use this command in concert with styles from your own HTML pages or linked files. You can also use this rule to import rules based on other media types. So, for example, using the following rule

```
@import "stylesheet_name.css" tv
```

would import this style sheet when rendering to a TV-based browser. I cover media types in more detail in Chapter 15.

Part III

Putting CSS to Work for You

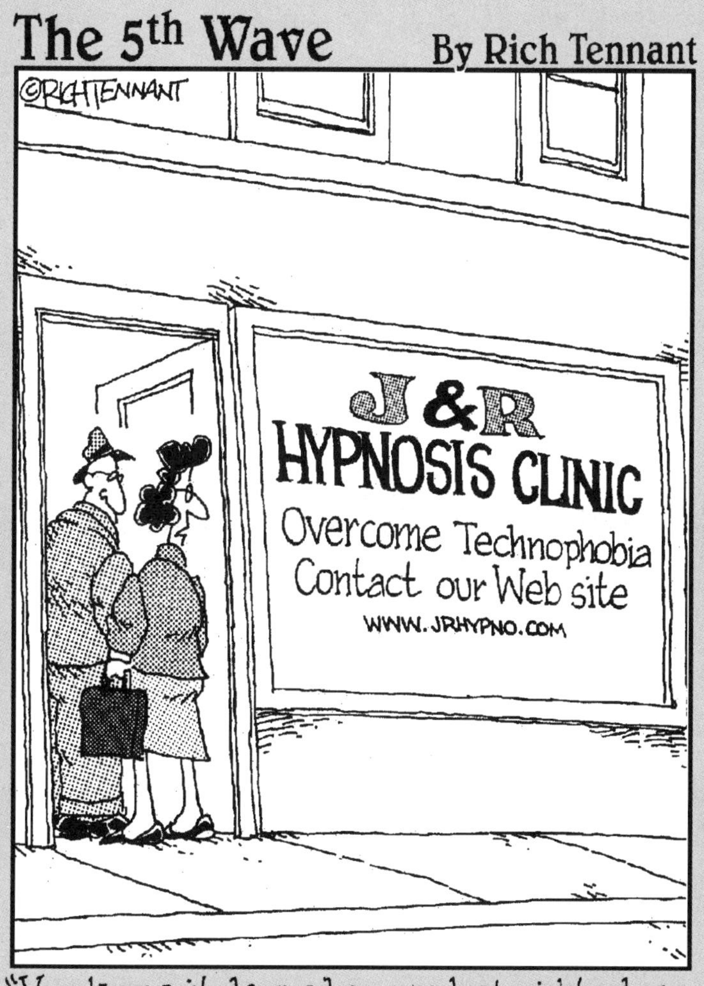

The 5th Wave
By Rich Tennant
©RICHTENNANT
J & R
HYPNOSIS CLINIC
Overcome Technophobia
Contact our Web site
WWW.JRHYPNO.COM

"You know, it dawned on me last night why we aren't getting any hits on our Web site."

In this part . . .

Suit up and grab your gear. Every good game needs its rules and regulations. From the skills you can acquire in Part II, it's time to hit the field running for real in Part III.

This part is jam-packed with all kinds of ideas to help you design your Web site using good old Cascading Style Sheets (CSS). After you breeze through this section, you'll know when to use more than one CSS, how to make your style sheets play nicely together, how to use more than one style sheet on the same page, and how to get over those darn inheritance rules.

Even if you're not starting your site from scratch, read here to discover how and when to enhance your existing content by adding CSS to your current Web site.

The CSS game is about to begin. The quarter is tossed, the fans await, the whistle blows. . . .

Chapter 10

Designing with Style Sheets

In This Chapter

- Deciding how much to use Cascading Style Sheets in your site
- Creating style sheets that work well together
- Discovering what to avoid when using Cascading Style Sheets
- Determining the best places to go inline with your styles

Cascading Style Sheets (CSS) are great in theory, but what really happens when you want to build a site from the ground up using style sheets? Should you just forget about everything you know about HTML and use CSS from start to finish? Or can you find a happy medium to get you up and running faster?

Answering those types of questions is precisely what I do in this chapter. Pretend that you don't have an existing Web site or that you want to get rid of your site altogether and start over again. Here I arm you with you a host of tips and questions to ask yourself as you begin to construct your site, and I give you the tools to make good decisions about the way your site should be designed with style sheets.

Disclaimer time! Although this chapter is a good primer to help you determine what should go into structuring your style sheets, every site understandably has different requirements, be it e-commerce or a simple site with pictures of the kids — and as the requirements change, so should the design of the style sheets.

Just How Deep Is the Deep End?

Your first step to designing or redesigning your site — and thus determining how much you want to use style sheets — is to think about the basic structure and needs of your site. Ask yourself a number of questions, such as

- How many pages do I need?
- How is the Web site organized?

- What do I need to apply styles to?
- What are my browser requirements?
- Who is my audience?

Questions like these will get you thinking about how you should begin to approach working with style sheets in your site. Check out a deeper discussion of these considerations in Chapter 3.

Before you decide, however, to use CSS at every possible place in your site, consider the following facts about Web developing with CSS:

- No browser out there is fully compliant with CSS2, and most aren't fully compliant with CSS1.
- Although Microsoft (Internet Explorer, or IE) is increasingly dominating the browser landscape, Netscape (Navigator) still owns upwards of 20 percent of the overall browser market. Considering that AOL owns Netscape, you can't discount its presence — Netscape may likely end up being absorbed by AOL in short order. No matter how much you'd like to convince yourself otherwise, you usually have to develop for both browsers.
- The more CSS you choose to implement, the more work you have to do to support the non-CSS browsers: that is, Netscape 3.*x* and below, and IE 3.0.
- The Macintosh operating system isn't going away anytime soon, despite the critics and pundits. So plan on developing for at least two browsers and two platforms (for PCs and for Macs).
- A lot of the whiz-bang properties in CSS (including dynamic menus, positioning, and visibility) require the use of other code to really make them useful, usually JavaScript.
- Worse yet, some of these same features require using Dynamic HyperText Markup Language (DHTML) and the Document Object Model (DOM), which will add a tremendous amount of development time and frustration to the process.

DHTML is beyond the scope of this book, but it isn't out of the scope of *this* book: *Dynamic HTML For Dummies*, 2nd Edition by Michael Hyman, published by Hungry Minds, Inc. I have a copy of it myself; it's a great book for getting to the root of all things DHTML.

Safety in the basics

When it comes to designing with CSS, you should begin with the basics because those properties are the best supported and some of the easiest to use. I don't mean to imply that you should just forget about some of the more cool and interesting properties, but seriously consider the impact of using these properties before you begin.

To help you choose the more basic (and safe) toys, I list 15 of the most commonly used CSS properties in Table 10-1. I also tell you just how safe they are, and which browser versions you should avoid if they're not very well supported.

Table 10-1 The CSS Top 15

Property	*Safety Factor*	*Issues*
font-family	Safe	None.
font-size	Safe	Try to avoid the absolute and relative sizes. Stick to length and percentage.
font-style	Safe	None.
font-weight	Safe	Netscape 4 for the Mac doesn't like a couple of the font-weight values (bolder and lighter).
color	Safe	None.
padding	Pretty safe	Older versions of browsers have some issues on inline properties, including padding.
position	Pretty safe	Because IE and Netscape use different positioning algorithms, don't try positioning with CSS and an HTML background image.
visibility	Pretty safe	This property can be buggy in some earlier 4.0 versions of Netscape.
text-decoration	Safe	Blink, however, is not supported by any of the major browsers.
text-align	Safe	None.
background-color	Safe	This can be buggy on Netscape 4 for the Mac.
border	Pretty safe	Older versions of browsers have some issues on inline properties, including border.

(continued)

Table 10-1 (continued)

Property	*Safety Factor*	*Issues*
z-index	Pretty safe	You can get into trouble using this with older versions of Netscape and getting the wrong index position for elements.
:visited	Safe	Netscape 4 for the Mac doesn't like this pseudo-class.
:link	Safe	Netscape 4 for the Mac doesn't like this pseudo-class.

Diving in deep

After you define your needs and plan your style sheets on the basics of CSS, dive in a little deeper. Consider the practicality of relying too heavily on CSS, making sure to factor in the cost of your development time. The truth is that you can't eliminate HTML — you still need to use a number of basic HTML elements. If you decided to commit to a heavily CSS intensive site, however, you could eliminate the need for the following HTML elements. This isn't a complete list, but these are the most common elements that CSS makes obsolete.

- <TABLE> and all its related elements, such as <TD> and <TR>
- <H1> through <H6>
- <FONT>
- <B>
- <I>
- <STRONG>
- <CENTER>
- <OL>, <UL>, and <LI>

In terms of additional work, the only one of these elements that requires significantly new thinking is how to build tables in CSS. Most Web developers are taught how to build tables in HTML first, and then learn how to embed tables within tables. In CSS, table design is very different, so it takes a little time to retrain your brain to use CSS tables.

I discuss approaches for building CSS tables in Chapter 13; thumb through this chapter for tools to use to get away from the traditional way of building tables in HTML.

The biggest risk when committing to a CSS-only site is the potential loss of users who have an older Web browser. Choosing a CSS-only construction route means that you make your site basically inaccessible — or, at the very least, ugly — to those people who use older browsers. What's the risk in that? According to sources like StatMarket (a leading Internet usage watchdog), the number of people globally using older browsers that are not CSS-enabled is below 5 percent.

However, as you can glean from Table 10-1, not all CSS-capable browsers support even the most basic of CSS properties equally. Your challenge changes from losing a small portion of your audience to having to do more work to support the audience that is CSS-capable. And, unfortunately, for that problem, there's no good answer.

Finding the happy medium

For most of us who develop Web sites, the end result is trying to find the happy medium marrying HTML and CSS usage. Check out the BART (Bay Area Rapid Transit) Web site in Figure 10-1 (`www.bart.gov`). This extremely unique site is both CSS- and DHTML-intensive, but also addresses the needs of older browsers and text-only readers. Because it's a government agency, BART has to comply with rigid ADA (Americans with Disabilities Act) requirements for Web browsing that are strict requirements for content and HTML design. The site serves dynamic menus using CSS to the vast majority of CSS-capable browsers on the market (both IE and Netscape), but also degrades nicely to the non-CSS capable browsers, as well as browsers on different platforms such as Unix and Linux. The result is a very well-planned and well-balanced site that uses CSS and HTML in a complimentary way.

Don't underestimate how much time and effort you need to invest building and supporting a CSS-intensive site for both IE and Netscape. In fact, supporting both platforms is more time consuming than just building the site for only CSS-capable browsers.

Sites such as BART (refer to Figure 10-1) show where the conventional thinking lies with the use of CSS and HTML together. CSS is used for a host of items throughout the site, but the fundamentals of HTML are still being used in the architecture of the site, as well as supporting the older browsers. Weigh your design options: For your site needs, you have to decide where you're comfortable making the switch to CSS.

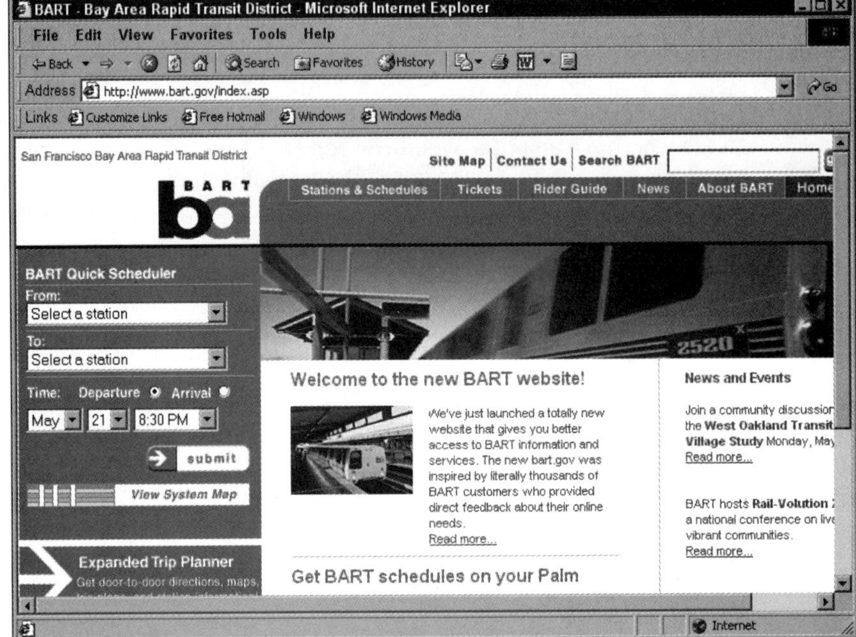

Figure 10-1: The BART Web site is a model for combining CSS and HTML.

Another good place to check out how CSS and HTML can be blended is the Excite site at `www.excite.com`. Go there to take a look at some of the underlying HTML (in IE, choose View➪Source; in Netscape, choose View➪Page Source). Excite is a very simple site that still uses both CSS and traditional fonts together. Although the implementation here is nothing fancy, it will give you an idea of how a portal site determined its happy medium between CSS and HTML.

Structuring Your Style Sheets for Success

After you decide how deep you're willing to invest in CSS, the next big task looming on your design horizon is structure. Good or bad, most Web sites follow a very similar structure of a home page and a series of subsections that users can navigate back and forth from via a series of buttons, rollovers, or links. The subsections (sometimes called Level 2 pages) also tend to have deeper subsections, and navigation within a subsection is usually handled via some form of secondary navigation. Most sites also have third level sections and navigation, but as a rule, this level is not nearly as consistent as other either the first-level or secondary-level navigation. Check out the diagram outline of this structure in Figure 10-2.

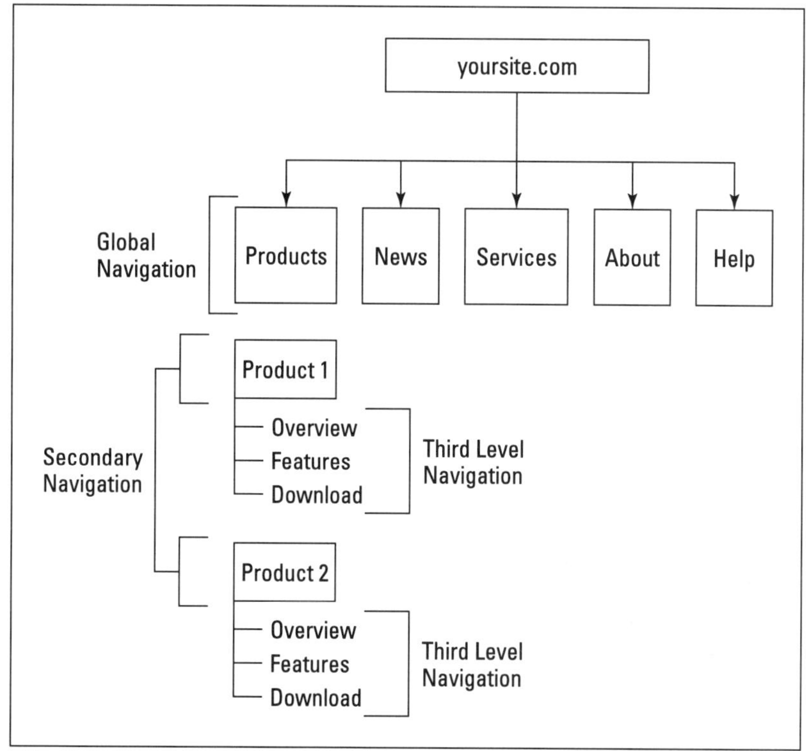

Figure 10-2: A typical site structure.

When developing styles for any kind of Web site, but particularly ones with different levels and subsections, keep in mind these goals before creating the architecture of your style sheets:

1. **Always work from the top down.**

   Start with the most broad elements first, and then work your way down to the one-of-a kind cases and weird anomalies for your site.

2. **Think about the future.**

   If we were playing Web Consultant Buzzword Bingo, I'd be throwing out words like *extensible* and *scalable*. In regular human-speak, this translates that you should always try to design your styles (and your site) with future growth in mind. That growth may mean moving from a static site to a database-driven site, or it may just mean adding pages and sections. In either case, try to think about how your site may eventually grow after millions of people are looking at it!

3. **Keep it simple.**

   The more complexity you add, the greater the chances that something will go wrong.

In the next few sections, I walk you through some good approaches to developing style sheets that keep these goals in mind, and set you up for success!

Go external!

Just throwing your styles into a style sheet inside an HTML document is so, *so* tempting. In the modern world of Web development, however, you're begging for a sure-fire headache later on. Instead, use external style sheets (a style sheet that's loaded from the HTML document when it's rendered to the screen). Consolidating and streamlining your style sheets into a central location will

- Make maintaining the site easier
- Enable you to use styles across sections and pages more easily
- Decrease the complexity of your site

Even if your site is tiny, your best bet is to go external from the start.

As I discuss in Chapter 3, you can link to a style sheet in your HTML document by using the following syntax:

```
<LINK href="filename.css" rel="stylesheet" type="text/css">
```

Segment your style sheets

One of the great things about style sheets is that you can have more than one of them in a document at the same time. The home page is usually the most dynamic and unusual page on your entire site. If you're like me, you want to get your visitors' attention right off the bat to let them know that your site is different and unique. The home page is your first, and sometimes only, chance to make that impression. As such, a lot of your styles may be needed for only that one page.

Similarly, different sections of your site may be more graphically or text intensive than others, resulting in different style needs for those sections. The answer, in many cases, is to segment your style sheets. Check out the following snippet of HTML code:

```
<head>
   <title>Welcome To My Site</title>
   <!-- Always put the global style sheet on top -->
   <LINK href="global.css" rel="stylesheet" type="text/css">
   <!-- And then the local one beneath it -->
   <LINK href="home.css" rel="stylesheet" type="text/css">
</head>
```

Always be careful about the cascade in your code. (Follow along with my comments in the code block.) In general, you want your local styles to overwrite your global styles. Because the browsers give priority to the last style loaded, your global styles should be written first, and then the local styles.

Here are two different style sheets being loaded for the home page of this site. In this case, the `global.css` style sheet could carry things like the default font and text settings for the site, as well as basic positioning elements for things such as the site's primary navigation. In the `home.css` style sheet, you could put font and text styles that are specific to the home page, as well as any positioned elements for that specific page.

When you use external style sheets, you have to save them someplace within your site's directory structure. The question is where? I recommend that the style sheets stay with their pages. If the pages of a section are in their own folder, then the section style sheet should go with them to that folder. If all your section pages are in a single directory, then the sheets should remain in that single directory, or perhaps get their own directory, to eliminate clutter and confusion.

Form versus function when naming your styles

I wish I could tell you of a set standard for naming styles. Most people choose whether to name styles according to their *format* (`.arial10black`, for example), or their *function* (`.newsheadline`, for example).

Realistically, either way is fine — in fact, even a mixture of both is okay. Keep consistency in mind, and take care not to name yourself into a corner. I like to use the main segments of my site as my guide. With the following three sections in my site:

- Home
- News
- About Us

a good method for naming is to have three different basic style structures combining form and function:

- Global text styles named by *format* (`.arial10black`)
- Global styles named by *function* (`.rightcolum`)
- *Section-specific* styles (`.homecallout`, `.newsrelease`, `.aboutdirections`)

You should name your styles by what makes the most sense for your site.

Start with the basics

The last major rule for structure is to begin with the basic global elements first. Generally, global elements include the following:

- The baseline styles for each of the major HTML elements
- The baseline styles for links
- The baseline styles for the site content
- The baseline rules for the global or site-wide navigation

Remember to think far ahead of what your site is going to look like, and how you plan to use it. The sample style sheet below shows how the a simple three-section site might construct a global style sheet taking these four things into account:

```
/* Theses are the base style for the HTML elements */
BODY    {
   font-family: Arial, Helvetica, Geneva, sans-serif;
   font-size: 12px;
       }

P {
   font-size: 10px;
   }

H1 {
   font-family: Times New Roman, Times, serif;
   font-size: 30px;
   }
DIV {
   font-style: bold;
   }

/* Theses are the base style for the Links */

A:link {
   color: red;
   text-decoration: none;
}
A:visited {
   color: red;
   text-decoration: none;
}
```

```
A:hover {
   color: blue;
   text-decoration: none;
}

/* Theses are the base styles for the site */

.black10 {
   color: #000000;
   font-family: Arial, Helvetica, Geneva, sans-serif;
   font-size: 10px;
   font-style: normal;
}

.black10bold {
   color: #000000;
   font-family: Arial, Helvetica, Geneva, sans-serif;
   font-size: 10px;
   font-weight: bold;
}

.black10boldital {
   color: #000000;
   font-family: Arial, Helvetica, Geneva, sans-serif;
   font-size: 10px;
   font-style: italic;
   font-weight: bold;
}

/* Theses are the base styles for Navigation */

.homebutton {
   position: absolute;
   left: 50px;
   top: 50px;
   }

.newsbutton {
   position: absolute;
   left: 150px;
   top: 50px;
   }

.aboutbutton {
   position: absolute;
   left: 250px;
   top: 50px;
   }
```

Wow! That's a lot of rules just to set up a simple site. Indeed it is, but this is not an uncommonly sized style sheet for a site with three sections, and more evidence that it's always good practice to begin with the basics!

The Big Don't List (And a Few Do's, Too)

This wouldn't be a *For Dummies* book if I didn't throw in a big "No, don't do that!!!!" list. Consider this the short-and-sweet-things-to-avoid list for Cascading Style Sheets. These handy tips will hopefully help you avoid getting into trouble when building your style sheets.

- **Don't try to do too much with one style.**

  You're better off mixing and matching styles than trying to create two styles that do everything on the site.

- **Don't mix position properties with text and font properties.**

  Yes, you can mix these, but it's always easier to maintain your site when you've got these two properties split.

- **Don't position base HTML elements.**

  Why not? Well, what if all your `P` elements have the same position? Unless every `P` element has its own ID with an offset that moved it away from the `P` element position, then all the `P` elements would end up on top of one another. You should always create the position style on its own and then apply that rule to a `P` element.

- **Don't apply styles to the `TABLE` element.**

  Explorer and Netscape have really different implementations for their `TABLE` element. With IE, you can apply a style easily, and it cascades down to the `TR` and `TD` elements. With Netscape, no such luck! So, rather than tear your hair out, apply individual text styles (such as `.arial10black`) to a `TD` element directly.

- **Don't try to do too much with the HTML elements.**

  Although it's nice to be able to apply styles to HTML elements, you'll always have more flexibility with your own styles. And, much like the `TABLE` element in the previous bullet, you get mixed results when you apply styles to an HTML element.

- **Don't kill yourself designing for every browser and platform.**

  Face it, some styles that you create are just not going to work in IE or Netscape, no matter how hard you try. Be prepared that some browsers will not support some properties, and design your site with that in mind.

- **Don't put all your styles in an external style sheet.**

  This advice may seem contradictory because I do recommend using external style sheets. However, using an inline style or a style in the HTML document is the better way to go, like when you want to apply a style to a single piece of content within a specific HTML document.

- **Don't just add styles just because they're nifty.**

  Some developers want to have an entire library of styles in one sheet. This attraction is a dangerous seduction for the developer because too many styles can be detrimental for the end user. Style sheets are loaded on every page, and those pages can get quite large, causing downloading delays.

- **Don't forget about case sensitivity.**

  According to the CSS specification, case doesn't matter. That's not entirely accurate, though: If you're pointed to a file location (say for a background image) on a Unix server, then case usage most certainly does matter.

- **Don't forget about redundancy!**

  You can save yourself a lot of time if you associate multiple HTML elements with a single style rule. Wherever possible, try to consolidate your styles!

The Right Time to Go Inline

In addition to all the tools you have at your disposal to create some killer styles for your site, you can also use inline style. In some ways, inline style is the most powerful style mechanism you have because you're assured that the style will always be applied. The downside is that inline styles are not reusable, so using the inline style is really inefficient.

I recommend that you only use inline styles when really necessary. Here's a good example. Suppose that I have the following style set up for my P elements:

```
P {
font-family: Arial, Helvetica, sans-serif;
font-size: 10px;
color: blue;
   }
```

And, somewhere in my site, I've got a paragraph that needs to be red and italicized. I could create a whole new style for that P element or give the P element an ID and apply it that way. Both ways are completely acceptable. However, using the following inline style is just as easy:

```
<P style="color: red; font-style: italic;">
```

You're assured that it'll end up the way you like it if you haven't messed with anything else in the site except that one element.

When you get a rash of these one-offs, consider creating a style rule that accounts for it. A good number to shoot for is five. If you call an odd style more than five times across your entire site, then it probably deserves a style of its own.

Chapter 11

Getting Existing Content into Style Sheets

In This Chapter

- Using SPAN instead of obsolete HTML
- Applying font and text properties
- Using a pseudo-element or two
- Dropping that main table
- Changing the background game

Building a site from the ground up is one thing. Taking the big old lug of an existing site you've got right now and making it sing again with style sheets . . . well, that's a little more challenging. You've already got your fonts set, with HTML tags all over the place and tables so complex that they make your head spin. So, just how can you work through this maze of existing content in short order and start seeing the value of Cascading Style Sheets (CSS) in your site?

Getting that content up to CSS snuff is precisely my focus here in Chapter 11. Truthfully, layering CSS on top of your existing site isn't all that hard even though sites are different all around the world, and no two sites are identical. As such, the goal here is to hit the big problems that you're most likely to come across as you try to introduce style sheets into your existing Web site.

I give you lots of good stuff in Chapter 10 about designing with style sheets and working with more than one at a time. Check it out for some of the basics, including questions to ask yourself before you make the change to CSS, good tips on how to architect your style sheets, the most often-used properties, as well as some pitfalls to avoid. Even though this chapter is about getting style sheets into existing content, all those same fundamentals apply!

Is your site right for a facelift?

Is it possible that you have a site that you really shouldn't be attempting to improve upon using Cascading Style Sheets? Maybe. Maybe not. A couple of kinds of sites may not really need to use CSS, such as:

- **Heavy Flash sites:** Sites that are almost entirely made up of Flash tend to not need style sheets because, well, the site's in Flash. All your styles will be in the Flash movie and not in the HTML document itself. So, if you're currently working in Flash, then your need for adding style sheets is definitely mitigated. If the site is a combination of Flash and HTML, then that's a different story, and you definitely want to include CSS in the site.
- **Sites with big accessibility requirements:** CSS2 is geared toward making sites much more flexible and accessible by a larger number of user agents. However, a lot of these features aren't yet implemented in the major Web browsers, so if your site is already ADA (Americans with Disabilities Act) compliant, then you need to be careful in the number and kind of style properties you use on your site. You'll want to steer clear of anything added in the CSS2 specification.

Cast Away That Obsolete HTML

One of the quickest and easiest ways to get some style into your site is to get rid of HTML that is rapidly become obsolete with the advent of CSS. Specifically, these include HTML tags such as:

- `<B>`: The bold tag
- `<I>`: The italics tag
- `<STRONG>`: The emphasis tag

The `FONT` element is also obsolete, but that's a larger and separate issue that I discuss in the upcoming section.

Each of these elements can be replaced easily with a `SPAN` element and an inline style. Consider the following snippet of HTML that includes all these near-obsolete elements:

```
<p>This is some old fashioned HTML text that uses the
          <i>italics tag</i>, the <b>bold tag</b> and some
          obscure tag called <strong>strong.</strong>
</p>
```

This same text can be represented easily with the following inline CSS styles, utilizing a `SPAN` element:

```
<p>This is some old fashioned HTML text that uses the <SPAN
        style="font-style: italic">italics tag</SPAN>, the
        <SPAN style="font-weight: bold">bold tag</SPAN>
        and some obscure tag called <SPAN style="font-
        weight: bold">strong.</SPAN></p>
```

The two side-by-side lines of HTML are shown rendered to the screen in Figure 11-1.

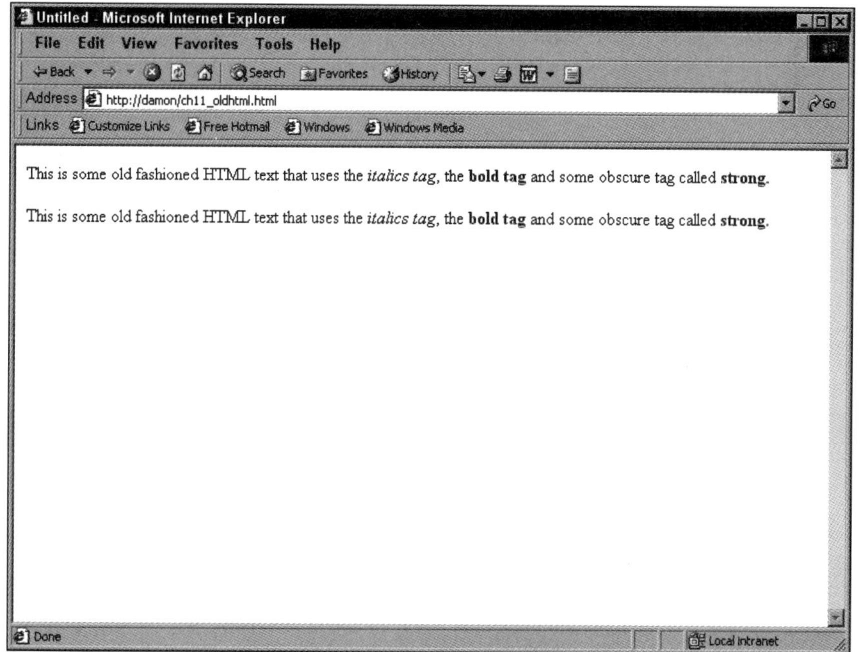

Figure 11-1: Old school and new school, side by side.

This isn't necessarily the most efficient way to go about adding styles to your page. Overloading an HTML document with `SPAN` elements and inline styles isn't good design, and it's hard to maintain because you're always looking through your HTML trying to figure out where your inline styles are. You should always have a plan for implementing style sheets across your site. This should be viewed only as a short- term fix!

Getting Your Font Properties in Order

Fonts are a tricky business in the move from strict HTML `FONT` elements to using CSS. You need to set the size of the font as well as the application of the font to the proper element. In this section, I help you get past both, in short order!

Trying to find like sizes

Converting from HTML font sizes to CSS font sizes appears, at first, to be a serious pain. The FONT element has no concept of a true font size. In HTML, the font properties use a numbering scale from 1 to 7, and can be either absolute by using one of the values, or can be relative if a value is preceded by a + or a -. Table 11-1 describes this relationship in more detail.

Table 11-1 Font Sizes in HTML

Values	*Description*
1 to 7	Values are an absolute size, moving from smallest to largest, based on the basefont (default size) for the page. The default value for basefont is 3.
+1 to +7	Increments the font size for the current element against the parent font element. Ranges in scale from 1 to 7; no value higher than 7 is allowed.
–1 to –7	Decrements the font size for the current element against the parent font element. Ranges in scale from 1 to 7; no value lower than 1 is allowed.

In contrast, when you move to style sheets, you have to give your fonts a size, as I describe in Chapter 6. Because fonts vary in size and dimension, calling all your fonts' sizes can be a somewhat painstaking task. In the end, you will need to make your own determination about the right size to convert to and from: Check out Figure 11-2 to see how the traditional HTML Arial font sizes translate on the PC to CSS and pixel heights.

In addition to the Arial font, this same bit of code works fine for Times, Verdana, Geneva, and Helvetica fonts.

Building your font styles for existing content

If you thought size was fun, wait until you build styles for a page! I promise that I'll walk you through this topic, too. If you've never used a style before or you've relied on an HTML editor to generate your code, most of your content would either have font attributes generated by a FONT element, or the content would just accept the default font styles.

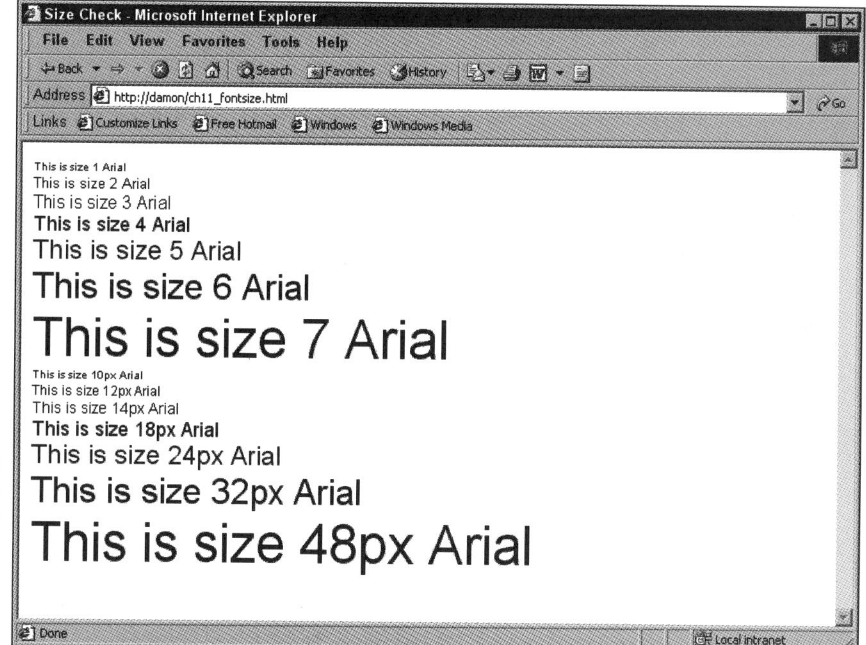

Figure 11-2: Old font sizes on the top; new CSS pixel sizes on the bottom.

Consider the following HTML code:

```
<body>
<table width="400" border="0" cellspacing="0"
          cellpadding="0">
<tr>
   <td width="200"><img src="images/spacer.gif" width="200"
          height="1" border="0"></td>
   <td width="200"><img src="images/spacer.gif" width="200"
          height="1" border="0"></td>
</tr>
<tr>
   <td colspan="2"><font face="Arial, Times, Geneva"
          size="6">What I plan to do when I'm done with this
          book.</font></td>
</tr>
<tr>
   <td valign="top" align="left" width="200">
   <font face="Arial" size="2">After finishing my second For
          Dummies book, I plan on getting some sleep. Then,
          after that's complete, which should take a few
          weeks, I'd like to go on a vacation to get some
          time to wind down. Nothing too extravagant,
          probably just a trip to someplace tropical. Then,
          upon my return, I hope to do it all again.
          </font></td>
```

```
    <td valign="top" align="left"><br><img
            src="images/happy.gif" width="134" height="139"
            border="0" ></td>
</tr>
</table>
</body>
```

Note the two different FONT styles I use in the block of code, which could reasonably be considered some average HTML that might appear in anyone's site. See the output in Figure 11-3.

You could apply a style sheet to this HTML document by a number of ways. In the real world, you'd very likely have the following goals in mind:

- The HTML document should have a consistent default style.
- The styles should mirror the existing styles in the HTML document as closely as possible.
- The site does not need to keep the old <FONT> tags around after the CSS makeover is complete.

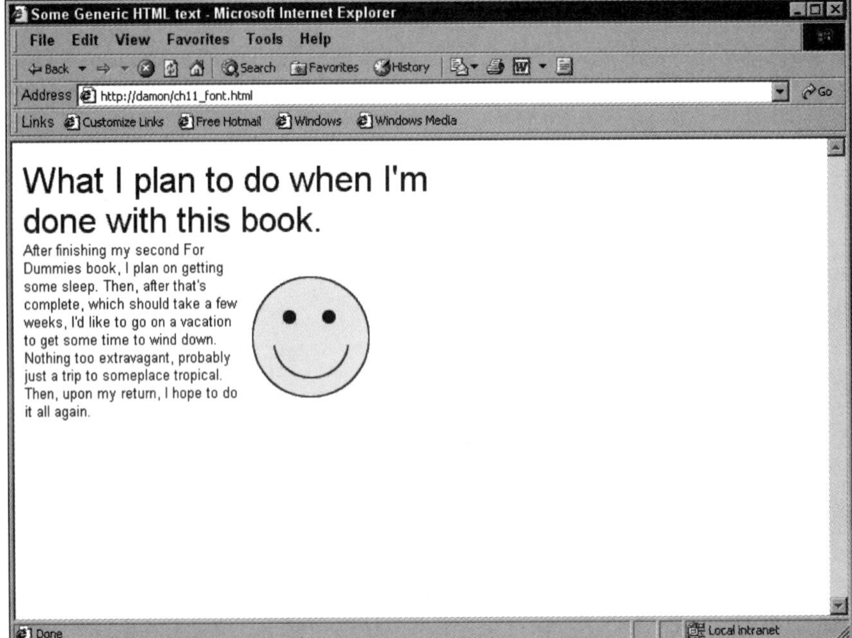

Figure 11-3: Some average HTML with no CSS.

Keeping that in mind, here's how you can compose a style sheet to render this page with CSS:

1. **Remove all the `<FONT>` tags.**

   Removing all the `<FONT>` tags may seem controversial, but if you've made the decision to leave the older browsers behind, then this is a reasonable thing to do. If you leave the `<FONT>` tags where they were, then you'd have to build styles specifically for the `FONT` element because it will always have the greatest specificity in the document hierarchy. Simply put, any styles you created for the `BODY`, `TABLE` or `TD` elements would never be inherited by the content when the `FONT` element was present. The result of all this removal is in Figure 11-4.

2. **Set a default `BODY` style.**

   Because the font for the majority of the content in the page is Arial, the best bet is to make that font the default font. As for size, the content in the table cells is all listed as `size="3"`, which is a fairly standard size. Note that I include the equivalent `font-size` property in the default style. The rule looks like this:

   ```
   BODY {
   font-family: Arial;
   font-size: 12px;
      }
   ```

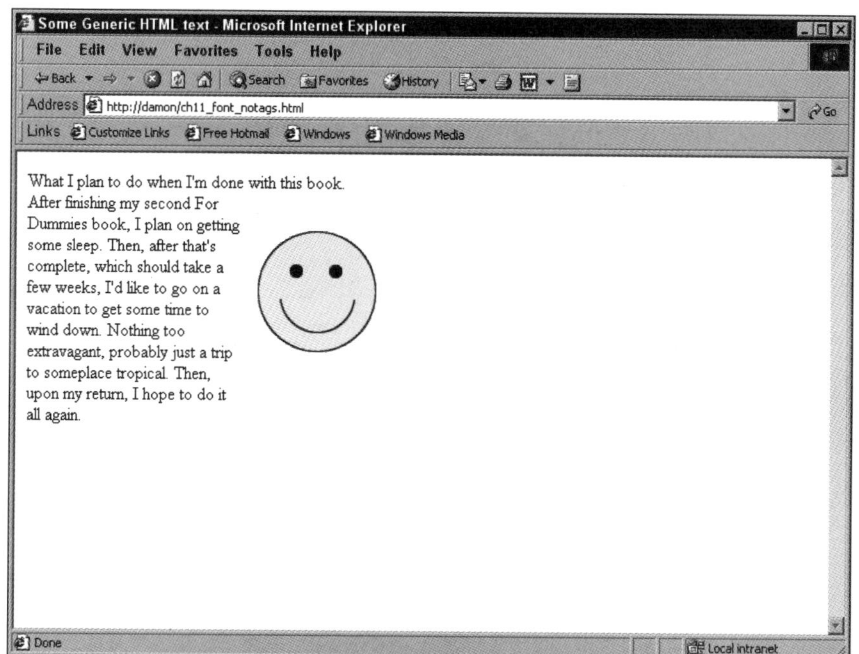

Figure 11-4: HTML, stripped to the bone.

See the resulting page in Figure 11-5. Although the rendered result is an improvement, the image is still a long way away from looking as good as its predecessor.

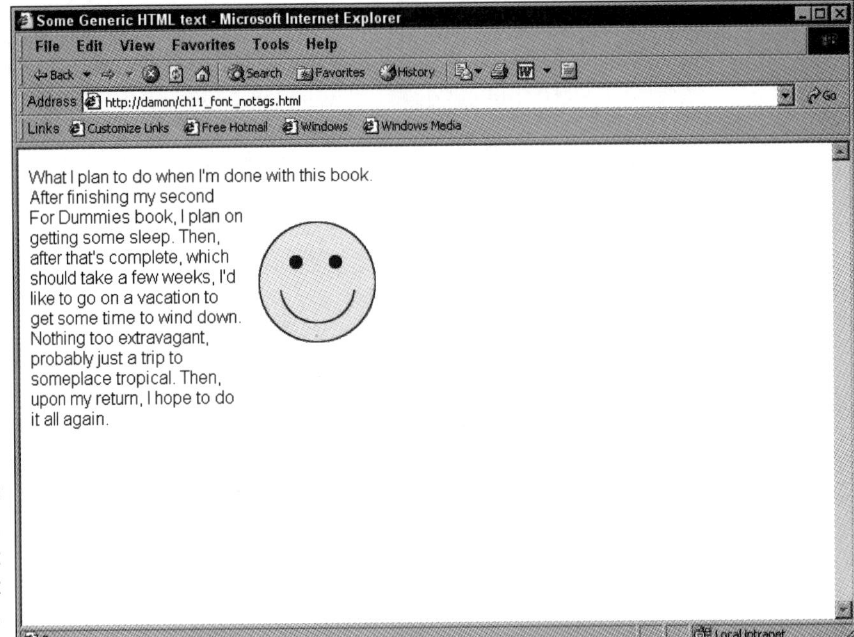

Figure 11-5: Better, but still not there.

3. **Create a default** TD **element and apply it to the left text content.**

   Look closely at Figures 11-3 and 11-5, and you can see that the left column text is larger now than it was before. That's because in the HTML-only version, you apply a style to the TD element as follows:

   ```
   TD {
   font-size: 12px;
   }
   ```

   I put all this code — including the various versions with fonts turned on and off — on the CD that accompanies this book so that you don't have to keep adding and deleting the <FONT> tags to see what I describe here.

4. **Create a headline style and apply it to the headline.**

   Because I already created a style for the TD element, I need a specific style to apply to the headline. Because the previous headline was a <FONT> tag with size="6", I can create an equivalent style with the following syntax:

```
.headline{
   font-size: 32px;
   }
```

and apply the style to the TD element containing the headline as follows:

```
<td class="headline" colspan="2"><font face="Arial,
        Times, Geneva" size="6">What I plan to do when
        I'm done with this book.</font></td>
```

Figure 11-6 shows the final page, rendered now completely with CSS.

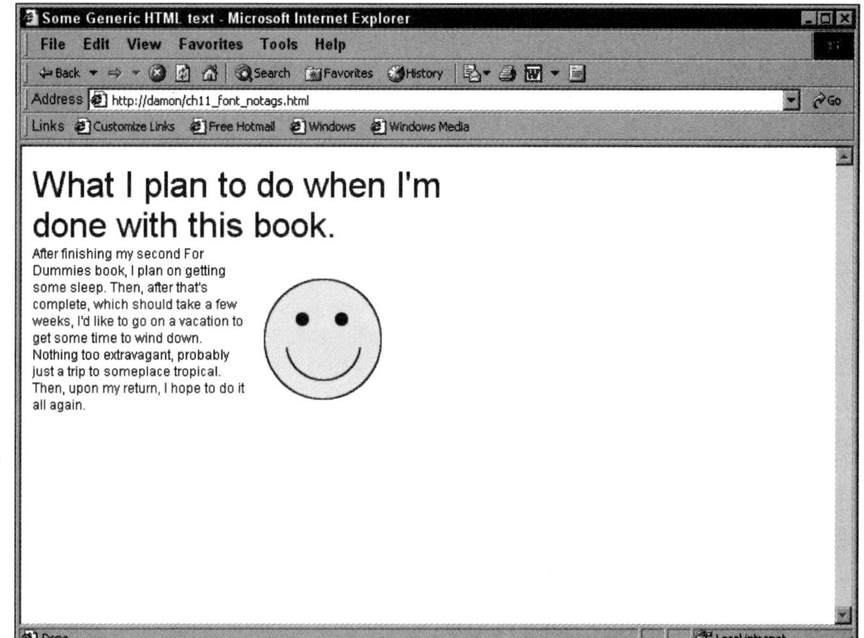

Figure 11-6: Fonts are gone, and CSS is throughout.

Hey, What about a Pseudo-element?

You have so many different ways at your disposal to do rollovers in Web pages. The most common way is to use a JavaScript rollover, which works great when you want to swap images for rollovers. But what if you just want to change colors on a rollover? It's easy and it's effective. Well, you don't really need any fancy JavaScript for that. Instead, you just need a quick hit of CSS.

Most Web pages have HTML similar to the following for links:

```
<p>Here I am, just waiting to <a href="page.html">link</a> to
        some page besides this one. </p>
```

which is to say, some HTML element, surrounded by an `A` element that defines the link.

With style sheets, you can easily transfer this rather lackluster linking scheme with a simple set of `A` pseudo-elements.

Here's how you can do it with the existing HTML:

1. **Create a style tag for your HTML document.**

   If you're using style sheets in your document, this isn't necessary. If not, it really just means adding the following syntax to the `HEAD` element of your HTML document:

   ```
   <style>
      </style>
   ```

2. **Within the style tags, create a pseudo-element for the link state of the `A` element.**

   To do this, all you need to do is grab the `A:link` pseudo-element and give it the following properties and values:

   ```
      A:link {color:blue}
   ```

   You don't necessarily need to use blue. You can use any color or size. My example is just for demonstration purposes.

3. **Within the style tags, create a pseudo-element for the visited state of the `A` element.**

   To do this, all you need to do is grab the `A:visited` pseudo-element and give it the following properties and values:

   ```
      A:visited {color:red}
   ```

4. **Create a pseudo-element for the hover state of the `A` element.**

   To get this pseudo-element working, all you need is the `A:visited` pseudo-element. You can give it the following properties and values:

   ```
      A:hover {color:gray}
   ```

   Although this little trick is great in theory, it only works in the new browsers: that is, IE 4.0 and above and Navigator 6.0 and above!

Your completed style should, in total, look a bit like this:

```
<style>
A:link {color:blue}
A:visited {color:red}
A:hover {color:gray}
</style>
```

Lose That Extra Table!

If you have a site with embedded table upon embedded table, something's got to give because they're hard to maintain and can begin to affect performance. And from where I sit, the thing that's got to give is a table or two. This sentiment may make lots of Web developers mad, and this may not be the most perfect implementation yet, but you can make your life a whole lot simpler in the new world Web order by eliminating that big structuring table that everyone depends on. And here's the great thing — it's super easy!

Here's some HTML that describes what I'm getting at:

```
<table width="600" border="0" cellspacing="0"
           cellpadding="0">
<tr>
   <td width="200"><img src="images/spacer.gif" width="200"
           height="1" border="0"></td>
   <td width="400"><img src="images/spacer.gif" width="200"
           height="1" border="0"></td>
</tr>
<tr>
   <td><table cellspacing="0" cellpadding="0" border="0">
      <tr>
          <td></td>
          <td></td>
      </tr>
      <tr>
          <td></td>
          <td></td>
      </tr>
      </table>
      </td>

   <td>
   <table cellspacing="0" cellpadding="0" border="0">
      <tr>
          <td></td>
          <td></td>
          <td></td>
      </tr>
      <tr>
```

```
            <td></td>
            <td></td>
            <td></td>
        </tr>
        </table>
    </td>
</tr>
</table>
```

The code, which describes the common HTML structure for most Web sites, includes a basic two-column table with two rows 200 pixels and 400 pixels wide, respectively. Within each of those columns is a nested table: The left one is 200 pixels wide, and the right one is 400 pixels wide. Using this type of structure, I can build the upside-down-L shaped navigation that I describe in Chapter 8.

Although this structure is very common, it's also very cumbersome and can be relieved by two very simple CSS properties — `position` and `width`. Now, without even having seen what I'm proposing, the purists would jump up and exclaim that:

- This design doesn't support older browsers, meaning any browser below 4.0 on either Explorer or Netscape.
- This design isn't supported by a number of newer browsers, meaning the early 4.*x* versions of Netscape.
- This design gets complicated if you have background images (`.gif` files).

I agree with the critics on the first two points. However, they're only correct insofar as the older browsers represent a small portion of the active browsers in use. And more modern browsers all support the positioning schemes laid out in CSS2 (Netscape 4.7 and above, and IE 4.0 and above). The last point, while true, really just requires that you change your background positioning scheme. You can easily accomplish this by using the `background-image` property. I discuss this property in the next section, and other background properties in Chapter 7.

To eliminate the controlling table in the code, follow these steps:

1. **Create two style rules,** `.leftcolumn` **and** `.rightcolumn`**, as follows:**

```
<style>
.leftcolumn {
   position: absolute;
   left: 0px;
   top: 0px;
   width: 200px;
   }
```

```
    .rightcolumn {
       position: absolute;
       left: 200px;
       top: 0px;
       width: 400px;
       }
    </style>
```

2. **Create two** `DIV` **elements and call the** `leftcolumn` **and** `rightcolumn` **classes:**

   The syntax for that would be as follows:

```
       <DIV class="leftcolumn"></DIV>
       <DIV class="rightcolumn"></DIV>
```

3. **Put the embedded tables into the** `DIV` **elements and remove the surrounding table.**

   After you complete the procedure, your HTML should look as follows:

```
<DIV class="leftcolumn">
<table cellspacing="0" cellpadding="0" border="1">
      <tr>
          <td> </td>
          <td> </td>
      </tr>
      <tr>
          <td> </td>
          <td> </td>
      </tr>
      </table>
</DIV>
<DIV class="rightcolumn">

   <table cellspacing="0" cellpadding="0" border="1">
      <tr>
          <td> </td>
          <td> </td>
          <td> </td>
      </tr>
      <tr>
          <td> </td>
          <td> </td>
          <td> </td>
      </tr>
      </table>
</DIV>
```

See how the two tables (in Figure 11-7) are effectively equal after the conversion is complete.

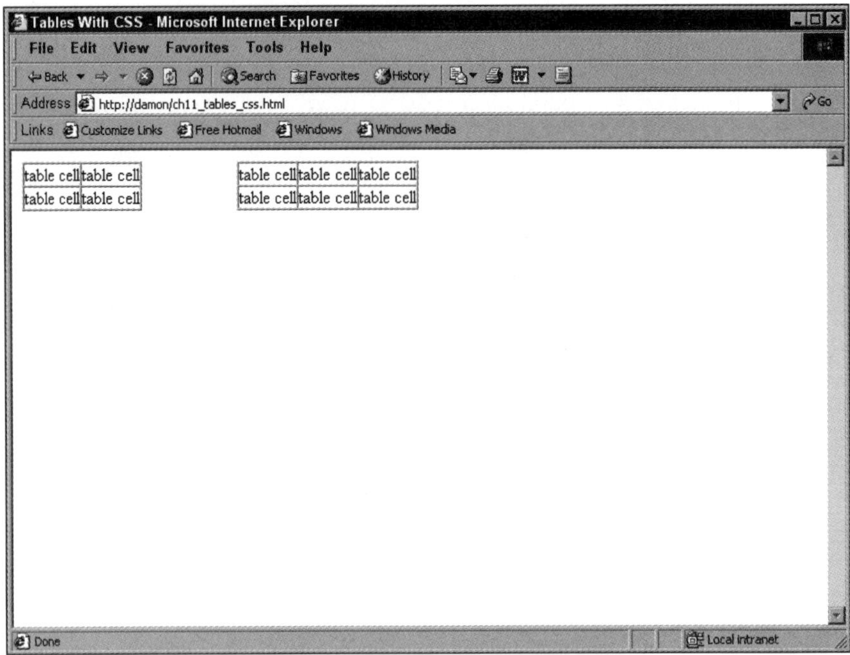

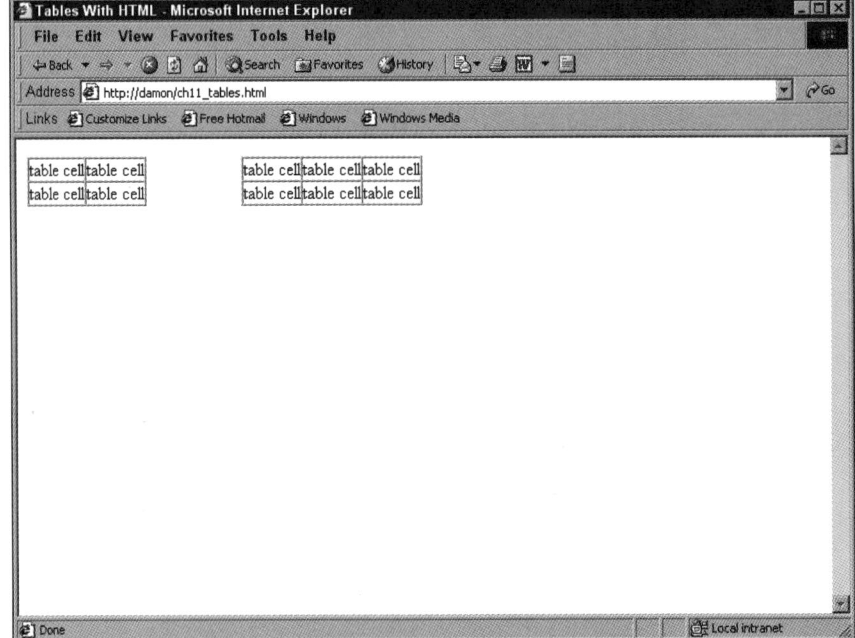

Figure 11-7: CSS and regular tables side by side!

If you were doing this in an HTML editor, you may have noticed that the tables don't quite match up. That's because an HTML table has padding that a `DIV` element doesn't have. However, you can use the CSS passing properties to make the two match by adding 10px of padding to the `DIV` element.

Changing the Background Game!

If you make the change to `DIV` elements instead of `TABLE` elements, you also need to change your background images if you have them in your HTML page. If you have an image in a background using HTML, it probably looks a little something like this:

```
<BODY background="image.gif">
```

With CSS, to make everything line up, you need to replace that tag with the following style rule:

```
    BODY { background-image: url("image.gif") }
```

To make it all work, you may need to offset your `BODY` by a pixel. Why? Well, because IE and Navigator don't like the 0, 0 position. I know, I know — it sounds weird, but it's true. So, if you're having problems with your background matching up, try this little trick and see if it works for you:

```
    BODY {
       position: absolute;
       left: 1px;
       top: 1px;
       }
```

Part IV

Getting Your Advanced CSS Degree

"Oh, we're doing just great. Philip and I are selling decorative jelly jars on the Web. I run the Web site and Philip sort of controls the inventory."

In this part . . .

If you're reading this part of the book after plowing through all the earlier sections (you know . . . you don't have to read this book cover to cover), you hopefully haven't caught a case of senior-itis. Remember that time in your life, when it was so hard to avoid that debilitating sickness that plagues millions of high school and college seniors each year? Always most prevalent during the months preceding graduation, victims of senior-itis feel that they've garnered all they can and have done enough work.

Don't get lulled into thinking that you're done blossoming in your use of Cascading Style Sheets. After you've become more than capable of creating a basic CSS Web site, you will probably want to go beyond the basics. Discover how to take your Web site to the next level with what you can find in this part.

In this part, I show you how to become more sophisticated through advanced ways of using CSS in your Web site. With the information in this part, you can create the type of accessible and superior Web site that gets noticed by your audience and the Web community. Among other things, I discuss how to generate content, how to integrate XML into your site, how to create style sheets for different types of media, and how to create tables using CSS.

All readers can benefit from this part. Your Web site can grow a step above what it is, and your audiences will "Ooooh and "Ahhhhh" over your expert use of CSS. You know it's true: Those sad people who catch senior-itis never seem to make it past the bush leagues. Consider this part as your graduate degree in CSS — sort of like a senior-itis vaccine.

Chapter 12

Generating Content

In This Chapter

- Working with the `content` property
- Using the `:before` and `:after` pseudo-elements
- Making quotes not so simple
- Looking to the day when you can add counters and automatic numbering
- Creating lists with CSS

Like any good sequel, the CSS Level 2 specification had to include all the elements that made the first specification so good, and then also include a bunch of new elements that made the whole spectacle bigger, larger, and more over-the-top than the original. Generated content — content created by the style sheet at the time of rendering — comprises the explosions and car chases scenes of the CSS Level 2 specification.

Although a number of these features are gratuitous and not really needed for the average everyday Web site, they're fun and even futuristic. Explore them with an eye toward moderation for use in your Web site.

Before I even crack the first section of this chapter, I feel compelled to lay down the proverbial law. Generated content is a hornet's nest when it comes to the browsers. Most of the older 4.0 browsers on both platforms don't support these elements, and even the Internet Explorer (IE) 5.0 and 6.0 families are best described as sketchy. I could post warning flags every couple of paragraphs, but rather than do that, I'm just going to toss this big one out first. Consider yourself forewarned! These properties are not browser friendly!

Show Me the Content!

The term *generated content* is a bit of a misnomer. Kind of like the CSS designers left something out, generated content comes from the style sheet, and you add it to different places in the document. All right, so it doesn't exactly roll right off the tongue, but that is precisely what the `content` property enables you to do. Try to break yourself of the mindset that content should be contained in the document and not in the style sheet.

The `content` property is a clever little invention, even if it does break the paradigm of keeping the styles separate from the content in the document. Here are just some of the diverse ways you can use this property:

- Add content to the document tree
- Specify counter increments
- Pass variables to applications
- Standardize URLs and pass them to the document
- Pass quotes to the quote property that will then include them in the document

The `content` property is unique in the sense that it works differently than most properties and is used differently than most properties in the CSS specification. It has a greater degree of variety in the values it can accept than any other property in the specification, which is part of the reason that it's so flexible. The following list includes the different values that the `content` property can accept.

- `string`: A string is good old-fashioned text content. It must be included in either single or double quotes.

  ```
  content: "Here is some content"
  ```

- `url`: This value specifies a URL to a file.

  ```
  content: url("http://wherever.com")
  ```

- `counter`: This works in conjunction with the CSS counter properties to place incremented values in a document.

  ```
  content: counter(somevalue)
  ```

- `open-quote`: This works in conjunction with the CSS quote properties to place quotes in a document.

  ```
  content: open-quote
  ```

- `close-quote`: This works in conjunction with the CSS counter properties to place incremented values in a document.

  ```
  content: close-quote
  ```

- `no-open-quote` or `no-close-quote`: Working in conjunction with the CSS counter properties to place incremented values in a document, this value inserts nothing, but increments or decrements the level of nesting for quotes.

```
content: no-open-quote or content: no-close-quote
```

- `attr(x)`: This passes a variable to the document that can then be used by a language such as JavaScript.

```
content: attr(var)
```

When using the `string` value for content, you can generate line breaks in the content by using the `\A` command. To put each word of the sentence *I like coffee* on a separate line, use the following syntax:

```
content: "I \A like \A coffee"
```

Although URLs and text strings are valid values, that doesn't mean you can pass HTML with the `content` property. For all practical purposes, you can't because the URL value is really designed for things like playing audio files. The `string` values, although able to pass HTML to the screen, do not pass said HTML to the renderer — if you try to give the browser HTML, you'll end up seeing that HTML right up on the screen.

In addition to being value flexible, the `content` property is also usage flexible. You can use `content` with the `:before` and `:after` pseudo-elements directly to place content into the document tree. It can also be used by other properties (counters and quotes primarily) to grab content and place it in the document. The following sections show how these interactions take place to generate content and place it on the screen.

The Appetizers and Desserts of the CSS Family

Pseudo-elements comprise a class of selectors that refer to sub-parts of elements, such as the first letter of a paragraph. Use them to generate style changes dynamically to a document element. (For a more detailed discussion on pseudo-elements, thumb through Chapter 4.)

I'm particularly fond of two nifty little pseudos: `:before` and `:after`. Like other pseudo-elements, `:before` and `:after` get attached to document-level elements such as `P`, `DIV`, and `SPAN`. And they do pretty much what you'd expect them to do, which is to include content either before or after a document element. The `:before` and `:after` pseudo-elements don't work at all, however, until the `content` property gets involved. Use this property to specify what content will be placed at the beginning or the end of the document element.

To attach content to the beginning of all `P` elements in a document, use the following syntax:

```
P:before
```

Similarly, if you want to attach content to the end of all `P` elements in a document, use the following syntax:

```
P:after
```

Adding content to the document element is accomplished by including the `content` property in the pseudo-element rules. If, for example, I want to add the word *Example:* to the beginning of every `DIV` element in a document, the syntax would look remarkably similar to this:

```
DIV:before {
   content: "Example:";
   }
```

To see it in action, here's a simple math example in HTML that shows how this might be applied.

```
<body>
Here are some examples of easy multiplication:
<DIV><br>2 x 2 = 4</DIV>
<DIV><br>3 x 3 = 9</DIV>
<DIV><br>4 x 4 = 16</DIV>
</body>
```

The resulting output, as shown in Figure 12-1, confirms that indeed the word *Example:* was generated and inserted before each of the math examples.

Unfortunately, `:before` and `:after` don't work in IE 5.5, meaning that this set of pseudo-elements is really only for the new Netscape Navigator 6.0 groupies.

The `:after` pseudo-element works exactly the same way as `:before`.

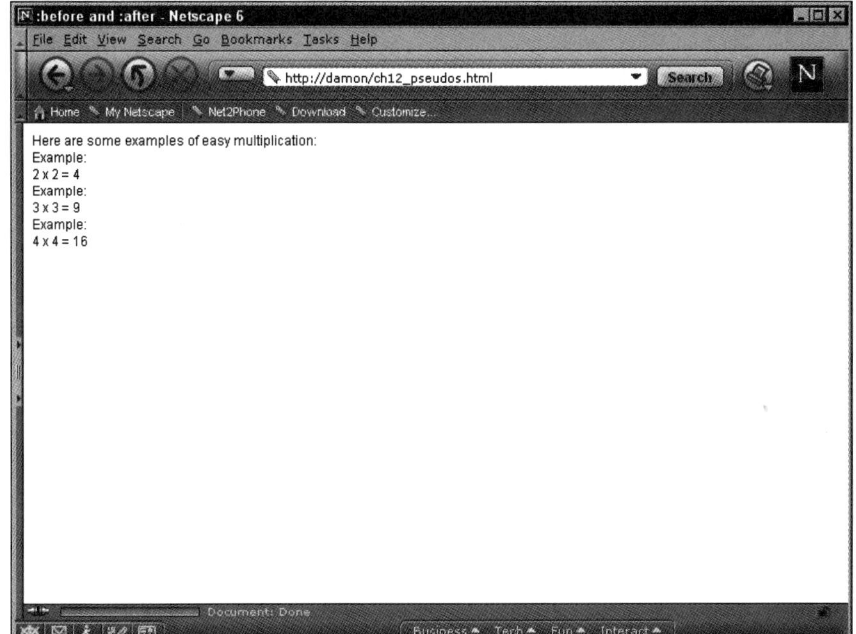

Figure 12-1: Examples of :before in action!

Can I Quote"s" You on That? No!

Here's your trivia for the day: HTML has a Q element that puts content in quotes. Who knew? 'Fess up — did you actually know that? This is a cool tool to generate quotes, as shown in Figure 12-2, and here's the syntax on how:

```
<body>
<Q>Why sir, I do believe I've never heard the word
          <Q>yankee</Q> used in such a friendly fashion
          before,</Q> the General said.
</body>
```

Surprise, surprise. The Q element doesn't work in Explorer, even the new versions. Certainly, inserting quotation marks is one of the more obscure properties in both HTML and CSS. And, to be honest, it shows in both the HTML and CSS implementations. There's nothing wrong with putting double and single quotes directly into your document, so the need for an element dedicated to quotes is severely diminished. When working with multiple languages, however, the CSS quotes property can be a practical way to provide different characters based on the language.

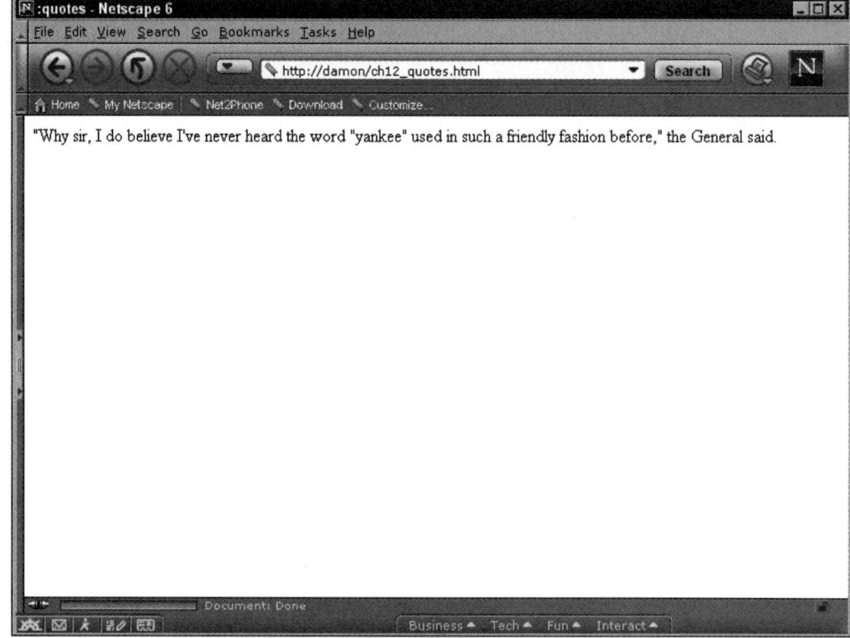

Figure 12-2: You can quote anything you want with the Q element!

In concept, the `quotes` property is similar in structure to the `text-shadow` property in that you can pass it more than one value. The property takes `string` pairs (it groups values in twos). When it comes across a `content open-quote` value, it takes the first `string` value; when a `close-quote` value comes along, it displays the second value in the HTML. When a second call is made to a `content` property with the `open-quote` value before the first one is closed with a `close-quote` value, then the second set of `string` values would be used if you specify more than one set of quotes. Again, in theory, you can go as deep as you like with the pairs. So, for example, if I want to use double quotes and then single quotes, the syntax for the property would look as follows:

```
quotes: '"' '"' "'" "'"
```

I intentionally include the phraseology *in theory* with this property. Despite repeated attempts with nearly every element type available to HTML, I can't get the `quotes` property to work properly in Navigator.

The `quotes` property, like the `:before` and `:after` pseudo-elements, needs a healthy dose of the `content` property to make it go. All that the `quotes` property does on its own is specify how the quotes should look. It's the `content` property that ensures that they get placed happily in the document.

You can use the `quotes` property with the `Q` element, but it's not required. Here's a way you can use the `Q` element to recognize and put the proper quote in the proper place in a document structure.

Start with the following set of styles:

```
Q  { quotes: '"' '"' "'" "'" }
Q: before {content: open-quote;}
Q: after {content: close-quote;}
```

Throw in a little HTML to see it in action. Try this:

```
<body>
<Q>Why sir, I do believe I've never heard the word
            <Q>yankee</Q> used in such a friendly fashion
            before,</Q> the General said.
</body>
```

All set? Hmmm . . . maybe not. Check out Figure 12-3. Because Explorer doesn't support the `Q` element or `:before` or `:after`, I have to show you the results in Navigator 6.0 (see Figure 12-3). The observant ones of you will notice that even Figure 12-3 is wrong. Although Netscape does support the `quotes` property, it only supports the first `string` value set, thus limiting the usefulness of the property even further.

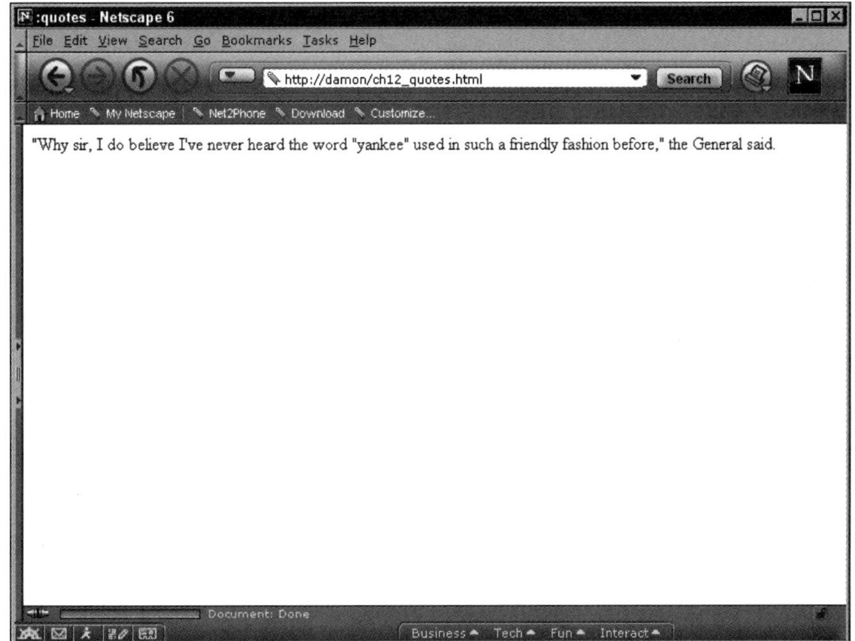

Figure 12-3: Just how useful is this property anyway?

Count Me in . . . or Out!

Considering that generating content with quotes was a bit of a bust, allow me to continue exuding confidence by introducing the CSS counting properties.

And although no major browser yet supports the counting properties, these properties could be reasonably handy. In the interest of eventual adoption on the part of Microsoft and Netscape, play along with me and assume that there is browser support for these properties.

The two counter properties are `counter-increment` and `counter-reset`. Like the quotes, they use both the `content` property as well as the `:before` and `:after` pseudo-elements. Thus, you know right off the bat that I won't be discussing Explorer again in this section.

The `counter-increment` property enables you to name a counter, and then specify with an integer the amount of the increment. Building on the scenario in the section "The Appetizers and Desserts of the CSS Family" where I add the word *Example:* to the simple multiplication examples, here I show you how to number those examples. Follow these steps to add the counter to the document:

1. **Name the counter.**

   You end up using the name in two places, so remember to be consistent in name, capitalization, and so forth, and make sure that your name doesn't contain any spaces. I name my counter `number`.

2. **Add the counter to the `content` property in the `DIV:before` rule.**

   The content property already looks like this:

   ```
   content: "Example:";
   ```

   Because I'm going to append the `counter` value and include the name number, the overall content syntax changes to the following:

   ```
   content: "Example #" content(number) ":";
   ```

   Note that the `counter` value is not included in quotes. You can also have more than one item in quotes, and the `content` value will be placed in-between them.

3. **Add the `counter-increment` property to the `DIV:before` rule.**

   Again, here you need to include the name of the counter and the increment value. In this case, the `counter-increment` is 1, which is the default value for the property, so you don't need to specify it. If the increment value were more than 1 (say 2), put it right after the name of the counter. In this case, the property is as follows:

```
counter-increment: number;
```

The resulting `DIV: begin` rule, in its entirety, is:

```
DIV:before {
   content: "Example"  counter(number) ":";
   counter-increment: number;
   }
```

and would result, in theory, in the output of Figure 12-4.

I manufactured the result that you see in Figure 12-4; no browser yet supports the `counter` property.

The `counter-reset` property theoretically works in conjunction with a named counter, and then by default, resets that counter to 0. Like `counter-increment`, though, you can specify the reset value by including it after the counter name in the property. For example, if you have a counter named `section` and you wanted to reset it to 2, then use the following syntax:

```
counter-reset: section 2;
```

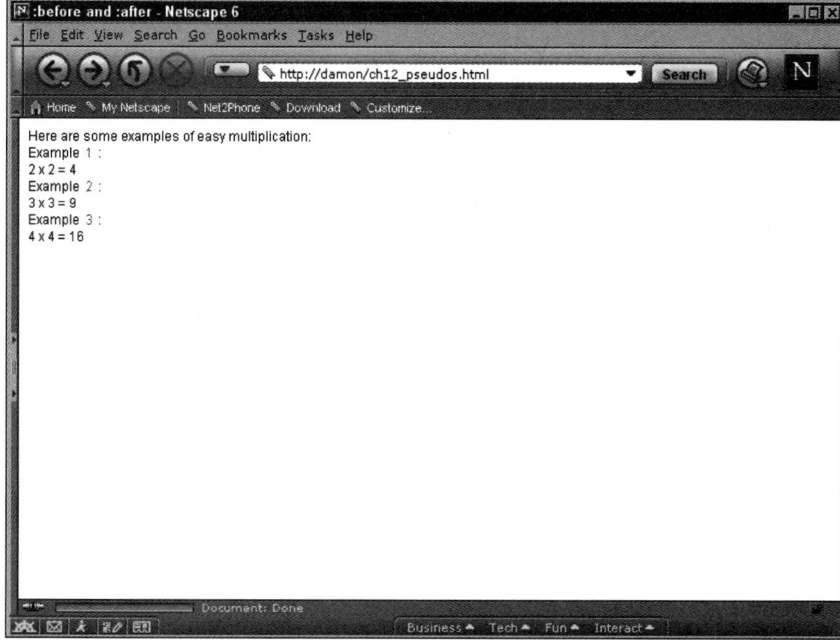

Figure 12-4: The potential of when browsers support counter properties.

So, Do the Lists Work?

Most definitely, yes, the lists do work, but that's because they've been around since the CSS Level 1 specification, and the browser companies have had the chance to get them all worked out . . . well, mostly worked out. *Lists* are exactly what you think they'd be — compiled pieces of data presented either in bulleted or numerical formats.

The four major properties in the list family include:

- `list-style-type`: Use these to specify the type of list marker, whether a number, letter, or character.
- `list-style-image`: This handy little property enables you to use images rather than numbers, letters, or characters when generating a list.
- `list-style-position`: Use this property to determine where text will reside on subsequent lines after the first line of a list item.
- `list-style`: This is a shorthand property that enables you to roll up the values of the previous three properties into one single property.

All these properties are valid when applied to a `display: list-item` property in a rule; `list-style-type` is the most common of the properties.

Many styles to choose from!

Use the `list-style-type` property to specify what kind of bullets you want in your list, and whether those bullets will be of the number or character variety. The values that you can pass to the `list-style-property` include:

- `disc`: A solid black disc
- `circle`: A white circle with a black border
- `square`: A solid black square
- `decimal`: 1, 2, 3, and so forth
- `lower-roman`: i, ii, iii, and so forth
- `upper-roman`: I, II, III, and so forth
- `lower-alpha`: a, b, c, and so forth
- `upper-alpha`: A, B, C, and so forth

One of the interesting things about this particular property is that it blurs the line drawn in HTML between ordered (`<OL>`) and unordered (`<UL>`) lists. You can define a `style-type` to both `OL` and `UL` elements and have them look identical. For example, when the following style is applied to the following two different sets of HTML code

```
LI  {
   display: list-item;
   list-style-type: disc;
   }
```

it yields the same result, as shown in Figure 12-5.

```
<body>
This is an ordered list
<ol>
<li>This is Item 1</li>
<li>This is Item 2</li>
</ol>
This, however, is an un-ordered list
<ul>
<li>This is the first item</li>
<li>This is the second item</li>
</ul>
</body>
```

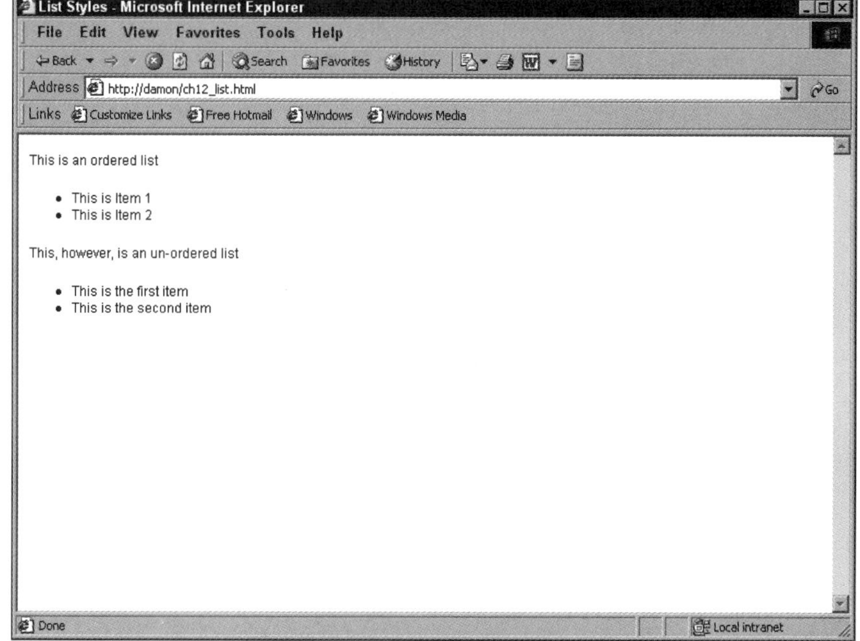

Figure 12-5: Ordered or unordered, they both get discs.

Smile, your list is in pictures!

The `list-style-image` property is pretty effective in changing the way you think about a traditional list. Usually, I think of lists as collections of numbers and bullets. But, using this property, you can effectively turn lists into pictures and captions. How often is that really necessary? Not very, but hey, if you're converting from HTML to CSS, then this is the way to go!

The value for the `list-style-image` property is a URL, which points to an image, as in the following example:

```
LI  {
   display: list-item;
   list-style-image: url("http://damon/images/happy.gif")
   }
```

That style, when added to an ordered or unordered list, will add the happy graphic where the bullet or number previously would have been. The following HTML shows a typical list, and you can see the resulting output in Figure 12-6:

```
<body>
How many different ways can one be happy?
<ul>
<li>I can be happy when it's sunny outside</li>
<li>I can be happy when I'm at the beach</li>
<li>I can be happy when I'm watching TV</li>
</ul>
</body>
```

What's my position?

I have to be honest. The `list-style-position` property makes no sense to me, but I think that's because I'm just a Type A, anal person. This property enables you to decide whether you want your content in a list item to be flush left against itself or flush left against the bullet or number. Now, why you'd ever want to be flush against the bullet or number is beyond me, because that's a completely non-standard convention, but hey — I didn't write the specification, I'm only trying to figure it out!

The two values for this property are `inside` and `outside`. Use `inside` to indent the bullet or number and place it flush with the content, and use `outside` to place subsequent lines of content flush with the first line. Here are two styles that highlight the different properties:

```
LI.correct  {
   display: list-item;
   list-style-position: outside;
   }
LI.kooky  {
   display: list-item;
   list-style-position: inside;
   }
```

Can you tell which one of the following list items in the HTML will look better? Just to be sure, check out Figure 12-7:

```
<body>
Now which of these do you think looks correct
<ul>
<li class="correct">The nice clear bullet<br> where
           everything is flush, or</li>
<li class="kooky">The kooky bullet where everything looks<br>
           messy. Come on, would you put this in your resume?
           </li>
</ul>
</body>
```

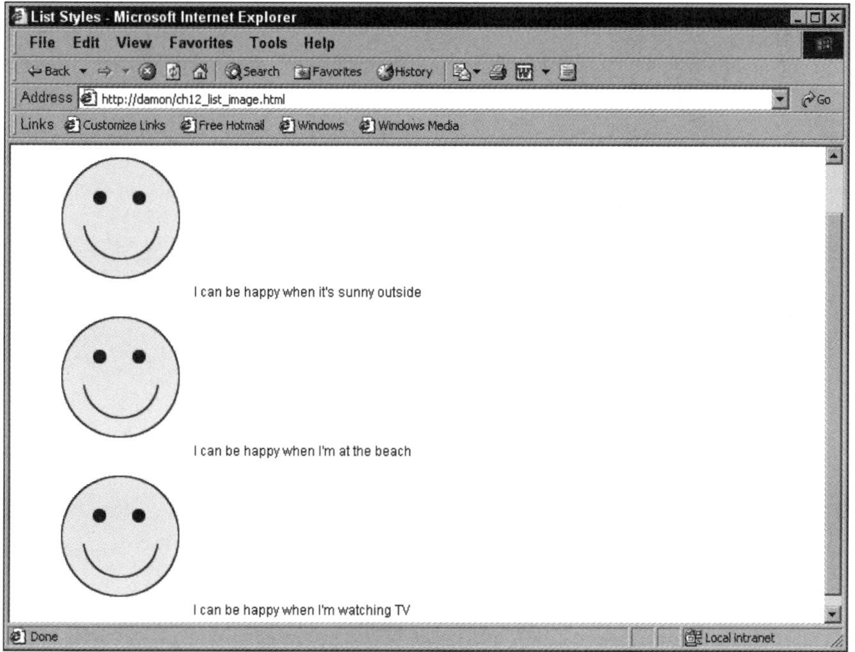

Figure 12-6: That's a lot of smiling faces!

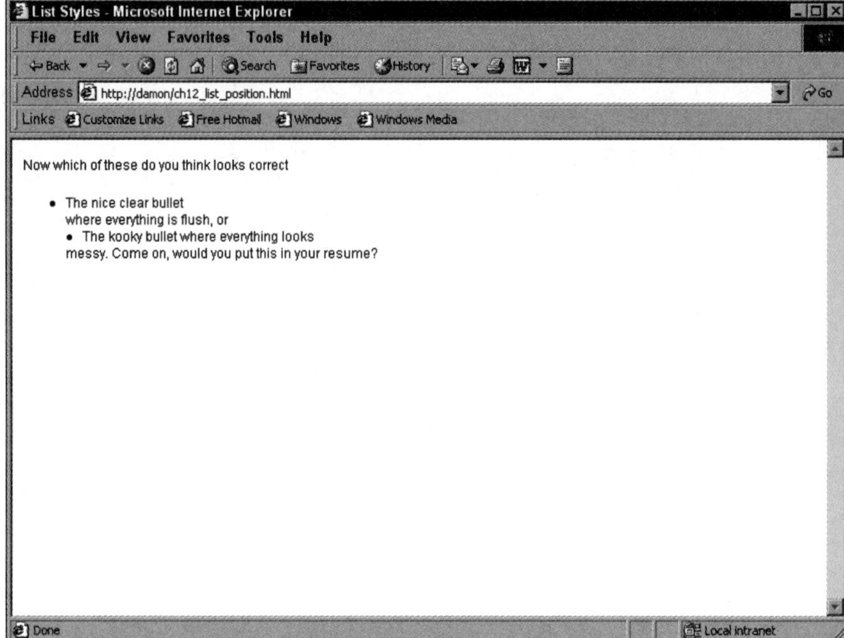

Figure 12-7: The top is smoooooth; the bottom . . . eeeew!

The summary list-style property

The summary element `list-style` eliminates the need for using more than one list property! Like other summary properties, the `list-style` property enables you to roll up other properties into one clean statement. Why would you want to roll up the `list-style-image` and `list-style-type` properties? Won't they overwrite one another? Well, yes, the image will take precedence over the bullet or number, unless the image is unavailable, in which case the marker will show up.

To roll up all the styles I've used thus far into a single style would look as follows:

```
LI   {
   display: list-item
   list-style: disc  url("http://damon/images/happy.gif")
            outside
   }
```

And just like that, you have six pages wrapped up into two very neat paragraphs!

Chapter 13

Mr. Smith, Your Table Is Ready

In This Chapter

- Using the tables cascade tool
- Playing with captions
- Having fun with table tags
- Configuring columns in Internet Explorer
- Applying borders
- Setting table rows and table data styles

When you see all the nifty things that Cascading Styles Sheets (CSS) can do for tables — like eliminating nested tables — you gotta say to yourself, "Cool beans! Look at all this neat stuff that I can do!" Unfortunately, the fact that you *can* do something in CSS doesn't mean that it's a practical application. It's a bit frustrating when you have these great tools at your disposal and then your crafted element doesn't work at all, works inconsistently or in only one browser, or works in a very limited set of circumstances. Try not to think of this as intentional teasing, like the big CSS kids on the playground are tossing your hat back and forth over your head. Try to anticipate the exciting possibilities that lie in the future.

In this chapter, I start out with the general table attributes that you're used to seeing. As with most HTML elements, basic text style attributes can be assigned to any of the standard table elements.

For example, all three of the following examples work pretty much the way you'd expect. For more on fonts, read through Chapter 6.

```
TD   {color: blue}
TD   {font-family: Helvetica}
TD   {text-align: left}
```

Remember that some CSS elements only work in one browser or another. Every time I introduce an element, I'll say something about which browser, if any, it actually works in.

Tables from the (HTML) Crypt

To begin to understand just how CSS can change the way you design tables, you must first understand the basic concepts of table design in HTML. I realize this will be a review for some, but nonetheless, it bears repeating. Here is a basic table layout:

```
 <table>
<caption>Here are some words describing the table</caption>
<tr>
<th>Here is a header for the first row</th>
<td>1</td>
<td>2</td>
   </tr>
<tr>
<th>Here is a header for the second row</th>
<td>3</td>
<td>4</td>
   </tr>
<tr>
<th>Here is a header for the first row</th>
<td>1</td>
<td>2</td>
   </tr>
</table>
```

In Internet Explorer (IE), you also have the options of using the `COLGROUP` and `COL` elements, which don't exist in Netscape (Navigator). Read through the upcoming section "Take Two Aspirins, and Column Me in the Morning" for the CSS rule on what you can use these elements for — but keep in mind that they only work in IE.

One of the most important things to remember when you're working with tables is that this is another place where the *cascading* part of Cascading Style Sheets comes into play. If you have one style set for an entire table and another style set for a table row, the table row set is *closer* to the stuff in the table row, and will thus override the general table settings. And, things that are assigned to the table data are even closer. If you have a background color set for a whole table, both the table row and table data it contains cannot have a background color in order for the table color to show through.

Before I dive into building tables, I first want to look at the `CAPTION` element because you can create style rules specifically for this element, and treat it as if it were a `P` or a `DIV` element. The following sections will show you the different kinds of properties that can be applied to this versatile HTML element.

Caption, I'm giving her all I've got!

Suppose that you want to have some text at the top of every table describing it. This is the time to use the <CAPTION> tag. You can do some pretty cool things with caption tags.

First, meet your new friend `caption-side`, which in theory enables you to determine whether you want the caption to appear at the top, bottom, left, or right of the table. Unfortunately, `caption-side` doesn't work in any browser I've tested, so you're stuck with a caption at the top of the table, which really isn't such a bad thing. However, if it worked, you'd assign the value like this:

```
CAPTION   {caption-side: top}
```

And your options would be `top`, `bottom`, `left`, and `right`.

Width and height: When size matters

You want your table caption to be functional: that is, readable and attention-catching but not distracting. No need to irritate the presbyopics further (enough with the commercials, already!) by making your caption too teeny to read. You refine the styles of your table caption by setting its width and height. Set the caption width with the following:

```
CAPTION   {width: 40px}
```

However, this only seems to work in Netscape. Explorer doesn't care what you set the `width` value to — your caption will always be the width of the table.

Now set the table caption height. Unfortunately, this property doesn't work in any browser yet, but you set it the same way as you do width:

```
CAPTION   {height: 40px}
```

Sigh. Someday, Toto.

Margins are not something you put on toast

You can only set table caption margins in Internet Explorer. Basically, if you want to have a little buffer space around your caption, you can set the left and right margins independently from the rest of the table. Follow this syntax:

```
CAPTION   {margin-left: 40px;
     margin-right: 40px}
```

Here's a nifty thing: If you give `margin-left` or `margin-right` negative values (such as –3), they will theoretically make your caption stick out over the edges of your table, so that your caption is actually wider than the table itself. Unfortunately, I haven't found a browser yet that this works on, but I keep hoping. . . .

I need a chiropractor to work on my vertical alignment

Strike up the band! Here are two things that work in both major browsers — text alignment and vertical alignment! Maybe IE and Netscape were trying to make up for all the rest of this CSS disappointment. Anyway, these are two things you've seen before. You set them this way:

```
CAPTION   {text-align: right;
     vertical-align: middle}
```

You can see the result of using these properties on the `CAPTION` element in Figure 13-1. Your options for `text-align` are right, left, center, and justified. I go into more detail about each of these in Chapter 6, so I won't go into too much detail here, other than to say, "Yippee!" — they work just the way you'd expect!

If you think of your caption in an invisible box at the top of your table, set the vertical-alignment to determine where it's going to show up inside that invisible box. To set where you want your caption to sit at the top of the box, use `vertical-align: top`; to set the caption in the middle, use `vertical-align: middle`; and to make your caption sit on the bottom like a carp, use `vertical-align: bottom`.

In Table 13-1, I list caption properties and values, and which browsers support each.

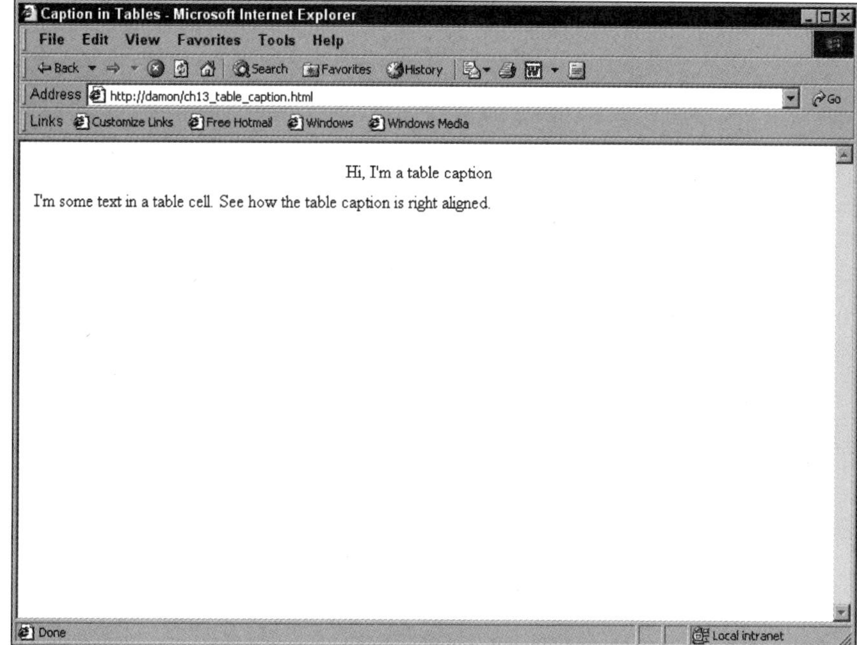

Figure 13-1: Using text-align with the CAPTION element.

Table 13-1 Caption Properties in CSS

Property	*Values*	*Browser Compatibility*
caption-side	top, bottom, right, left	None
width	integer	Netscape only
height	integer	None
text-align	right, left, center, justify	All
vertical-align	top, middle, bottom	All

Table Tags — Do Not Remove under Penalty of Law

I wish that I could show you how to replace those nagging `TABLE` elements once and for all. I truly do! However, because the CSS table properties are so new, these elements aren't universally supported by the browsers. This section is a good primer on building tables, but don't expect to be able to toss out those TABLE elements quite yet. Here I cover the basic table-layout property, which you can use to get going designing your first tables. The table-layout property is really pretty simple: It just refers to table widths. You set a table width inside a normal <TABLE> tag in HTML, like this:

```
<table width="500">
```

You have three table layout options at your disposal: auto, fixed, and inherit. These names are deceptively clever, eh, Clouseau? Explorer, and only Explorer, supports these.

- **auto:** The simplest table layout option is the auto value. When you see this:

  ```
  table-layout="auto"
  ```

  in effect you're stating, "Hey, set this table just as you would if I *didn't* tell you to do anything." Why would you want to do that? Hey, maybe your cats don't listen to you, but you talk to them anyway, don't you? Actually, the biggest reason to set table-layout to auto is that if you've done something wacky and you just want it to go back to the default setting, auto comes in handy.

- **fixed:** Use the fixed value with the table-layout property to make the table exactly the size outlined inside the <TABLE> tag.

  Building on the example in the previous section where width=500, setting table-layout to 500 keeps that table at exactly 500, no matter what the rest of the page is set at. You'd use this when you want to lock down the size of your tables to ensure that they're a given size, no matter what size the user has his or her browser set at.

- **inherit:** Use the inherit value with the table-layout property if your table is inside something else (like another table), and you just want it to inherit the settings from that other thing it's inside.

  Children do take after their parents, after all. Using this value can be handy if, for example, you wanted to nest a table and inherit the table size from the cell size you're embedding the table in.

Of these three layouts, the fixed value makes your page load the fastest. When an HTML page loads in a browser, it has to figure out how much space to leave on the page for each of the things it's loading. If your table-layout is set to auto or inherit, the browser doesn't know exactly how much space the table is going to take up — it has to wait until more things load so it can figure it out. If your table-layout is set to fixed, the browser knows exactly how much space the table is going to take up, and can start placing the other things on the page even before the table finishes loading.

This property is only supported in Internet Explorer 4.0 and above.

Take Two Aspirins, and Column Me in the Morning

Use <COL> tags to give some information at the top of your table, telling the browser a little bit about how you want the table set up. For example, if you want three columns in your table, with widths of 8, 10, and 15 pixels, set these column widths at the top of the table, like this:

```
<colgroup>
<col width="8"><col width="10"><col width="15">
</colgroup>
```

The <COL> and <COLGROUP> tags only work in IE.

Set the width of your table's columns so that you don't have to worry about formatting every single table data element in your table. To set this in the style sheet, you simply write:

```
COL   {width: 80px}
```

Other things you can change per column are the background color, border, and visibility.

Background check

Imagine that you want to create a grid of features in which you want to offset the columns from one another. One way to accomplish this would be to change the background color of a table column. To set the background color of a column (blue, in this example), you simply type:

```
COL   {background: blue}
```

and the browser will render a blue background for your column. Remember, though, that a <TD> tag is considered closer to the data it encloses, so setting a column color only works if the <TD> tags it encloses have a transparent background (if you haven't set a background color, then it defaults to transparent).

You should always remember to choose a different text color than your background color so that you can see the text.

You can also apply borders to the COL element. The same rules apply for setting background color. So, the following syntax

```
COL   {border: 2px;}
```

puts a 2-pixel wide border around the table. I discuss borders more later in this chapter in the section "Tables without (and with) Borders."

Visibility — we have shrinkage!

You only have one option available to you for visibility, which is `visibility: collapse`. Use this to essentially make the column disappear. This is a neat option when you want to have a column not show up if there are no values for the cells that make up the table, and then have all the other columns collapse upon it and take up its position. For example, I can have a 16-column wide table with only 8 columns containing data. Using this property, the table would display as if it were only 8 columns wide!

To make this happen, you type the following:

```
COL   {visibility: collapse}
```

Any space that the column took up will disappear, so don't be surprised when your table shrinks up. And, if some of the text in this column overflowed into another one, it will also disappear. To read how `visibility: collapse` can be used for `TR` and `TD` elements, skip to the upcoming section "Generating table content."

Check out Table 13-2 for column properties and their browser compatibilities.

Table 13-2 Column Properties in CSS

Property	*Values*	*Browser Compatibility*
width	integer	IE only
background	color	IE only
border	integer	IE only
visibility	collapse	IE only

Tables without (and with) Borders

Time to put those borders to work — and jazz 'em up while you're at it. You can set different widths, colors, and patterns.

First I tell you about the border things that actually work — and then I tell you more about what CSS provides that just isn't utilized yet. I start with the ones that only work in Explorer.

Border widths and colors

Border widths and colors are simply set with the <BORDER> tag, pretty much the way font sizes and colors are. In order to set a border width/color, use syntax like this:

```
TABLE    {border: 2px;}
```

or

```
TABLE    {border: blue}
```

Border styles and other designer table fashions

Your border style choices only work in IE, and you write them like this:

```
TABLE    {border: none}
```

You also have the value options of none, hidden, dotted, dashed, solid, double, groove, ridge, inset, and outset. I describe these values in more detail in Chapter 7.

Suppose that you don't want to use the same border everywhere you set one. You can either make one line per element, like this:

```
TABLE    {border: blue;
       border: dotted}
```

or you can put them all in one line, separated by spaces, like this:

```
TABLE    {border: 2px blue dotted}
```

See the result of using these properties in Figure 13-2.

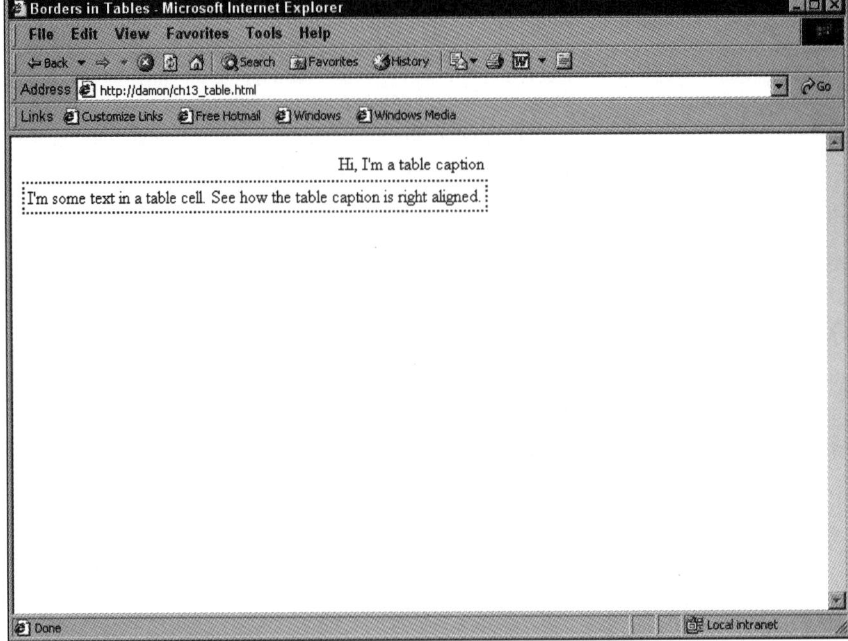

Figure 13-2: Put a nice dotted border around a table.

Border-collapses not in the Middle East

Here's another nifty tool, but again, yet another that works only on IE: `border-collapse`. Use this property to specify how you want the borders of different table elements to interact with one another. You refine border-collapse with one of these three values:

```
TABLE   {border-collapse: separate}
TABLE   {border-collapse: collapse}
TABLE   {border-collapse: inherit}
```

- **`separate`:** The result of applying the `separate` value is the easiest one to see. If you have `border-collapse` set to `separate`, instead of having an intersecting gridline, each individual cell has a little square box around it.
- **`inherit`:** A `border-collapse` style of `inherit` means that the table you're working on keeps the same `border-collapse` style as whatever it's sitting inside. In other words, when you nest tables, this table takes on the `border-collapse` style of the table it's inside.
- **`collapse`:** Collapsing borders is basically a way of telling the borders what to do in the case of border conflict. (No, border conflict has nothing to do with clashes in Eastern Europe.) If you have more than one border style set for different elements on your page and two borders are

in the same place, using the `collapse` value dictates that the more eye-catching border wins.

Dashed or dotted borders, for example, are considered more eye-catching than your run-of-the-mill 1-pixel solid black line. While the term *eye catching* is actually printed in the specification, the truth is that there's a fairly complex algorithm that the browsers are supposed to use to determine eye-catchiness. That formula applies greater priority to those borders that are wider first, and then (if they're equal in width) to those that are more visually interesting, in the following order: double, solid, dashed, dotted, ridge, outset, groove, and inset.

Empty cells — something to hide?

The last border element is `empty-cells`, which looks like this:

```
TABLE   {empty-cells: show}
```

and your options are `show`, `hide`, or `inherit`. Set these to tell the browser what to do with cells that don't have anything in them. Do you want to see a border outlining the cell anyway, or do you want it to look like there's a hole in your table where something should be?

Use the `show` value to make the cell visible, even though the cell holds nothing. Use the `hide` value to make the cell invisible. And, use the `inherit` value to set the cell to use whatever style belongs to the thing it's inside.

Check out Table 13-3 for border properties, values, and browser compatibilities.

Table 13-3 Border Properties in CSS

Property	*Values*	*Browser Compatibility*
border-collapse	collapse, separate, inherit	IE only
border-spacing	<length><length>	None
border sizes	pixels	IE and Netscape 6.0
border colors	colors	IE and Netscape 6.0
border styles	none	IE and Netscape 6.0
border	outset, inset	IE and Netscape 6.0
empty-cells	show, hide, inherit	None

Headers, Rows, and Data Are Our Friends

Theoretically, any of the border elements listed previously can be assigned to TH, TR, and TD elements as well. I've found that they only work, however, in IE and not in Netscape.

CSS has two really spiffy data alignment settings that don't work in any browser I tested, but if they ever do come into fashion, they'd be really useful. Still dreaming of that far-off CSS Utopian society, here's text-align and :before.

Aligning text to a character

This great tool enables you to line up a column of numbers by their decimal points. A column that looks like this can be pretty annoying and difficult to read:

$1.04

$10.04

$.04

To make your numbers straighten up, use this syntax:

```
TD {text-align: "." }
```

Now (theoretically), numbers will align by decimal point. This tool would be exceptionally handy for listing prices, or generating an online invoice. This part of the text-align property (and it's geared specifically for the TABLE element) isn't yet supported by either browser.

Generating table content

The other spiffy little pseudo-element is the :before rule, which basically tells the browser to put whatever you write here before every element inside the table data. Why would you use this? If you have a whole table full of dollar amounts, use this to eliminate having to type all of those pesky little dollar signs over and over. Instead, in the style sheet, you could just type the following:

```
TD:before  {content: "$"}
```

and it would put a dollar sign in front of everything between the `<TD></TD>` tags. This property is currently only supported on Netscape 6.0 on the PC. For more information on generated content, check out Chapter 12.

Again, the `visibility:collapse` property can also theoretically be assigned to `TR` and `TD` elements. Unfortunately, this application is only theoretical because it doesn't actually work in any of the browsers I tested. Read about table data properties, values, and browser compatibilities in Table 13-4.

Table 13-4 Table Data Properties in CSS

Property	*Values*	*Browser Compatibility*
text-align	character (string)	None
:before{content:}	character	Netscape 6.0 for the PC
visibility	collapse	None

Chapter 14

CSS and XML: The Perfect Match?

In This Chapter

- Understanding XML
- Structuring an XML document
- Building a page with XML and CSS

As the Web has evolved over the past few years, more and more companies are turning toward eXtensible Markup Language (XML) to manage documents and data. XML, like HTML, is a structured language that enables you to categorize data according to properties that you define. Simply put, XML combines content (words, images, and other documents) and a logical structure for what that content is supposed to represent in the structure of a document. And because of its wide range of applications, from document management to data management, companies are adopting XML as a standard left and right.

XML is not all that different from HTML; two main differences separate them. First, HTML contains some design and stylistic elements (`TABLE`, `STRONG`, `FONT`, `B`, and `I`), whereas an XML document contains none. Second, with an HTML document, you're limited to one single document structure — namely, the one defined by the HTML elements. In XML, you can structure a document in an infinite number of different ways.

XML is more appropriately designed to use CSS than HTML because XML uses no design whatsoever: just content and attributes. The result is that you can use style sheets to design the entire presentation of an XML document. And in this chapter, I show you how!

Although CSS is perfect for the aesthetic layout of an XML document, displaying that document is a different matter. Netscape Navigator 6.0 has the best implementation of CSS2 to make this display possible, but it's far from perfect. Many of the features I describe in this chapter won't work on even the latest versions of Internet Explorer (IE). So, proceed with caution!

XML Gives Your Documents Structure and Meaning

In this section, I give you a very — and I mean *very* — brief primer on the XML concept. XML was designed to provide a way for richly structured documents to be presented on the Web. HTML, although a good language for basic construction, lacks a mechanism for extending itself to include more detailed and fine grain information. I can't, for example, describe a stock transaction in HTML that has any relation to another stock transaction. The best that I could do is to input the data manually into an HTML table, as follows:

```
<TABLE>
<TR>
   <TD>Stock</TD>
   <TD>Shares</TD>
   <TD>Sell Price</TD>
</TR>
<TR>
   <TD>Motorola</TD>
   <TD>100</TD>
   <TD>20.25</TD>
</TR>
</TABLE>
```

The result is just an output of some bits of data. I couldn't use this HTML, for example, to add a whole bunch of stock transactions to tally how many stocks I sold today. There's no structural logic behind it, except that it's contained within a `TABLE` element in an HTML document.

With XML, you have the flexibility to create structures that include vast amounts of information, with as much detail as you're inclined to provide. I could create a document structure, for example, that represented my entire portfolio, all the way from the summary information down to an individual stock. See how that structure might look in Figure 14-1.

With XML, you define your own document structures, which means that you're not limited by any other language.

In this portfolio, a stock has structure and meaning, which is based on both its position in the document hierarchy and the attributes (ticker symbol, sales price, shares, and so forth) that are associated with it. In this structure, I could represent that same stock transaction from the example in the following fashion:

```
<STOCK ticker="MOT" name="Motorola" sellprice="20.25"
        shares="100" />
```

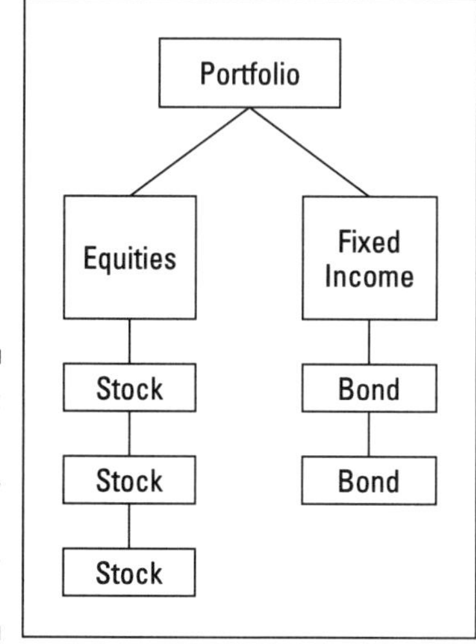

Figure 14-1: A possible XML structure for a stock portfolio.

Notice a difference in the tag structure between the HTML and the XML. XML has two different kinds of tagging structures:

- Tags, just like in HTML, that use an opening and closing tag for an element: `<HTML>...</HTML>`.
- Self-contained single tags, which include all the needed information within the brackets. These always follow this format: `<tag data="something" moredata="somethingelse" />`.

XML really gives you the flexibility to design documents and data the way you want to achieve a desired effect.

I'm only scratching the tip of the proverbial iceberg here on XML. To get a more in-depth view of XML, check out Ed Tittel's *XML For Dummies,* 2nd Edition, published by Hungry Minds, Inc.

Building an XML Document

The best way to get the concept behind XML is to go ahead and build an XML document from scratch. Follow along as I go through this process.

Suppose that I'm getting out of the big city and building a home on the shores of Bora Bora. My architect, interesting fellow that he is, prefers to have his documents delivered in XML format, so I have to specify how I want my living room to look in my new house using XML. Hmmm.

Step one: Create a framework

Before I even deliberate what I want in each individual room, I have to think through the kinds of things that I want and need to deliver to my architect. If my goal is to deliver a document to him that adequately describes the rooms in the house, then I want to at least give him the following:

- The name of the room
- A brief description of the room
- The furnishings for that room
- A floor plan for how I want the room to look
- Any notes about the room that I want to convey

Always begin your framework at the highest level, and then drill down later. That way, your framework is easily applied to every room in the house. You'll see how this becomes important later as you read through this chapter.

Step two: Take inventory

After I create an initial information framework for my rooms, the next step is to go through each of the categories I created in the previous section to see what content I need to flesh out for each category. Instead of being generic, though, now I need to think about one room in particular — the living room. Getting to this level of detail gives me a full inventory of everything that I need to include in my XML document, and it also provides me with all the data I need to create an XML structure. In Table 14-1, I include each room category and what content goes with each. In this example, I use a subcategory for the furnishings (under furniture).

Table 14-1 Living Room Elements

Category	*Subcategory?*	*Content*
Name	No	Text
Description	No	Text
Floorplan	No	Image
Furniture	Chair, table, lamp, and hutch	Text
Notes	Note	Text

Always try to put your content into categories because it's easier to come up with a structure that represents all the different kinds of content elements you may have in your document structure.

Step three: Build a document structure

After I have a complete inventory for everything that I want in my living room, I begin to map a structure for my XML document. Take a look at Figure 14-2, which shows a representation of the document hierarchy.

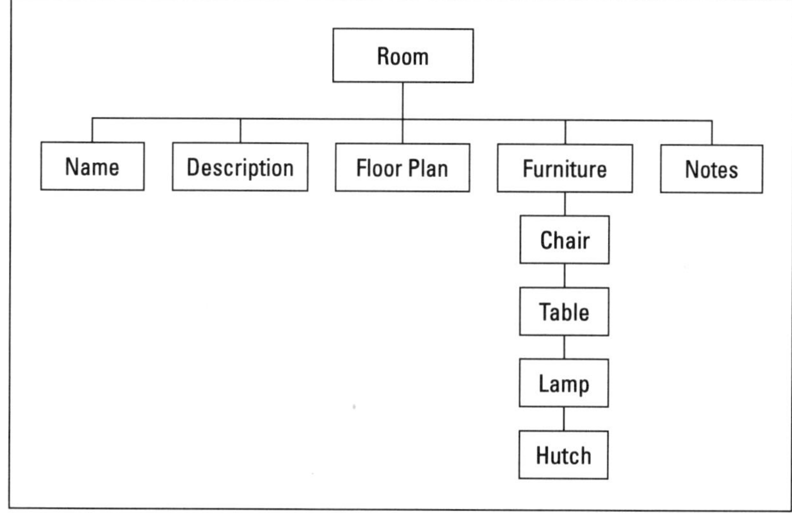

Figure 14-2: The document hierarchy.

With this logical structure, and the content types from Table 14-1, I can create an XML structure that represents the entire room, as shown in the following code:

```
<ROOM>
   <NAME>...</NAME>
   <DESCRIPTION>...</DESCRIPTION>
   <FLOORPLAN />
   <FURNITURE>
      <CHAIR>...</CHAIR>
      <TABLE>...</TABLE>
      <LAMP>...</LAMP>
      <HUTCH>...</HUTCH>
   </FURNITURE>
   <NOTES>
      <NOTE>...</NOTE>
   </NOTES>
</ROOM>
```

Most of the tags in the XML structure allow for text because most of the content in the document will be text. The exception to this is the `<FLOORPLAN>` tag, which is a single tag because all it does is signify an image that accompanies the document.

In addition to the tags, I need to identify the document as an XML document. This syntax would *precede* the `ROOM` element in the document:

```
<?xml version="1.0" encoding="utf-8" ?>
```

Here's a little puzzle for you: What if I have more than one chair? In XML, depending upon how you structure your document, you can have as many instances of a tag as you like; just take care to use consistent identifiers for elements. To include more than one chair, for example, include a `type` value for the `CHAIR` element that describes the chair: wicker, ottoman, recliner, and so forth. Accomplish this with the following syntax:

```
<CHAIR type="wicker">This is chair of type wicker</CHAIR>
```

Step four: Populate the XML

For the living room in my Bora Bora retreat, I've decided that I want the following furniture items (I can dream, can't I?):

- A Johnson wicker chair
- A leather ottoman
- A South Sea glass oblong table
- A tropical halogen lamp
- Soft white recessed track lights
- Jim's House of Teak Super Hutch

In addition to the furniture, I also have a few notes for the architect that I'll include in the Notes area. I also need to fill out the name of the room and its description, and provide an image for the floor plan (in `.gif` format), shown in Figure 14-3.

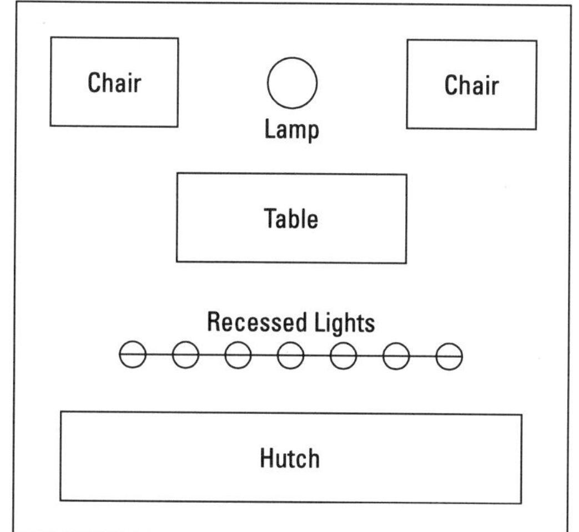

Figure 14-3: The floor plan for the living room.

When complete, my XML document is going to look like this:

```
<?xml version="1.0" encoding="utf-8" ?>

<ROOM>
   <NAME>THE LIVING ROOM</NAME>
   <DESCRIPTION>This is how I'd like the living room to look
          for my new home on Bora Bora. I've gone to great
          lengths to design a style that is both tropical
          and functionally pleasing!</DESCRIPTION>
   <FLOORPLAN description="This is the floorplan for the
          room" type="image" />
   <FURNITURE>
      <CHAIR type="wicker">Johnson Wicker Chair</CHAIR>
      <CHAIR type="ottoman">Leather Ottoman</CHAIR>
      <TABLE type="coffee">South Sea Glass Oblong</TABLE>
      <LAMP type="floor">Tropical Halogen Lamp</LAMP>
      <LAMP type="recessed">Soft White Recessed Track
           Lights</LAMP>
      <HUTCH type="entertainment">Jim's House of Teak Super
           Hutch</HUTCH>
   </FURNITURE>
   <NOTES>
      <NOTE>Get the blue wicker chair if you can!</NOTE>
      <NOTE>Can you please make sure the ottoman is a light
           leather?</NOTE>
      <NOTE>Don't go cheap on this lamp!</NOTE>
   </NOTES>
</ROOM>
```

All this code is on the CD that accompanies the book, so you don't have to worry about having to retype any of this!

Using CSS to Design an XML Document

I've created and delivered my XML document to my architect. Because he's in Bora Bora and I'm in California, we figured it would be better to share our work on the Web. Wanting a consistent look and feel across all rooms, he decides that he wants to format my XML document using Cascading Style Sheets. That means no HTML!

Thankfully, the latest browsers (IE 5.*x* and Netscape 6.0) can process XML documents directly in the browser, and a style sheet can be applied directly from the XML source file using the following syntax:

```
<?xml-stylesheet href="xmlstyle.css" type="text/css" ?>
```

where `xmlstyle.css` is the name of the style sheet that will apply styles to the XML document. Check out the desired output in Figure 14-4. In the following sections, I describe the steps to create this.

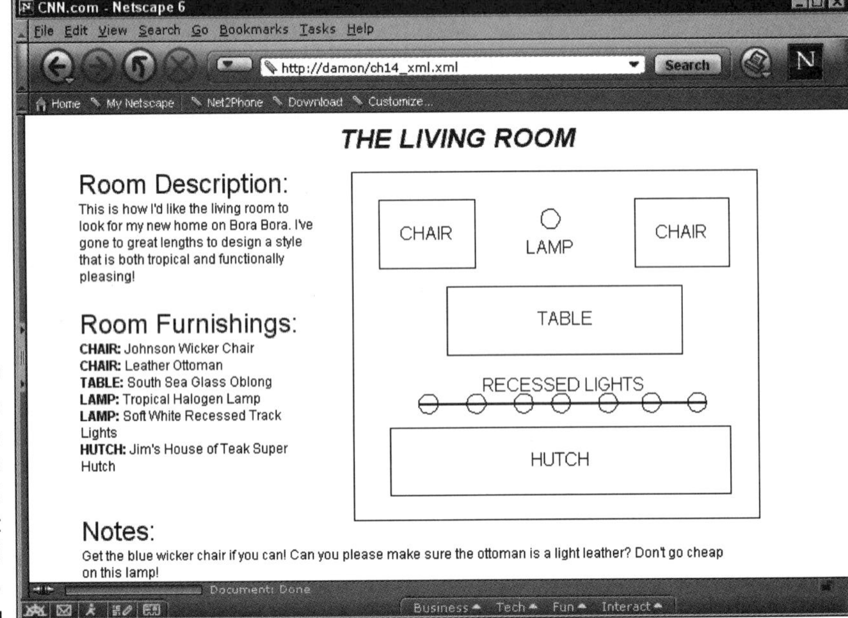

Figure 14-4: This is what the eventual layout should look like.

Step one: Develop a base font for the document

Unlike an HTML document, an XML document has no default styles, so your first step is to develop a baseline font style for the entire document. For this example, a 12-pixel-high Arial font should serve quite nicely. The default font style then can be applied to the highest element in the document structure (the ROOM element) as follows:

```
ROOM {
   font-family: Arial;
   font-size: 12px;
   }
```

Setting this font style will ensure that no matter what, all child elements to the ROOM element will display Arial 12-pixel text.

Step two: Establish positions for each of the major elements

The display of the XML document has five major areas:

- The Room title
- The room Description
- The room Furniture
- The floor plan
- The Notes section

Before worrying about the styles of the content with those major areas, you first need to establish position. Because each of the items above is an element (NAME, DESCRIPTION, FURNITURE, FLOORPLAN, NOTES) within the XML document, position can be placed on each individually, as follows:

```
NAME {
   position: absolute;
   top: 10px;
   left: 50px;
   width: 700px;
   }

DESCRIPTION {
   position: absolute;
   top: 50px;
   left: 50px;
```

```
    width: 220px;
    }

FLOORPLAN {
    position: absolute;
    top: 50px;
    left: 300px;
    }
FURNITURE{
    position: absolute;
    top: 175px;
    left: 50px;
    width: 220px;
    }
NOTES{
    position: absolute;
    top: 360px;
    left: 50px;
    width: 600px;
    }
```

This is just one approach to the layout. You could also create a header rule for the `NAME`, a left column rule for `FURNITURE` and `DESCRIPTION`, a right column rule for the `FLOORPLAN`, and a footer rule for the `NOTES`.

Step three: Create the headers

One thing that you want to make sure you do when you're creating a reusable style is to minimize the amount of customization or duplication in either the style sheet or the XML document. For example, you can reasonably assume that the other rooms in the house will also include `Room Description`, `Room Furnishings`, and `Notes` in their layouts. Instead of continually including them in your XML document, use the CSS `:before` pseudo-elements and the `content` property to create a single set of headers that can be applied to all XML documents delivered for this house.

IE doesn't yet support the `:before` or `:after` pseudo-elements, and by association, the `content` property.

Here's how you do it:

1. **Create a `:before` pseudo-element for the `DESCRIPTION`, `FURNITURE`, and `NOTES` elements.**

   The empty rules would look as follows:

```
DESCRIPTION:before {
    }
FURNITURE:before {
    }
NOTES:before {
    }
```

2. **Add a `font-size` property value of `24px` to each of the `:before` pseudo-elements.**

   This will ensure that each of the `:before` pseudo-elements will have the larger font size than the content in the regular element.

   You could consolidate the rules to one `:before` rule for text size if there were no other `:before` elements in the document. The syntax for that is:

```
*:before { font-size: 24px; }
```

3. **Add the header to each of the `:before` pseudo-elements by adding a `content` declaration to each.**

   Each of the content declarations would look as follows:

   For the `DESCRIPTION` pseudo-element:

```
content: "Room Description:";
```

   For the `FURNITURE` pseudo-element:

```
content: "Room Furnishings:";
```

   For the `NOTES` pseudo-element:

```
content: "Notes:";
```

   Ideally, I would also include a `\A` at the end of each of those descriptions to create a line break. However, this syntax isn't supported by Explorer or Netscape, so it wouldn't work even if I did put it there.

4. **To create a line break, set the display to `list-item` for each of the `:before` pseudo-elements.**

   Ideally, you wouldn't need this property, but it's the only reasonable way to create a line break. If you didn't put it in, the text would run together, as shown in Figure 14-5.

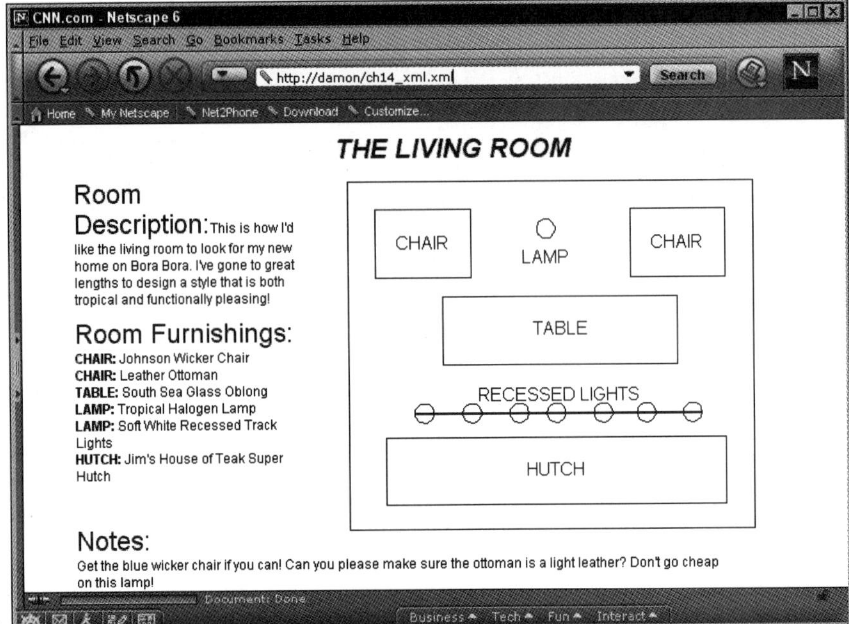

Figure 14-5: Avoid run-in text like this by creating a list-item.

After you complete these steps, the headers are good to go, and the resulting style rules would look as follows:

```
DESCRIPTION:before {
   font-size: 24px;
   content: "Room Description:";
   display: list-item;
   }
FURNITURE:before {
   font-size: 24px;
   content: "Room Furnishings:";
   display: list-item;
   }
NOTES:before {
   font-size: 24px;
   content: "Notes:";
   display: list-item;
   }
```

Step four: Format the furniture descriptions

All the furniture elements (`CHAIR`, `LAMP`, `HUTCH`, and `TABLE`) work identically, but they're a tad quirky as a result of that line break feature (`\A`) not being implemented in Navigator 6.0.

Each of the FURNITURE elements requires a :before pseudo-element to insert the name of the element before the furniture description. The following rule — specified here for the TABLE element — also needs to be applied to CHAIR, LAMP, and HUTCH in the style sheet:

```
TABLE:before   {
   font-weight: bold;
   content: "TABLE: ";
      }
```

with the caveat that the content value should match the name of the element.

In addition to the :before pseudo-element, however, the CHAIR, TABLE, HUTCH, and LAMP elements all need to be set to display: list-item in order to make sure that they break properly. That creates the following rules:

```
CHAIR   {display: list-item;}
TABLE   {display: list-item;}
LAMP    {display: list-item;}
HUTCH   {display: list-item;}
```

Step five: Lay the floor plan

Even the floor plan isn't totally intuitive! I create the positioning for the floor plan in the section "Step two: Establish positions for each of the major elements." However, because standard ways exists to embed an image in a XML document, you have to use CSS to get it done! That's okay, though, because with an :after pseudo-element, it's a piece of cake.

Just follow these two quick steps:

1. **Add the :after pseudo-element to the FLOORPLAN element, as shown in this code.**

   ```
   FLOORPLAN:after{ }
   ```

2. **Add the floorplan.gif to the :after pseudo-element using a content property.**

   Here's the syntax:

   ```
      FLOORPLAN:after{
   content: url('images/floorplan.gif');
   ```

You have other ways to get content into the document using XML itself, but those properties aren't yet as well supported as the content property, so although you have alternatives, this is the easier way to go!

Step six: Stylize the header

The only other thing left to do is to apply the style rules to the NAME element. I set the positioning earlier in the section "Step two: Establish positions for each of the major elements." However, in order to make the name 24 pixels high, bold, italic, and centered, add the following properties to the rule:

```
    font-size: 24px;
    font-weight: bold;
    font-style: italic;
    text-align: center;
```

The overall NAME rule should look like this:

```
NAME {
    font-size: 24px;
    font-weight: bold;
    font-style: italic;
    text-align: center;
    position: absolute;
    top: 10px;
    left: 50px;
    width: 700px;
    }
```

And voilà! — I turned my XML document into a designed page in a Web browser!

Is This an Efficient Way to Design Pages?

You can argue that this wasn't the most efficient way to design a page in a browser. Then again, if you were to substitute another XML document with the same structure as the Living Room, as shown in Figure 14-6, you'll see that the style sheets effectively serve both documents equally.

My example is admittedly limited. After the various browsers have fully adopted CSS2, then using style sheets to design XML documents will be a more user-friendly endeavor. But, even then, CSS will have limitations of what you can reasonably do with it. Another effort being undertaken by the World Wide Web Consortium is the development of the eXtensible Scripting Language, or XSL.

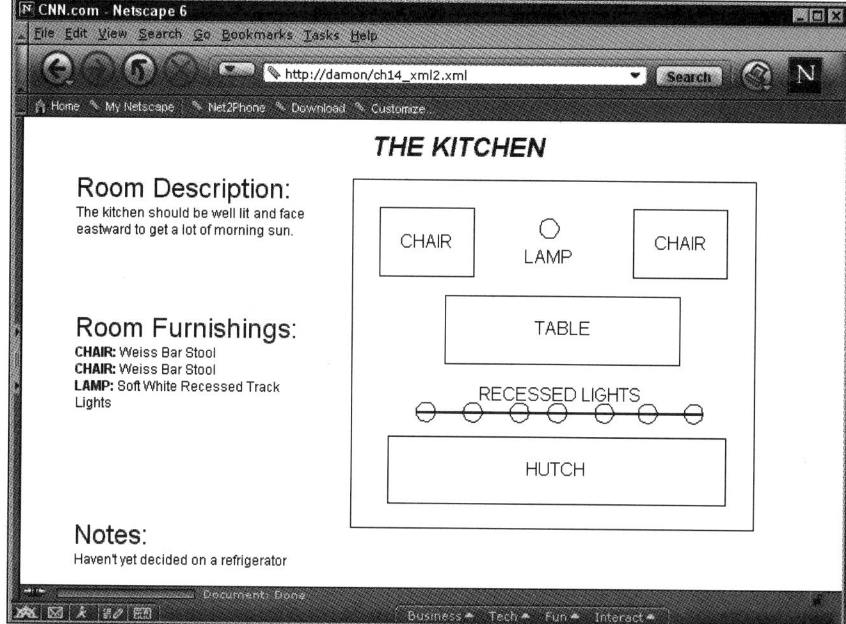

Figure 14-6: Different XML document, same style sheet.

XSL does some of what CSS had problems doing in the previous example (such as creating headers, inserting images, and lines breaks), plus a whole lot more. With XSL, you can perform a number of cool functions on any number of XML documents. So, will XSL make CSS obsolete for styling CSS documents? It can't really because although XSL can more easily create headers, footers, and variables and perform functions that CSS can't, the basics of design (style, position, font, and text) are not included in the XSL specification.

Thus, the answer lies in the development of both languages to be supported fully by all the browsers. Only then will using CSS with XML truly become a more developer-friendly venture.

Chapter 15

Styles and Other Media

In This Chapter

- Introducing media types
- Discovering aural style sheets
- Using aural style sheet properties for your user's aid

Sure, Cascading Style Sheets can do amazing things for you and your Web site, but CSS can be used for other media types, such as Palm Pilots and even the TV. One of the most important features of style sheets is how your information is going to be presented to other people, and what the needs of those users are.

Aural style sheets, for those that are visually impaired, are also an important media consideration in your Web development because this is a growing area for Web development. Is your Web site just going to be on-screen? Or will your Web site need to go through a speech synthesizer or Braille device? Life just got a little more complicated!

In this chapter, I describe different media types, the nuances of aural style sheets, and how to use these properties and values to the benefit of your user.

Using CSS for Different Media Types

Cascading Style Sheets aren't just for visual presentations anymore! Use style sheets to include several different types of media and change your data presentation for a number of different media types, even if the data source is the same. Check out Table 15-1 for all the media types that are included in the CSS2 specification.

None of the media types listed in Table 15-1 has been adopted by any major browser yet. The two most significant ones — the ones that are likely to be implemented first — are `print` and `aural`.

Table 15-1 Media Types

Media Name	*Definition*
all	Suitable for all devices.
aural	Intended for speech synthesizers.
braille	Intended for Braille tactile feedback devices.
embossed	Intended for paged Braille printers.
handheld	Intended for handheld devices (typically small screen, monochrome, with limited bandwidth).
print	Intended for paged, opaque material and for documents viewed on-screen in Print Preview mode.
projection	Intended for projected presentations, such as projectors or print-to-transparencies applications.
screen	Intended primarily for color computer screens.
tty	Intended for media using a fixed-pitch character grid, such as teletypes, terminals, or portable devices with limited display capabilities. Authors should not use pixel units with the tty media type.
tv	Intended for television-type devices (low resolution, color, limited-scrollability screens, sound available).

To specify a different media type, begin to familiarize yourself with the `@media` rule. The `@media` rule enables you to specify different properties for data elements, depending on the media type. In the following example, the author is describing a different set of rules for the `P` element, depending upon whether the user is viewing the content in print format or on the computer screen. The syntax for the rule is as follows:

```
@media print {
    P { font-size: 10pt }
  }
  @media screen {
    P { font-size: 12px }
  }
  @media screen, print {
    P { font-family: Times }
  }
```

I describe paged media (media destined to be printed like a book or a magazine, which you specify with the `print` value), in more detail in Chapter 16.

What's the practical application of using the `print` value with the `@media` property? When users with alternative media capabilities (not a Web browser) visit your Web site, they will then be able to decipher the information on your Web page.

Although using HTML is a good start for other media types, eXtensible Markup Language (XML) will eventually drive the `@media` rule. Most wireless and set-top applications use derivations of XML to collect and strucutre data; HTML is becoming used more and more for browser-only applications.

Defining Aural Style Sheets

In order to make your Web site accessible to vision-imparied users, develop style sheets that enable aural rendering. I recommend that all Web sites should be made available to those with sight impairments. Aural style sheets are designed to go beyond the current generation of text readers by enabling content generation geared specfically for those who cannot see well but who can hear. The aural presentation of your information occurs when a special software reader scans through the text, and literally reads it back to the visitor. Pretty cool when you think about it.

Increased Web accessibility for the disabled is really just the tip of the iceberg for using aural style sheets. Let your mind run with the fantastic possibilties that you can create with this technology: Imagine that you're in your car heading to the airport with your laptop sitting on the passenger seat. You're running late and need to get some information about your flight. You check your flight, and your airline's Web site *tells* you your flight information. Or imagine that you're in the kitchen up to your elbows in flour and bread dough *listening* to recipe instructions instead of having to turn cookbook pages with your nose.

Aural style sheets can also be a great resource for those who have literacy or secondary language deficiencies, for home entertainment, and for anyone who'd rather listen than read.

Aural style sheets are really defined by sounds. The sounds are categorized by common sound file formats that are reasonably safe for aural style sheets and the various browsers:

- **AIFF** or **AIF:** The Audio Interchange format, common to both platforms
- **AU:** A sound file native to the Sun platform; has grown in support on other platforms
- **SND:** A sound file format most greatly associated with the Macintosh
- **MIDI** or **MID:** One of the oldset sound file formats, supported by both Windows and the Macintosh environments
- **WAV:** A sound file format more closely associated with Windows than other platforms

Quite unfortunately, although aural style sheets offer Web development a new plane of user services, the reality is that very few applications currently support these kinds of features.

Aural Style Sheet Properties: Making Your Sound Behave

When you use aural style sheets, you define space: both a physical space and a temporal space (because sound temporarily surrounds). The CSS properties enable your site to vary the quality of the synthesized speech, such as voice type, frequency, inflection, and so forth. Think of Stephen Hawking's computerized voice.

For your aural style sheets, CSS provides a host of properties to give you control of nearly every aspect of the spoken word. You need rules in your styles so that your visitor's reader doesn't speak every little bit of code that's on your site. You don't want your visitor to hear every meta tag and painstakingly written line of HTML. Check out Table 15-2 where I list a number of the most common aural style sheet properties, as defined in the CSS2 specification, and their accepted values.

If the following table seems a tad daunting, don't worry! I describe each of the major properties in more detail throughout this chapter. To help you research the ones that I don't discuss (those properties that aren't that useful yet), check out the W3C Web site at `www.w3.org`.

All your properties for an aural style sheet will be contained within an `@media aural` rule.

Bouncin' and behavin' volume

No, *defining volume* does not refer to some shampoo product, but rather setting volume parameters through an aural style sheet. For example, suppose that you to want to define a median volume so the user doesn't get scared to death by a hard rockin' speech synthesizer. Users will probably be able to adjust the volume themselves, but you still want to define the initial volume. Properties of volume include `lather`, `rinse`, `repeat`. Just kidding!

Table 15-2 Properties of Aural Style Sheets

<table>
<tr><th>Property</th><th>Value</th><th>Initial Value</th><th>Applies To</th><th>Inherited?</th><th>Percentages</th></tr>
<tr><td>volume</td><td><number> | <percentage> | silent | x-soft | soft | medium | loud | x-loud | inherit</td><td>Medium</td><td>All elements</td><td>Yes</td><td>Refer to inherited value</td></tr>
<tr><td>speak</td><td>normal | none | spell-out | inherit</td><td>Normal</td><td>All elements</td><td>Yes</td><td>N/A</td></tr>
<tr><td>pause-before</td><td><time> | <percentage> | inherit</td><td>Depends on user agent</td><td>All elements</td><td>No</td><td>N/A</td></tr>
<tr><td>pause-after</td><td><time> | <percentage> | inherit</td><td>Depends on user agent</td><td>All elements</td><td>No</td><td>N/A</td></tr>
<tr><td>pause</td><td>[[<time> | <percentage>]{1,2}] | inherit</td><td>Depends on user agent</td><td>All elements</td><td>No</td><td>N/A</td></tr>
<tr><td>cue-before</td><td><url> | none | inherit</td><td>None</td><td>All elements</td><td>No</td><td>N/A</td></tr>
<tr><td>cue-after</td><td><url> | none | inherit</td><td>None</td><td>all elements</td><td>No</td><td>N/A</td></tr>
<tr><td>cue</td><td>[<cue-before> || <cue-after>] | inherit</td><td>Not defined for shorthand properties</td><td>All elements</td><td>No</td><td>N/A</td></tr>
<tr><td>play-during</td><td><url> mix? repeat? | auto | none | inherit</td><td>Auto</td><td>All elements</td><td>No</td><td>N/A</td></tr>
<tr><td>azimuth</td><td><angle> | [[left-side | far-left | left | center-left | center | center-right | right | far-right | right-side] || behind] | leftwards | rightwards | inherit</td><td>Center</td><td>All elements</td><td>Yes</td><td>N/A</td></tr>
</table>

(continued)

Table 15-2 *(continued)*

<table>
<tr><th>Property</th><th>Value</th><th>Initial Value</th><th>Applies To</th><th>Inherited?</th><th>Percentages</th></tr>
<tr><td>elevation</td><td><angle> | below | level | above | higher | lower | inherit</td><td>Level</td><td>All elements</td><td>Yes</td><td>N/A</td></tr>
<tr><td>speech-rate</td><td><number> | x-slow | slow | medium | fast | x-fast | faster | slower | inherit</td><td>Medium</td><td>All elements</td><td>Yes</td><td>N/A</td></tr>
<tr><td>voice-family</td><td>[[| <generic-voice>],]* [|] |</td><td>Depends on user agent</td><td>All elements</td><td>Yes</td><td>N/A</td></tr>
<tr><td>pitch</td><td><frequency> | x-low | low | medium | high | x-high | inherit</td><td>Medium</td><td>All elements</td><td>Yes</td><td>N/A</td></tr>
<tr><td>pitch-range</td><td><number> | inherit</td><td>50</td><td>All elements</td><td>Yes</td><td>N/A</td></tr>
<tr><td>stress</td><td><number> | inherit</td><td>50</td><td>All elements</td><td>Yes</td><td>N/A</td></tr>
<tr><td>richness</td><td><number> | inherit</td><td>50</td><td>All elements</td><td>Yes</td><td>N/A</td></tr>
<tr><td>speak-punctuation</td><td>code | none | inherit</td><td>None</td><td>All elements</td><td>Yes</td><td>N/A</td></tr>
<tr><td>speak-numeral</td><td>digits | continuous | inherit</td><td>Continuous</td><td>All elements</td><td>Yes</td><td>N/A</td></tr>
</table>

In Table 15-3, I include the different value types and definitions that you can apply to the `volume` property.

Table 15-3 Volume Values and Meanings

Name	*Definitions*
<number>	Any number between 0 and 100. 0 represents the *minimum audible* volume level, and 100 corresponds to the *maximum comfortable* level.
<percentage>	Percentage values are calculated relative to the inherited value, and are then clipped to the range 0 to 100.
silent	No sound at all.
x-soft	Same as 0.
soft	Same as 25.
medium	Same as 50.
loud	Same as 75.
x-loud	Same as 100.

The value `0` does not mean the same as `silent`; calling a value of `0` gives you a sound level of `x-soft`. Remember that `0` is the lowest audible value, which is different than `silent`.

The following code snippet displays the proper syntax for the aural `volume` property.

```
volume: x-soft;
```

Speaking only when told to

The `speak` properties define what content will be read out loud or not. As I mention earlier, you don't want every tag ("`<font size=-2>`," for example) to be read aloud. Define in your style sheet only what you want to be heard, and what's best left unsaid. The syntax for the property is defined like this:

```
speak: none
```

Here's the full list of the values that are acceptable for the `speak` property:

- `none`: Using this value keeps all styles non-aural: That is, no data with this property applied is spoken (rendered), making the whole listening experience that much faster.

- `normal`: This value uses the language selected for the User Agent to speak the proper pronunciation for that element and all its siblings.
- `spell-out`: Use this value to spell out the text one letter at a time (think acronyms and abbreviations).

Watch your speed!

After you style your text to be read aloud, choose the language, and set the volume level, then you need to decide the speed at which your text will be synthesized on a user's machine. (Speech rate is one of two voice characteristics properties in CSS; read about the other — voice family — in the upcoming section "Whose voice is that, anyway?")

Use the `speech-rate` property to set the number of words per minute that a synthesizer should speak. You can amend the rate of speech with the following values:

- `<number>`: This value is an integer that specifies the number of words per minute that a syntesizer should speak.
- `x-slow`: This value is equal to 80 words per minute (wpm).
- `slow`: This value is equal to 120 wpm.
- `medium`: This value equals between 180 and 200 wpm.
- `fast`: This value equals 300 wpm.
- `x-fast`: This value is equal to 500 wpm.
- `faster`: This value adds 40 wpm to the inherited value.
- `slower`: This value subtracts 40 wpm to the inherited value.

The syntax for the property is as follows:

```
speech-rate: 40;
```

Pausing for effect

After you set the language rendering speed, you can further refine the delivery speed of aural material on your Web site for a more effective presentation for your users. For example, if you post a bus schedule on your site, you would want that information read to users in a way they could use — you would want to slow down the way this information is presented. The pause family has three properties that enable you to slow down the vocalization of aural text.

- `pause-before`: Use this property to create a pause before an element.
- `pause-after`: Use this property to create a pause after an element.
- `pause`: Use this property to create a summary property that enables you to set the `pause-before` and `pause-after` values without using those properties.

When you use the `pause` summary property and give it a single value (`pause: 10ms`, for example), the pause you call applies to both the before and after times. If you give your `pause` summary property two values (for example, `pause: 10ms 20ms`), it will apply the first value before the element occurs and the second value after the element occurs.

The following are the accepted values for all three `pause` properties.

- `time`: This value expresses the pause in absolute time units of seconds (s) and milliseconds (ms).
- `percentage`: This value refers to the inverse of the value of the speech-rate property. For example, if the speech-rate is 120 wpm (thus, a word takes half a second, or 500 ms), then a `pause-before` of 100% means a pause of 500 ms, and a `pause-before` of 20% means 100 ms.

Right on cue!

Just like in the theatre where things happen because of directorial cues, different job functions in your production work together to create the complete story. Aural style sheets are similar because they take cues from the code to create sounds when needed. The tool you use to trigger an event is the `cue` property that, like the `pause` family of properties, supports these three different properties:

- `cue-before`: Use this property to cue a sound before an element.
- `cue-after`: Use this property to cue a sound after an element.
- `cue`: This is a summary property that enables you to set the cue-before and cue-after values.

The only values that can be accepted by the `cue` family of properties are sound files, and the properties obey the following syntax rules:

```
P {
cue-before: url("ding.wav");
cue-after: url("dong.wav");
```

To deny the inheritance of a sound on a specifically named element, set the `cue` value to `none`.

Two turnables and a .wav file

Cascasding Style Sheets also give you the ability to mix aural properties — mix sounds, that is. Use the `play-during` property to specify that a sound plays in the background while a content element is being read. The property is slightly different in that it can support values that will enable you to either mix two sounds or repeat a sound. Here are the accepted values for the property:

- **`url`:** When you call this value, it must point to an audio file to be played while the element is being read. The syntax for this is

  ```
  play-during: url("dong.wav");
  ```

- **`mix`:** This value is used in addition to the `url` value, and it mixes the parent element's sound with the sound specified in the URL. The syntax for this is

  ```
  play-during: url("dong.wav") mix;
  ```

- **`repeat`:** This value is similar to `mix` because it refers to a sound file. Use this value to repeat the file specified if it completes before the content element is completed being read. The syntax for this is

  ```
  play-during: url("dong.wav") repeat;
  ```

Whose voice is that, anyway?

The final aural property that I want to cover in this chapter is `voice-family`. This is one of two voice characteristics properties of CSS (read about the other, speech rate, in the earlier section "Watch your speed!").

The `voice-family` property is akin to the `font-family` property that I describe in detail in Chapter 6. Use this property to append several different voice family types in order to cover all the vairous platforms and possible voice types. Note that this property accepts the following generic values:

- **`male`:** A male voice
- **`female`:** A female voice
- **`child`:** A child's voice

The `voice-family` property also accepts specific values, and can be chained together, according to the following syntax rules.

```
voice-family: comedian, Bill, Steve, Bobcat, male;
```

Chapter 16

Working with Paged Media

In This Chapter

- Creating pages for printing
- Understanding the `@page` rule
- Learning how to create page breaks
- Using left, right, and first pages

Paged media, a new addition to the CSS Level 2 specification, hasn't been adopted by the major browsers as of yet. It does, however, represent a new leap forward in the way document management can be controlled on the Web, and as such, deserves some attention in this book.

Paged media properties, simply put, treat Web pages as printed pages instead of continuous scrolling media viewed through a Web browser. The intent is to produce pages for printing from a Web browser. I can hear the collective sigh of all of you out there who have ever had to create a printable version of a Web page. After paged media is fully adopted by browsers and Web developers, using these properties will make your life a *whole* lot easier.

Setting Up Pages with the @page Rule

CSS2 defines several different media types, such as handheld devices and TV, as I mention in Chapter 15. Print is one of those media types, and the basic organizing property for print media is the page. The architects of CSS created a rule that basically says, "Hey, if you're working in print, use this rule to define the size of the page." That rule is called `@page`, and it works identically to the any other rule you'd use in CSS, meaning

- The rule must be contained within the `<STYLE>` tag.
- The rule must have properties and values.
- Properties and values need to be book-ended by brackets: { and }.

The `@page` rule can accept several different properties, all of which I describe in more detail in this chapter, but the basic idea is to set up a printable page, usually as follows:

```
@page   {
   size: 8.5in 11in;
   margin: 2in;
   }
```

This rule doesn't actually exist yet! It's just a representation of how a page would look in a Web browser if the rule were supported.

One of the cool things about paged media — especially after it catches on — is that you can specify left, right, and first pages, much like in a book or a magazine. By default, the `@page` rule assumes that the first page is a left-hand (verso) page and that the second page is a right-hand (recto) page, and so on. In some cases, you may want to change the order, or even specify the first page in a series. You can control the positioning of left, right, and first pages by a few page media-specific pseudo-elements, namely `:left`, `:right`, and `:first`. Apply them directly to the `@page` rule in the following manner:

```
@page :left
```

Sizing Up Your Pages

`@page` is designed to be used primarily with two different property classes: `size` and `margin`. The size property is used to specify the size of the page that you'll eventually be printing to, like a piece of paper, for example.

After you set the page size, then you set the page's margins. Use these `margin` class properties:

- **`margin-left`:** Creates a margin on the left side of the page
- **`margin-right`:** Creates a margin on the right side of the page
- **`margin-top`:** Creates a margin on the top of the page
- **`margin-bottom`:** Creates a margin on the bottom of the page
- **`margin`:** A summary property that creates margins on two, three, or four sides of the page

The margin properties work identically with the way that they work on block HTML elements. The difference here is that the margin is on a page rather than on an HTML element. Check out in Figure 16-1 how the margins work on a page element.

You can read more about the margin properties and how they work in Chapter 7.

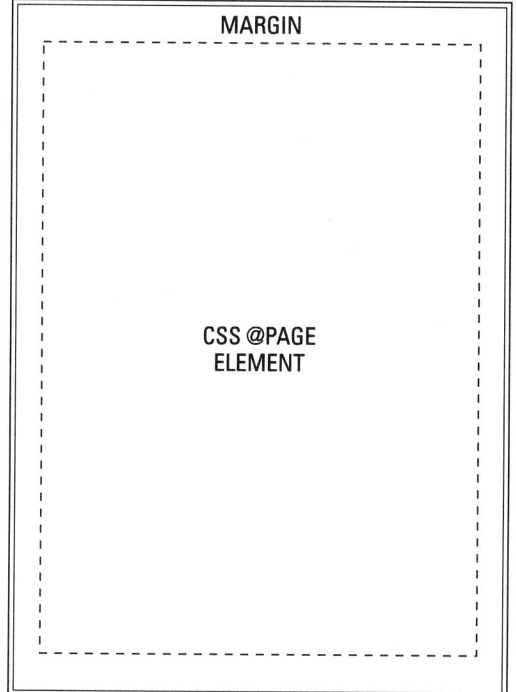

Figure 16-1: Margins on a virtual page.

The size class is just made up of one property, shockingly called `size`, which can support a number of different values, including

- `<length> {1,2}`: Enables the author to specify a width and length pair for the page using CSS accepted units

  Although you can use any of the CSS accepted units, stick with the standard conventions for page size, such as inches and centimeters.

- `auto`: Sets the page size and orientation to the target page as specified by the user's browser
- `landscape`: Overrides the browser's current orientation and sets the longer sides of the page to be horizontal
- `portrait`: A cousin to `landscape`, overrides the browser's current orientation and sets the longer sides of the page to be vertical

Breaking the Page

Paged media comes complete with five different ways to introduce page breaks into any page being rendered to the screen. These properties tell the application where to break to a new page, and then specify where the next set of content should go (that is, a left or right page).

The page-break properties

CSS specifies three different properties for traditional page breaks, namely:

- `page-break-before`: Creates a page break before the element
- `page-break-after`: Creates a page after before the element
- `page-break-inside`: Creates a page break inside the element

You apply each of these properties to a block element, such as a `DIV` element, for example, so that the User Agent (browser) can know when to insert a page break. The first two properties (`before` and `after`) work with all the possible values in the following list, and `page-break-inside` (which is designed to create page breaks within block elements) only uses the first two:

- `auto`: Neither forces nor denies a page break before, after, or inside the block element
- `avoid`: Avoids a page break before, after, or inside the block element
- `always`: Always forces a page break before or after the block element
- `left`: Forces one or two page breaks before or after the block element so that the next page is formatted as a left page
- `right`: Forces one or two page breaks before or after the block element so that the next page is formatted as a right page

Buzz through the following HTML to see how this works:

```
<html>
<head>
<title>pagebreak</title>
   <style>

   P.lastsection   {
      page-break-after: left;
      }

</style>
</head>
<body>

<P class="lastsection">Once this P element is complete, a
            page break will be generated</P>
<P>This should be on a second page.</P>
</body>
</html>
```

Now, although the older version 4.0 browsers don't support the page break feature, it does work in IE 5.5, as shown in Figure 16-2.

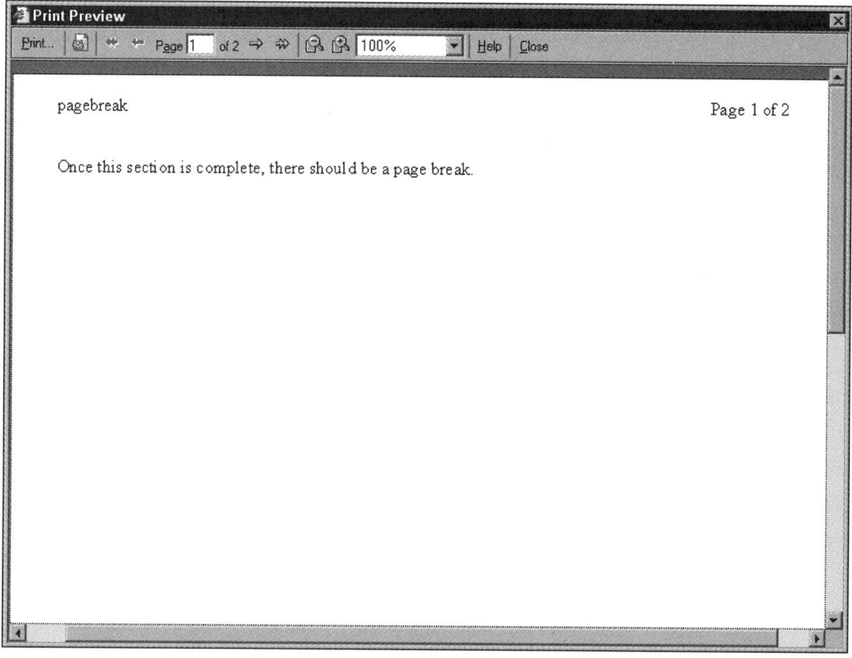

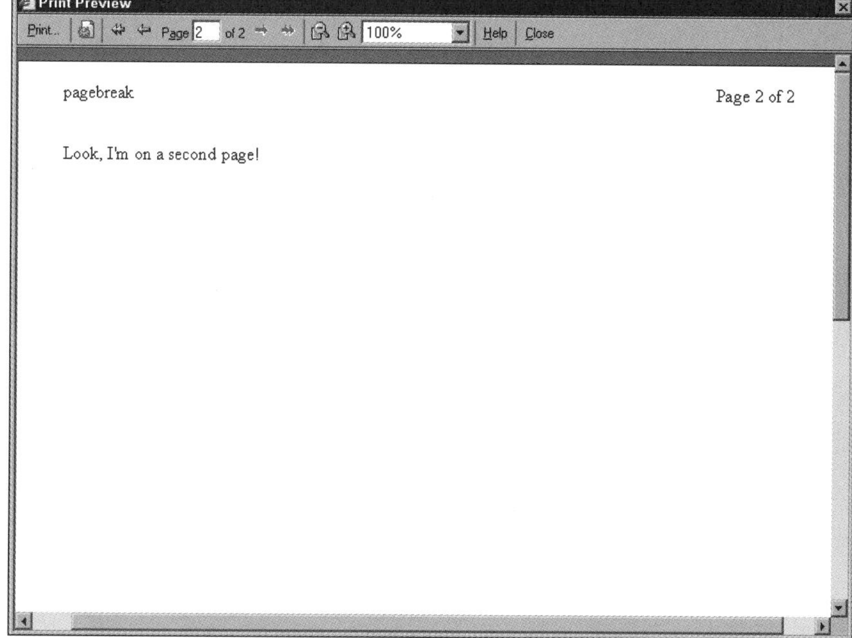

Figure 16-2: Wow, a paged media feature that works.

I've widowed my orphans!

For those of you who remember your typesetting days — what, no one out there? — *widows* refer to the minimum number of lines of a paragraph that must begin the top of a page, and an *orphan* specifies the minimum number of lines of a paragraph that must be left at the bottom of a page. The two corresponding CSS paged media properties — `widows` and `orphans` — can indirectly cause page breaks, and that's why I include them here. Both properties use integer values to specify the number of lines and would use the following syntax in a style rule:

```
DIV   {
   page-break-after: always;
   widows: 3;
   orphans: 5;
   }
```

There's @page, and now there's page

The last property paged media I want to mention here is the `page` property. This property enables you to name your pages and, depending upon your settings, cause a page break to occur between elements. Here's a brief example to help illustrate my point. In the following style sheet

```
   <style>
   DIV {page: skinny}
   TABLE {page: wide}
   @page skinny {size: portrait}
   @page landscape {size: landscape}
   </style>
```

what I've effectively done here is to give all my `DIV` elements the name `skinny` and the `TABLE` elements the name `wide`. Perhaps I've done this because I work for an accounting firm that posts really wide tables on the Web for clients to see. Now, in the normal flow of the page, I've got the following HTML:

```
<DIV>Here's some text in a DIV explaining how good the
          forecasts were</DIV>
<TABLE>Here's a table with some figures</TABLE>
<TABLES>Here's another table with some more figures</TABLE>
<DIV> And now my text just keeps on going.</DIV>
```

Because the `DIV` elements are named and get the skinny pages, and the `TABLE` elements are named and get the wide pages, the browser would read the `DIV`, create a page break, place the two tables on the landscape page, and then finally create another page break and continue on with the next `DIV` on a portrait page.

The `page` property will not accept any name containing spaces.

Part V
The Part of Tens

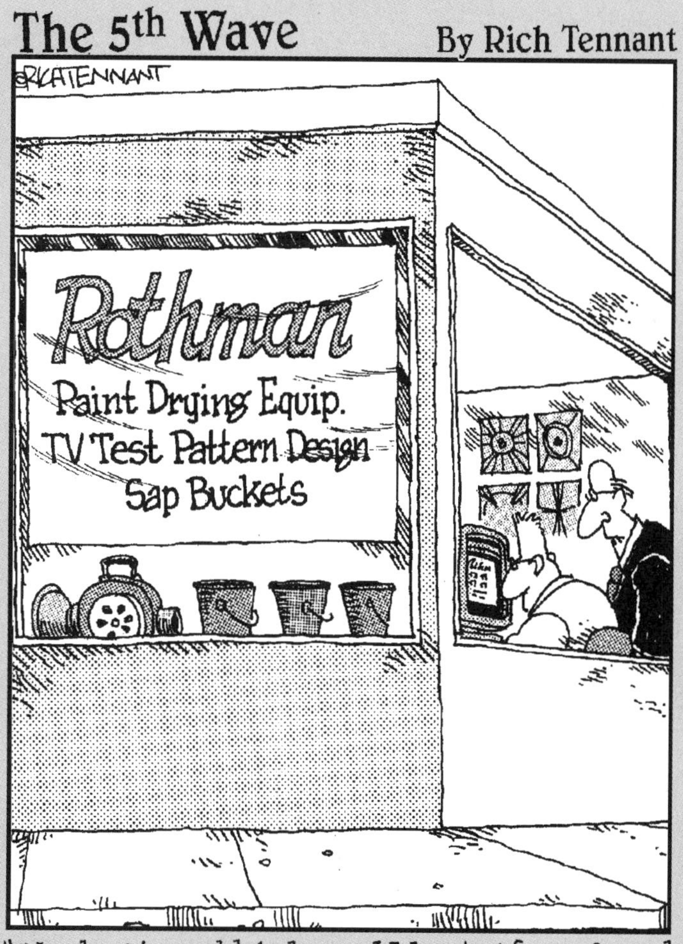

"Maybe it would help our Web site if we showed our products in action."

In this part . . .

Star Trek: Voyager has 7 of 9 and *Cascading Style Sheets For Dummies* has its Part of Tens. This part is like a CSS Trek: You will boldly go places to explore how to continue using CSS to your advantage. In particular, each chapter in this section will seek out ten different resources for you to view, observe, and use. You're your own captain, navigating through the Web in search of new and creative ways to use CSS.

When reading this part, stay near your Internet access so that you can immediately hop to those sites that most appeal to you. Read through these chapters to see examples of those sites that use CSS extremely well, and how you can emulate the applications that you see. I also show you resources to explore that can offer you more about using CSS. When you finish reading this part, you should better understand how to use CSS to improve your site.

With each chapter you navigate in your CSS Trek, you will observe new behaviors, discover more about CSS, and boldly go where others may have been before.

Chapter 17

Ten Web Sites That Use Cascading Style Sheets

In This Chapter

- CNN
- ESPN
- The Standard
- Ford Motor Company
- MSN
- Expedia.com
- 1-800-Flowers
- Entertainment Weekly
- Museum of Modern Art
- Morningstar

Use the Internet to research good examples of HTML and creative scripting in sites all over the world. Companies pump hundreds of millions of dollars every year into developing innovative ideas and advancing techniques into Web site design, and there's nothing wrong with taking a peak to see what other people are up to. Some folks may call this research approach "sneaky;" I call it Public Access Web Education.

CSS has been adopted in varying degrees by nearly every high-traffic site on the planet, so realistically, you could check out a variety of sites to find out how people are using style sheets. For this list, I compiled a number of sites from a variety of disciplines — news, entertainment, art, e-commerce, finance, and automotive — to give a good cross-section of implementations. Some of these sites don't use CSS extensively, but the one thing they all have in common is that they use CSS well, and that's what counts!

CNN

```
cnn.com
```

CNN.com is one of the best news reporting sites on the Internet, and if you spent any time there during the 2000 U.S. Presidential election, you probably noticed that the style and layout of this site changed almost hourly at times. With a great suite of styles and a very solidly designed basic structure, this site uses a mix of core styles and section-specific cascades. It's no accident that CNN has such great flexibility in being able to manipulate content around on its site.

The following bit of code shows just one simple example of how CNN uses a `<DIV>` to set an overall class, then embed another class for links, and then finally specify the link color using an inline style:

```
<div class="Threespaceindent">
<A href="http://fyi.cnn.com/fyi/" class="NavNormBlack"
           style="color:#000000">CNNfyi.com</a><BR>
<A href="http://europe.cnn.com/" class="NavNormBlack"
           style="color:#000000">CNN.com Europe</a><BR>
<A href="http://asia.cnn.com/" class="NavNormBlack"
           style="color:#000000">CNN.com Asia</a><BR>
</div>
```

ESPN

```
espn.go.com
```

There's a saying in the Web-design business: *When you want to see something done first, and best, you can find it at espn.go.com.* ESPN is home to some of the most advanced scripting, coding, and application development on the Internet, thanks to Disney's purchase and subsequent integration of Starwave. This is the same group that was also responsible for `ABCNEWS.com`, Mr. Showbiz, and Wall of Sound. In short, this design group is good — very, very, *very* good.

You really should check out the Spotlight sections in any of the ESPN Sport Sections areas. There you'll find great examples of using the `visibility` property in a useful, easy-to-understand way. Just by clicking a tab, different bits of content will either appear or disappear. Here's a cool clue: The designers of the ESPN site have been nice enough to embed some of these styles in the page, too, so you can see exactly how they work!

Even if you don't like sports, bookmark the ESPN site. You can often find interesting work-arounds to common browser problems on this site.

The Standard

`www.thestandard.com`

If you really dig into the code, you'll find that The Standard Web site is put together really rather simply, and its use of styles, although extensive, is pretty mainstream. Even though The Standard's use of styles is pretty conventional, the way in which those styles are created is not, and that's why it's cool.

Major sites commonly "sniff" your browser type when you hit the site. Sniff is just a fancy industry term for, "Psst, tell me what kind of browser this person is using!" The reason behind this sniffing is so that the site reads what kind of browser it's dealing with, and then provides the appropriate content. When it comes to styles, most sites either don't bother, or provide different `LINK` elements, depending on the browser type.

At The Standard, the designers have gone through the trouble of building a JavaScript function that decides (sniffs) which browser you're using. Then, based on that, the JavaScript puts the appropriate value for a property into the style sheet. What a clever alternative to loading two style sheets!

Ford Motor Company

`www.ford.com`

Over the past couple of years, nearly all the major automotive manufacturers have upgraded their Web sites and invested large amounts of money in their Web infrastructure. Some, including Ford, have gone so far as to link entire dealer inventories, making them available to Web users. Parallel to these upgrades are significant upgrades in the design and usability of sites, and, not surprisingly, a greater use of Cascading Style Sheets.

Ford's site uses CSS to position major content components on its home page. Through the use of absolute positioning (placing an element directly at a specific location on the screen) and the `<DIV>` tag, large blocks can be placed in very specific locations on the page, and the lion share of the page is composed using traditional HTML tables. The advantage to this method is that the site takes on a more modular feel, and the tables can be more self-contained and less nested within one another, making maintenance that much easier.

MSN

```
www.msn.com
```

You would expect a site like `msn.com` to use a lot of CSS. I mean, this is a Microsoft site, after all, and Microsoft loves to show off what its browser can do. If nothing else, MSN is worthy of a look because of the depth of functions used in this site. Strangely absent from its list of styles are any font attributes, but a modest number of pseudo-classes and pseudo-elements are used.

In short, the pages on this site look nice and simple, but show a depth of understanding of CSS that a number of other sites simply don't have.

This site is very Microsoft- and Windows-centric — which is okay for those environments — but side-by-side comparisons with a Netscape browser will yield very different results, almost purposefully so.

Expedia.com

```
www.expedia.com
```

If you're planning on doing some traveling, Expedia.com is a great place to nab a great fare. This site also happens to be a pretty good place to check out some Cascading Style Sheets in use, as well. The folks at Expedia.com are nice enough to have included their style sheets right there in the home page. Check out these style sheets for pseudo-classes and pseudo-elements in action, too.

Here is a small snippet of code that is somewhat unique among Web sites — you can find this at the Expedia.com site. In it, the developers use a rule, called `text1B`, to set the font and text properties of a form element.

```
<INPUT class=text1B id=idFcity1 maxLength=100
        name=Fcity1 value="">
```

1-800-Flowers

```
www.1-800-flowers.com
```

1-800-Flowers falls into the category of Best-All-Around-Site design. Although this site is not super glamorous, it is incredibly functional, with a broad use of basic CSS elements throughout the site. What's remarkable about the site is that it's very rich in terms of product content, partnerships, and the buying experience. That being said, the site uses a single style sheet to manage the entirety of the site. That style sheet may be a bear to maintain (only these

Web designers would know!), but from a development standpoint, these site gurus have done a remarkable job of coordinating the development under a single point of reference. Styles are segmented logically and efficiently, and although the use of `DIV` elements is frequent, it's not overwhelming. As a result, the site is able to maintain flexibility, and its entirety can be changed with a few edits to its style sheet.

Entertainment Weekly

`www.ew.com/ew/`

Entertainment Weekly (EW) is part of the Pathfinder series of Web sites. Traditionally, Pathfinder has had the opposite industry impression that a firm like Starwave has had. Pathfinder grew very quickly and was responsible for a number of sites, including *Time* magazine. (This was before Time and CNN were under the same roof, let alone under the even-larger roof of AOL.)

When the EW site first launched, it wasn't all that good, but it is much better now. The site reflects the print publication very well, with liberal use of `CLASS` and `ID` elements throughout the site. Because the style sheets are external, it's difficult to get an idea of the contents of the individual rules. However, you can see through the `CLASS` calls that this site (just like the 1-800-Flowers site) has been segmented nicely and can be managed easily from a minimal number of style sheets.

EW uses Vignette's StoryServer 5.0 as its development platform. Using this enables a lot of server-side scripting and page generation; thus, when you're looking at the source code for a page, you won't necessarily be able to trace where and how it was generated.

Museum of Modern Art

`www.moma.org`

The New York City Museum of Modern Art (MOMA) is one of the most well-known museums in the world, boasting some of the finest in contemporary artwork. MOMA has also got one downright kooky Web site. This site isn't all that complicated, but it's way more complex than it needs to be. (I'm guessing that it was probably created using Dreamweaver's built-in styling features.) This site does use, though, some identifiable style sheet components.

The MOMA site uses rollovers that show menu elements when you rollover a specific image on the home page. Some of these elements overlap one another, and to accomplish this, you need to use a lot of CSS to drive the process. Inline styles are used to absolutely position the menus, and then visibility features are used to turn those menus on or off depending upon where the mouse is on the screen. It's a simple, but nonetheless effective, way of building a menu system that works on the majority of browsers.

Morningstar

```
www.morningstar.com
```

Some financial firms also make good use of CSS features. Morningstar, which researches and rates mutual funds, provides a lot of content in various forms to a number of different financial institutions.

Morningstar easily wins the prize for the largest number of styles used in a page. Some of the other sites may use more styles, but because those style sheets are all external, they don't count. With Morningstar, you can easily see that its site uses a lot of styles, traditional as well as advanced CSS2 pseudo-elements.

Perhaps the most interesting part of the site though is the Scroller. The Scroller welcomes users to the site, and then offers a series of headlines and promotions for Morningstar services. The Scroller is almost completely defined using style sheets, in concert with DHTML. The result? Compelling, although I resisted the temptation to buy anything!

Chapter 18

Ten Great Web Resources for More about CSS

In This Chapter

- WebReview.com
- Builder.com
- msdn online
- World Wide Web Consortium (W3C)
- DevEdge Online
- Webmonkey
- WebReference.com
- EarthWeb
- HTMLHelp.com
- CSS Pointers Group

You know, as much as I'd love to believe that this *For Dummies* book could be your only source for information on Cascading Style Sheets, so much great information is out there at your fingertips — and well, I'm not quite *that* vain! Sort of like accessorizing a great-looking outfit, no great book is complete without tools that you can use to augment your learning process. In this chapter, I review some great Web resources you may find useful.

Although the Web addresses of these sites were current at the time of writing, the online world changes often. If you encounter difficulty accessing the URL I list for any of these sites, I suggest doing a search on the home page of the site, or through your favorite search engine.

WebReview.com

`www.webreview.com/style/index.shtml`

According to this Web site, "WebReview.com is the largest and longest-standing weekly site dedicated to Web professionals." The site is primarily geared toward Web development teams, which is great stuff for individual Web designers, too. Written by folks who work in the Web industry, this site is published each Friday and provides the insights of real-world professionals. Check it out for a handy-dandy one-stop area containing basic CSS information, support charts, and links to articles about CSS.

One of the superstars of this educational site is the WebReview.com Style Sheet Reference Guide's Browser Compatibility Charts! The Master List gets my gold star. The self-proclaimed "mother of all CSS charts," this list contains everything you need to know about CSS specifications, and how well those specs are supported by different browsers and operating systems. The Master List is based on CSS1 specs, but an addendum list that addresses CSS2 selectors.

Not to be outdone, I've also included a compatibility chart for CSS1 in Appendix A!

Don't miss the FAQ section where you can find answers to some of the most commonly asked questions about CSS. For a mini-tour of CSS specifications, you can view the page containing an Overview of CSS Specifications.

Builder.com

`www.builder.com`

Owned by CNET, the Builder.com site is the all-you-can-eat smorgasbord of Web development tools. From securing your domain name to Web development reference guides to a user's discussion forum to Web authoring downloads, Builder.com is the place to fill and refill your Web development plate.

Gluttony has its price, though, and the payment due at Builder.com is the constant barrage of myriad banner ads — blinking, offering this and that, and hogging real estate. If your eyes can handle the blankety-blank constantly blinkity-blink banner ads, you can gorge yourself on Web development information here and even come back for seconds!

Builder.com also offers all levels of CSS information, from just getting started to CSS editors. Don't miss the CSS Reference Table on the home page — this reference table links to the CSS recommendations and guidelines at `www.w3.org`. And kick yourself if you skip over the Style-O-Matic (the name alone is worth taking a peek). Use this cool tool to view the code for a style by typing in some text and applying properties to the style through drop down menus. Geek treat!

msdn online

`msdn.microsoft.com`

The msdn online (Microsoft Developer Network) site holds a plethora of Web development info. Similar to WebReview.com, the site's primary audience is Web development professionals, although msdn online is also a friend of the more technically minded. If acronyms like XML, ASP, ADO, MSMQ, ADSI excite you, then this is the place for you.

Even if you don't know your ADO from your ASP, this site is crammed with tons of useful information, including development articles, applications, news, technical columns, postings of developer training and events, and online courses.

msdn online prides itself on its online courses; consider taking its CSS course (posted October 1996). You can quickly access information about CSS from this course, which includes an introduction, ways to incorporate CSS in your site, and a style reference guide. Although the course is a great thumbnail sketch of CSS, it's not the whole enchilada, but still useful.

Another cool thing about this site is that msdn online is linked to the Microsoft Support Network, which is a network that answers questions from other developers and then posts those answers for all us kiddies to see. You'll find questions ranging the gamut from those just learning to crawl to marathon runners (Web developer-wise, that is).

This site is the place to go to determine whether Internet Explorer supports a particular CSS property.

World Wide Web Consortium (W3C)

`www.w3.org`

This consortium is the well from which Cascading Style Sheets sprung! If you just read the home page of the W3C, you'd probably turn and run the other way. "The World Wide Web Consortium (W3C) develops interoperable technologies (specifications, guidelines, software, and tools) to lead the Web to its full potential as a forum for information, commerce, communication, and collective understanding." Ick: This purpose statement has about as much character as a brown paper bag. Here's the scoop, in English.

The W3C is like the referee of the Internet. This consortium, comprising over 500 member organizations, set the standards by which development of the Web takes place. The intent is to set and maintain rules that Web developers follow so that the code and the browsers and the Internet all play nicely together.

This site offers lots of documents that define the skeleton of Web development. This skeleton is what gives life to the body of content that lives and breaths online. (Don't expect to find light reading here, though — when you have about 3,478 hours and some brain gigs free, peruse the technical reports and publications at the W3C site.)

Most important is that here's where you find the master CSS specifications document, which outlines in explicit detail everything CSS. Jump to the subject information you seek with handy links in the table of contents, and you're there!

You can find the CSS specifications at the `www.w3.org` Web site.

DevEdge Online

`http://developer.netscape.com/`

DevEdge Online is Netscape's arm reaching out to the Web developer community. Similar to msdn online, this site offers all the technical Webby information you need to create pages for this crazy mixed-up Internet world we live in.

The documentation at DevEdge Online includes a variety of references to guide and assist developers, including articles, manuals, sample code, and case studies. This is great stuff if you're trying to develop a site that you want to work in Netscape, which you'll discover can to be more than a challenge sometimes.

Check out the section dedicated to CSS (Cascading Style Sheets Developer Central), which is a great tool to complement your learning process. Highlights of the DevEdge Online commitment to CSS include newsgroups, compatibility info, tutorials, demos, and sample style sheets.

This site is the place to go to determine whether Netscape Navigator supports a particular CSS property.

Webmonkey

`http://hotwired.lycos.com/webmonkey/`

Lycos is becoming a veritable animal farm. The folks with the digging dog mascot now have a monkey. The Webmonkey site is the Lycos Web development network, where Web developers can share information, go through tutorials, and monkey around with emerging technologies.

In its own unique way, Webmonkey has a no-nonsense presentation to its information. Lycos means business, even if it is monkey business. The site boasts a complete how-to section, including design, authoring, multimedia, e-business, programming, backend topics, and even jobs. With its self-proclaimed "vicious posse of contributors," weird side projects section, staff hideout, Elbow Grease newsletter, and Webmonkey for Kids, this developer site is definitely top banana in the originality category.

Consistent with the rest of the Webmonkey site, the CSS tutorial you'll find here is made to be easy, original, and fun. Leaving no stone unturned, the tutorial takes you through five different lessons from making your first style sheet to developing special effects in your style sheets to controlling positioned elements. What a great place to practice your newly acquired CSS expertise!

WebReference.com

`www.webreference.com`

WebReference.com is one of the oldest Web development communities, developed when domain names were free and Netscape didn't support frames. Started around 1995, WebReference.com is equivalent to the wise old man in Web years.

This site was created by Anthenia Associates and is now owned by internet.com. Go here for all the design, authoring, and programming information you need as a Web developer. Just avoid getting lost in the internet.com ads, statistics, and news articles.

Search the home page for CSS information, and you'll find related articles, tutorials, and workshops that are predominantly links to other sites.

WebReference.com does contain a very helpful section outlining the history and basics of Cascading Style Sheets, but the real pearls exist in its Further Information section. Go there for links to other sites to help you supplement your CSS abilities.

EarthWeb

`www.earthweb.com`

EarthWeb is part of internet.com, a provider of "global real-time news and information resources for Internet industry and Internet technology professionals, Web developers and experienced Internet users."

The EarthWeb site is a great resource about CSS, including articles on the basics and CSS properties. One of the best things about EarthWeb is the specialized pieces about CSS. Read through these to help you learn about everything from borders to scrollbars. You'll also find links to tutorials, workshops, message boards, and style samples.

HTMLHelp.com

`www.htmlhelp.com`

Save your sanity at the HTMLHelp site run by the Web Design Group, which is an organization made up of experienced HTML authors that have banded together. HTMLHelp.com was formed to promote the use of valid and creative HTML documents with the hope of providing guidance and instruction to Web authors at all stages of development. Shop here for reference information on Web authoring, tools, FAQs, design elements, and more.

This site is also full of help on CSS, including a tutorial, CSS structure and rules, and CSS check lists.

CSS Pointers Group

`www.css.nu`

The CSS Pointers Group (the keeper of this site) is a newsgroup-turned-CSS-authority. Here you'll find many useful sources of information, examples, and links to other external resources. This information is for the advanced CSS player.

Stand-out sections for this site include CSS Pointers, a FAQ list, articles, example pages, experimental pages, and style sheets to study.

Here's your trivia for the day: What does `.nu` represent? (Think Scandinavian in design.)

Part VI
Appendixes

"Give him air! Give him air! He'll be okay. He's just been exposed to some raw HTML code. It must have accidently flashed across his screen from the server."

In this part . . .

Unlike the useless appendix organ of the human body, this part may end up being the section you use the most often, serving as your quick reference guide for everything Cascading Style Sheets (CSS).

Appendix A is your one-stop shop to all the property references you will need. I also include a compatibility chart in Appendix A to help you check quickly what browsers will play nicely with your CSS expertise.

Some of the best applications ever created are those nifty Web development editors out there. In Appendix B, I walk you through some of the more popular Web editors, with a specific focus on those that include CSS editors. The Internet may be a What-You-See-Is-What-You-Get (WYSIWYG) kind of place, but behind every beautiful Web site is a heck of a lot of code supporting it. These editors simplify the process.

Don't forget to check out the CD that came with this book. Hopefully, you weren't trying to play it in your car — that won't work. Put the thing in the CD-ROM drive on your computer, and then watch the magic that happens. The swell guy that I am, I included heaps of code on the CD for you to use to save you a little time and aspirin. (You're welcome!) Read through Appendix C for a walk-through on the information you can find on the CD.

Appendix A

CSS Property Index and Browser Compatibility Charts

In This Appendix

- Cacscading Style Sheets Index Chart
- Cacscading Style Sheets Browser Compatibility Chart

These two tables will eventually become your best friends, I guarantee it. The first table is a listing of the properties and values for the Cascading Style Sheets 2 specification. The second table provides a guide to let you know which properties are safe and unsafe when using CSS.

Browsers are being upgraded all the time, so use Table A-2 only as a reference guide to compatibility and not as the letter of the law! Results may vary, depending on the browser version.

Table A-1 Cascading Style Sheets Index Chart

<table>
<tr><th>Property</th><th>Value</th><th>Initial Value</th><th>Applies To</th><th>Percentage Values</th></tr>
<tr><td>background</td><td><background-color> || <background-image> || <background-repeat> || <background-attachment> || <background-position></td><td>Not defined for shorthand properties</td><td>All elements</td><td>Allowed on <background-position></td></tr>
<tr><td>background-attachment</td><td>scroll | fixed</td><td>scroll</td><td>All elements</td><td>N/A</td></tr>
<tr><td>background-color</td><td><color> | transparent</td><td>transparent</td><td>All elements</td><td>N/A</td></tr>
<tr><td>background-image</td><td><url> | none</td><td>none</td><td>All elements</td><td>N/A</td></tr>
<tr><td>background-position</td><td>[<percentage> | <length>]{1,2} | [top | center | bottom] || [left | center | right]</td><td>0%</td><td>Block-level and replaced elements</td><td>Refer to the size of the element itself</td></tr>
<tr><td>background-repeat</td><td>repeat | repeat-x | repeat-y | no-repeat</td><td>repeat</td><td>All elements</td><td>N/A</td></tr>
<tr><td>border</td><td><border-width> || <border-style> || <color></td><td>Not defined for shorthand properties</td><td>All elements</td><td>N/A</td></tr>
<tr><td>border-bottom</td><td><border-bottom-width> || <border-style> || <color></td><td>Not defined for shorthand properties</td><td>All elements</td><td>N/A</td></tr>
<tr><td>border-bottom-width</td><td>thin | medium | thick | <length></td><td>medium</td><td>All elements</td><td>N/A</td></tr>
<tr><td>border-color</td><td><color>{1,4}</td><td>The value of the color property</td><td>All elements</td><td>N/A</td></tr>
</table>

<table>
<tr><th>Property</th><th>Value</th><th>Initial Value</th><th>Applies To</th><th>Percentage Values</th></tr>
<tr><td>border-left</td><td><border-left-width> || <border-style> || <color></td><td>Not defined for shorthand properties</td><td>All elements</td><td>N/A</td></tr>
<tr><td>border-left-width</td><td>thin | medium | thick | <length></td><td>medium</td><td>All elements</td><td>N/A</td></tr>
<tr><td>border-right</td><td><border-right-width> || <border-style> || <color></td><td>Not defined for shorthand properties</td><td>All elements</td><td>N/A</td></tr>
<tr><td>border-right-width</td><td>thin | medium | thick | <length></td><td>medium</td><td>All elements</td><td>N/A</td></tr>
<tr><td>border-style</td><td>none | dotted | dashed | solid | double | groove | ridge | inset | outset</td><td>none</td><td>All elements</td><td>N/A</td></tr>
<tr><td>border-top</td><td><border-top-width> || <border-style> || <color></td><td>Not defined for shorthand properties</td><td>All elements</td><td>N/A</td></tr>
<tr><td>border-top-width</td><td>thin | medium | thick | <length></td><td>medium</td><td>All elements</td><td>N/A</td></tr>
<tr><td>border-width</td><td>[thin | medium | thick | <length>]{1,4}</td><td>Not defined for shorthand properties</td><td>All elements</td><td>N/A</td></tr>
<tr><td>clear</td><td>none | left | right | both</td><td>none</td><td>All elements</td><td>N/A</td></tr>
<tr><td>clip</td><td><shape> | auto</td><td>auto</td><td>Elements with the position property of type absolute</td><td>N/A</td></tr>
<tr><td>color</td><td><color></td><td>UA specific</td><td>All elements</td><td>N/A</td></tr>
<tr><td>display</td><td>block | inline | list-item | none</td><td>block</td><td>All elements</td><td>N/A</td></tr>
<tr><td>float</td><td>left | right | none</td><td>none</td><td>All elements</td><td>N/A</td></tr>
</table>

(continued)

Table A-1 *(continued)*

<table>
<tr><th>Property</th><th>Value</th><th>Initial Value</th><th>Applies To</th><th>Percentage Values</th></tr>
<tr><td>font</td><td><font-style> || <font-variant> || <font-weight>]? <font-size> [/ <line-height>]? <font-family></td><td>Not defined for shorthand properties</td><td>All elements</td><td>Allowed on <font-size> and <line-height></td></tr>
<tr><td>font-family</td><td>[[<family-name> | <generic-family>],]* [<family-name> | <generic-family>]</td><td>UA specific</td><td>All elements</td><td>N/A</td></tr>
<tr><td>font-size</td><td><absolute-size> | <relative-size> | <length> | <percentage></td><td>medium</td><td>All elements</td><td>Relative to parent element's font size</td></tr>
<tr><td>font-style</td><td>normal | italic | oblique</td><td>normal</td><td>All elements</td><td>N/A</td></tr>
<tr><td>font-variant</td><td>normal | small-caps</td><td>normal</td><td>All elements</td><td>N/A</td></tr>
<tr><td>font-weight</td><td>normal | bold | bolder | lighter | 100 | 200 | 300 | 400 | 500 | 600 | 700 | 800 | 900</td><td>normal</td><td>All elements</td><td>N/A</td></tr>
<tr><td>height</td><td><length> | <percentage> | auto</td><td>auto</td><td>Block-level and replaced elements, elements with position property of type absolute</td><td>Refer to parent element's height. If parent's height is auto, percentage of height is undefined.</td></tr>
<tr><td>left</td><td><length> | <percentage> | auto</td><td>auto</td><td>Elements with the position property of type absolute or relative</td><td>Refer to parent element's width. If parent's height is set to auto, percentage is undefined.</td></tr>
<tr><td>letter-spacing</td><td>normal | <length></td><td>normal</td><td>All elements</td><td>N/A</td></tr>
<tr><td>line-height</td><td>normal | <number> | <length> | <percentage></td><td>normal</td><td>All elements</td><td>Relative to the font size of the element itself</td></tr>
</table>

<table>
<tr><th>Property</th><th>Value</th><th>Initial Value</th><th>Applies To</th><th>Percentage Values</th></tr>
<tr><td>list-style</td><td><keyword> || <position> || <url></td><td>Not defined for shorthand properties</td><td>Elements with display value list-item</td><td>N/A</td></tr>
<tr><td>list-style-image</td><td><url> | none</td><td>none</td><td>Elements with display value list-item</td><td>N/A</td></tr>
<tr><td>list-style-position</td><td>inside | outside</td><td>outside</td><td>Elements with display value list-item</td><td>N/A</td></tr>
<tr><td>list-style-type</td><td>disc | circle | square | decimal | lower-roman | upper-roman | lower-alpha | upper-alpha | none</td><td>disc</td><td>Elements with display value list-item</td><td>N/A</td></tr>
<tr><td>margin</td><td>[<length> | <percentage> | auto]{1,4}</td><td>Not defined for shorthand properties</td><td>All elements</td><td>Refer to parent element's width</td></tr>
<tr><td>margin-bottom</td><td><length> | <percentage> | auto</td><td>0</td><td>All elements</td><td>Refer to parent element's width</td></tr>
<tr><td>margin-left</td><td><length> | <percentage> | auto</td><td>0</td><td>All elements</td><td>Refer to parent element's width</td></tr>
<tr><td>margin-right</td><td><length> | <percentage> | auto</td><td>0</td><td>All elements</td><td>Refer to parent element's width</td></tr>
<tr><td>margin-top</td><td><length> | <percentage> | auto</td><td>0</td><td>All elements</td><td>Refer to parent element's width</td></tr>
<tr><td>marks</td><td>crop || cross | none</td><td>none</td><td>Page context</td><td>N/A</td></tr>
<tr><td>overflow</td><td>none | clip | scroll</td><td>none</td><td>Elements with the position property of type absolute or relative</td><td>N/A</td></tr>
</table>

(continued)

Table A-1 *(continued)*

<table>
<tr><th>Property</th><th>Value</th><th>Initial Value</th><th>Applies To</th><th>Percentage Values</th></tr>
<tr><td>padding</td><td>[<length> | <percentage>]{1,4}</td><td>0</td><td>All elements</td><td>Refer to parent element's width</td></tr>
<tr><td>padding-bottom</td><td><length> | <percentage></td><td>0</td><td>All elements</td><td>Refer to parent element's width</td></tr>
<tr><td>padding-left</td><td><length> | <percentage></td><td>0</td><td>All elements</td><td>Refer to parent element's width</td></tr>
<tr><td>padding-right</td><td><length> | <percentage></td><td>0</td><td>All elements</td><td>Refer to parent element's width</td></tr>
<tr><td>padding-top</td><td><length> | <percentage></td><td>0</td><td>All elements</td><td>Refer to parent element's width</td></tr>
<tr><td>page-break-after</td><td>auto | allways | left | right</td><td>auto</td><td>Block-level elements outside of tables</td><td>N/A</td></tr>
<tr><td>page-break-before</td><td>auto | allways | left | right</td><td>auto</td><td>Block-level elements outside of tables</td><td>N/A</td></tr>
<tr><td>position</td><td>absolute | relative | static</td><td>static</td><td>All elements</td><td>N/A</td></tr>
<tr><td>size</td><td><length>{1,2} | auto | portrait | landscape</td><td>auto</td><td>Page context</td><td>N/A</td></tr>
<tr><td>text-align</td><td>left | right | center | justify</td><td>UA specific</td><td>Block-level elements</td><td>N/A</td></tr>
<tr><td>text-decoration</td><td>none | [underline || overline || line-through || blink]</td><td>none</td><td>All elements</td><td>N/A</td></tr>
<tr><td>text-indent</td><td><length> | <percentage></td><td>0</td><td>Block-level elements</td><td>Refer to parent element's width</td></tr>
</table>

<table>
<tr><th>Property</th><th>Value</th><th>Initial Value</th><th>Applies To</th><th>Percentage Values</th></tr>
<tr><td>text-transform</td><td>capitalize | uppercase | lowercase | none</td><td>none</td><td>All elements</td><td>N/A</td></tr>
<tr><td>top</td><td><length> | <percentage> | auto</td><td>auto</td><td>Elements with the position property of type absolute or relative refer to parent element's height</td><td>If parent's height is set to auto, percentage is undefined</td></tr>
<tr><td>vertical-align</td><td>baseline | sub | super | top | text-top | middle | bottom | text-bottom | <percentage></td><td>baseline</td><td>Inline elements</td><td>Refer to the line-height of the element itself</td></tr>
<tr><td>visibility</td><td>inherit | visible | hidden</td><td>inherit</td><td>All elements</td><td>N/A</td></tr>
<tr><td>white-space</td><td>normal | pre | nowrap</td><td>normal</td><td>Block-level elements</td><td>N/A</td></tr>
<tr><td>width</td><td><length> | <percentage> | auto</td><td>auto</td><td>Block-level and replaced elements, elements with position property of type absolute</td><td>Refer to parent element's width</td></tr>
<tr><td>word-spacing</td><td>normal | <length></td><td>normal</td><td>All elements</td><td>N/A</td></tr>
<tr><td>z-index</td><td>auto | <integer></td><td>auto</td><td>Elements with the position property of type absolute or relative</td><td>N/A</td></tr>
</table>

Table A-2 Cascading Style Sheets Browser Compatibility Chart

CSS Element	*IE 3.02*	*IE 4.0*	*IE 4.01 (Mac)*	*IE 4.5 (Mac)*	*IE 5.0 (Windows)*	*Netscape 4.x*	*Netscape 4.0 (Mac)*	*Netscape 6 (Windows)*
background	Partial	Partial	Partial	Safe	Safe	Partial	Partial	Safe
background-attachment	Unsafe	Safe	Safe	Safe	Safe	Partial	Partial	Safe
background-color	Unsafe	Safe	Safe	Safe	Safe	Partial	Partial	Safe
background-image	Unsafe	Safe	Safe	Safe	Safe	Safe	Safe	Safe
background-position	Unsafe	Safe	Safe	Safe	Safe	Unsafe	Unsafe	Partial
background-repeat	Unsafe	Partial	Partial	Safe	Safe	Unsafe	Partial	Partial
border	Unsafe	Partial	Partial	Safe	Partial	Partial	Partial	Safe
border-bottom	Unsafe	Safe	Safe	Safe	Safe	Unsafe	Unsafe	Safe
border-bottom-width	Unsafe	Safe	Safe	Safe	Safe	Partial	Partial	Safe
border-color	Unsafe	Safe	Safe	Safe	Safe	Partial	Partial	Safe
border-left	Unsafe	Safe	Safe	Safe	Safe	Unsafe	Unsafe	Safe
border-left-width	Unsafe	Safe	Safe	Safe	Safe	Partial	Partial	Safe
border-right	Unsafe	Safe	Safe	Safe	Safe	Unsafe	Unsafe	Safe
border-right-width	Unsafe	Safe	Safe	Safe	Safe	Partial	Partial	Safe

CSS Element	IE 3.02	IE 4.0	IE 4.01 (Mac)	IE 4.5 (Mac)	IE 5.0 (Windows)	Netscape 4.x	Netscape 4.0 (Mac)	Netscape 6 (Windows)
border-style	Unsafe	Partial	Safe	Safe	Partial	Partial	Partial	Safe
border-top	Unsafe	Safe	Safe	Safe	Safe	Unsafe	Unsafe	Safe
border-top-width	Unsafe	Safe	Safe	Safe	Safe	Partial	Partial	Safe
border-width	Unsafe	Safe	Safe	Safe	Safe	Partial	Partial	Safe
clear	Unsafe	Partial	Partial	Safe	Safe	Partial	Partial	Safe
clear/float	Unsafe	Partial	Unsafe	Partial	Partial	Unsafe	Unsafe	Safe
color	Safe	Safe	Safe	Safe	Safe	Safe	Safe	Safe
color units	Partial	Safe	Partial	Safe	Safe	Safe	Safe	Safe
display	Unsafe	Unsafe	Unsafe	Partial	Partial	Partial	Partial	Partial
first-line	Unsafe	Unsafe	Unsafe	Unsafe	Safe	Unsafe	Unsafe	Safe
first-letter	Unsafe	Unsafe	Unsafe	Unsafe	Safe	Unsafe	Unsafe	Unsafe
float	Unsafe	Partial	Partial	Partial	Partial	Partial	Partial	Safe
float/margin	Unsafe	Safe	Safe	Safe	Safe	Unsafe	Unsafe	Safe
float element in series	Unsafe	Safe	Safe	Safe	Safe	Unsafe	Unsafe	Safe
float on text elements	Unsafe	Partial	Partial	Safe	Safe	Partial	Partial	Safe
font	Partial	Partial	Partial	Partial	Partial	Partial	Partial	Partial
font-family	Partial	Safe	Safe	Safe	Safe	Safe	Safe	Safe

(continued)

Table A-2 *(continued)*

CSS Element	*IE 3.02*	*IE 4.0*	*IE 4.01 (Mac)*	*IE 4.5 (Mac)*	*IE 5.0 (Windows)*	*Netscape 4.x*	*Netscape 4.0 (Mac)*	*Netscape 6 (Windows)*
font-size	Partial	Partial	Partial	Partial	Partial	Safe	Safe	Safe
font-style	Partial	Safe	Safe	Safe	Safe	Partial	Partial	Safe
font-variant	Unsafe	Safe	Safe	Safe	Safe	Unsafe	Unsafe	Partial
font-weight	Partial	Partial	Partial	Partial	Partial	Partial	Partial	Safe
height	Unsafe	Safe	Safe	Safe	Safe	Unsafe	Unsafe	Partial
length units	Partial	Partial	Partial	Partial	Partial	Partial	Partial	Partial
letter-spacing	Unsafe	Safe	Safe	Safe	Safe	Unsafe	Unsafe	Safe
line-height	Unsafe	Safe	Safe	Safe	Safe	Safe	Safe	Safe
margin	Partial	Partial	Partial	Partial	Partial	Partial	Partial	Partial
margin-bottom	Unsafe	Safe	Safe	Safe	Safe	Safe	Safe	Safe
margin-left	Partial	Safe	Safe	Safe	Safe	Safe	Safe	Safe
margin-right	Partial	Safe	Safe	Safe	Safe	Safe	Safe	Safe
margin-top	Unsafe	Safe	Safe	Safe	Safe	Safe	Safe	Safe
padding	Unsafe	Safe	Safe	Safe	Safe	Safe	Safe	Safe
padding-bottom	Unsafe	Safe	Safe	Safe	Safe	Safe	Safe	Safe
padding-left	Unsafe	Safe	Safe	Safe	Safe	Safe	Safe	Safe
padding-right	Unsafe	Safe	Safe	Safe	Safe	Safe	Safe	Safe
padding-top	Unsafe	Safe	Safe	Safe	Safe	Safe	Safe	Safe

CSS Element	IE 3.02	IE 4.0	IE 4.01 (Mac)	IE 4.5 (Mac)	IE 5.0 (Windows)	Netscape 4.x	Netscape 4.0 (Mac)	Netscape 6 (Windows)
percentage units	Safe	Safe	Safe	Safe	Safe	Safe	Safe	Safe
text-align	Partial	Safe	Partial	Partial	Safe	Safe	Safe	Safe
text-decoration	Partial	Partial	Partial	Partial	Partial	Partial	Partial	Partial
text-indent	Safe	Safe	Safe	Safe	Safe	Safe	Safe	Safe
text-transform	Unsafe	Safe	Safe	Safe	Safe	Safe	Safe	Safe
URLs	Safe	Safe	Safe	Safe	Safe	Safe	Safe	Safe
vertical-align	Unsafe	Partial	Partial	Partial	Partial	Unsafe	Unsafe	Partial
white space	Unsafe	Unsafe	Unsafe	Unsafe	Unsafe	Partial	Partial	Partial
width	Unsafe	Safe	Safe	Safe	Safe	Partial	Partial	Safe
word-spacing	Unsafe	Unsafe	Safe	Safe	Unsafe	Unsafe	Unsafe	Safe

Appendix B

HTML Editors and Utilities with CSS Built In

In This Chapter

- AceHTML
- Arachnophilia
- BBEdit
- CoffeeCup HTML editor
- Dreamweaver
- Fireworks
- FrontPage
- GoLive
- HomeSite

In the Web world, you have your choice of HTML editors. You also have a wide array of editors that include CSS editing tools in them, as well. Here's a brief list of the more common editors and the CSS features they provide.

AceHTML Freeware

Hey, the price is right! AceHTML Freeware (formerly AceExpert) from Visicom Media, is a free HTML editor with many powerful features. This What You See Is What You Get (WYSIWYG) application enables you to add more than 100 pre-designed graphics. AceHTML also helps you get the most out of new technologies by providing an extensive help file system. This system includes references to JavaScript, CSS2, and SSI (server-side includes). Save a penny, get a lot!

Join Jack Benny at

```
www.visicommedia.com/acehtml
```

Arachnophilia

Calm down — no need to start panicking about attacks from mutant deadly spiders. (Thanks a lot, Spielberg and company!) Arachnophilia is another easy-to-use free HTML editor software program. One of the highlights of this application is its ability to prepare your text, tables, and indented outlines in your favorite word processor or other application. Then, all you have to do is use a simple drag-and-drop maneuver to plop in the result for immediate, effortless conversion to HTML. The application also supports CSS, Java, common gateway interface (CGI), and Flash.

Arachnophilia comes with a built-in intelligent FTP client that uploads changed files. It also has an HTML beautifier (cleans up your HTML for you!), macro support, and an error checker. Not sure how to do any of these things? Arachnophilia also includes tutorials on HTML, JavaScript, and the Internet. More bang for NO buck!

Spin your Web design skills (compliments of Paul Lutus) at

```
www.arachnoid.com
```

BBEdit

Mac lovers, here is the code editor for you: BBEdit, from Bare Bones Software. This editor has traditionally seen the most use among programmers as a source-code editor, but lots of other folks get a lot of good from it after they get around its busy interface.

BBEdit recognizes most Mac-friendly languages, and includes many Web-authoring tools. With an HTML tools window with buttons for commonly used tags, BBEdit also offers a Web-safe color palette built-in, a syntax checker, a spell checker, and a file transfer protocol (FTP) client. If you buy the Mac version of Dreamweaver, BBEdit is the default text editor. BBEdit is not a WYSIWYG editor, although you can preview your work in your preferred browser. This Web-authoring tool is for all those Mac-aholics out there.

Rattle your bones, Mac, at

```
www.barebones.com
```

CoffeeCup HTML Editor

Just in case you've been hankerin' for some caffeinated HTML, shinny on over to CoffeeCup HTML, from CoffeeCup Software. This HTML editor has everything you need to jolt your way to a better-looking Web site. CoffeeCup includes a spell checker, tag syntax highlighting, an Open-from-Web function, an Image Companion, and a well-stocked sound gallery.

This feature-heavy application has a split-screen preview so you can see your page change while you edit. It also includes editing support for your Cascading Style Sheets, eXtensible Markup Language (XML), ASP (Active Server Pages), and XHTML (the latest development standard for HTML). About the only stuff it doesn't come with are sweetener and a ceramic cow with milk pouring from its nose. (Ewww.)

Hey, Joe — top yours off at

```
www.coffeecup.com
```

Dreamweaver

Nope, Dreamweaver is not the 1976 pop hit "Dream Weaver" by Gary Wright, but rather, a way to write your own HTML. Dreamweaver is the WYSIWYG editor from Macromedia. Don't know much (or any) HTML? Don't worry, Dreamweaver doesn't care — it's the ultimate application when creating your Web site without having to know how to code it.

Dreamweaver works especially well with other Macromedia tools, including Flash and Fireworks. The application gives users an easy way to create rollovers, use JavaScript, and (hmmm) create Cascading Style Sheets. You can easily add most features for your Web site through a simple insert, and then preview them shortly after that. With its easy-to-use features, I would imagine the staying power of Dreamweaver will be a bit longer than that of Mr. Gary Wright.

Dream on at

```
www.macromedia.com
```

Fireworks

Macromedia has another HTML editor? I know . . . Macromedia already got its plug. However, Fireworks is different from Dreamweaver because it's more of a graphics creation tool, kind of like Photoshop. With the application, you can create graphics such as dynamic interfaces, and then convert these graphics into HTML! When you're trying to create Cascading Style Sheets that are more graphically oriented, Fireworks can be a great Web development tool.

Celebrate the Fourth early at

```
www.macromedia.com
```

FrontPage

According to the folks at `Builder.com`, more than a half million Web builders use FrontPage. FrontPage, from Microsoft, is one of the most popular HTML editors, and with good reason — it's one of the easiest editors on the market to use.

FrontPage is a jack-of-all-trades when it comes to WYSIWYG HTML editors. The application supports D(ynamic)HTML, JavaScript, and most importantly, Cascading Style Sheets (CSS).

One of the benefits of FrontPage is its tight integration with Microsoft Office. FrontPage can use Office rich text format (RTF) converters to convert all popular word-processing documents and spreadsheets to HTML. Further, you can use FrontPage to manage hyperlinks that you create within your Microsoft Office documents. FrontPage includes many of the same keyboard shortcuts and the same dictionary and thesaurus that you find in Office applications.

And although FrontPage is an easier application, I don't mean to imply that you can easily master it. For a little help with that, I recommend a wonderful book: *FrontPage 2000 For Dummies Quick Reference*, penned by yours truly (plug, plug) and published by Hungry Minds, Inc. (plug, plug, plug).

Make your own front page headlines at

```
www.microsoft.com
```

GoLive

GoLive from Adobe is a designer's friend. GoLive integrates very well with those other Adobe favorites, the popular design tools Photoshop and Illustrator. The application relies on the premise that layout is king when it comes to Web design. For all its graphic design-friendly features, GoLive does give you access to an HTML source code in its own editor.

GoLive has excellent support for Cascading Style Sheets, JavaScript, and Dynamic HTML. One standout feature of this Web-authoring tool is its QuickTime Editor, which enables you to edit your own movies. If you're using GoLive, you might as well use up a whole mess of bandwidth!

Go liven up your site at

```
www.adobe.com
```

HomeSite

Technically savvy Webmasters still create and edit pages in raw HTML code, despite the attractions of WYSIWYG page editors. HomeSite, from Allaire, is the code-based editor used by the savviest of Webmasters.

Those of you already familiar with HomeSite know the two-pane interface that has made it famous. This interface enables the user to navigate through the HTML. The left side consists of file lists, code snippets, site diagrams, and other resources. The right side enables the user to switch among code, preview, and view rudimentary edits.

HomeSite has its own built-in style sheet editor, called TopStyle Lite, for editing your CSS. TopStyle is an excellent CSS tool, with an accurate preview pane, support for future CSS features, and spreadsheet-style CSS tag inspectors that look and act exactly like the HMTL tag inspectors in HomeSite. For our code-loving friends, this is the application for you!

For more on HomeSite, go to

```
www.allaire.com
```

Appendix C

About the CD

In This Chapter

- System requirements
- Using the CD with Windows and Mac
- What you'll find on the CD
- Troubleshooting

In this appendix, I outline everything you'll find on the *Cascading Style Sheets* CD-ROM, what your computer needs to run the programs, and how to troubleshoot any problems you may have.

System Requirements

Make sure that your computer meets the minimum system requirements shown in the following list. If your computer doesn't match up to most of these requirements, you may have problems using the software and files on the CD. For the latest and greatest information, please refer to the ReadMe file located at the root of the CD-ROM.

- A PC with a Pentium or faster processor; or a Mac OS computer with a 68040 or faster processor
- Microsoft Windows 95 or later; or Mac OS system software 7.6.1 or later
- At least 32MB of total RAM installed on your computer; for best performance, I recommend at least 64MB
- A CD-ROM drive
- A sound card for PCs; Mac OS computers have built-in sound support
- A monitor capable of displaying at least 256 colors or grayscale
- A modem with a speed of at least 14,400 bps

If you need more information on the basics, check out these books published by Hungry Minds, Inc.: *PCs For Dummies,* 7th Edition, by Dan Gookin; *Macs For Dummies,* 6th Edition, by David Pogue; *iMacs For Dummies,* 2nd Edition, by David Pogue; and *Windows 95 For Dummies,* 2nd Edition, *Windows 98 For Dummies, Windows 2000 Professional For Dummies,* and *Microsoft Windows ME Millennium Edition For Dummies,* all by Andy Rathbone.

Using the CD with Microsoft Windows

To install items from the CD to your hard drive, follow these steps:

1. **Insert the CD into your computer's CD-ROM drive.**

   A window appears with the following options: HTML Interface, Browse CD, and Exit.

2. **Choose one of the options, as follows:**

   - **HTML Interface:** Click this button to view the contents of the CD in standard Dummies presentation. It'll look like a Web page.
   - **Browse CD:** Click this button to skip the fancy presentation and simply view the CD contents from the directory structure. This means you'll just see a list of folders — plain and simple.
   - **Exit:** Well, what can we say? Click this button to quit.

Note: If you do not have autorun enabled or if the autorun window does not appear, follow these steps to access the CD:

1. **Insert the CD into your computer's CD-ROM drive.**
2. **Click the Start button and choose Run from the menu.**
3. **In the dialog box that appears, type** d:\start.htm.

   Replace *d* with the proper drive letter for your CD-ROM if it uses a different letter. (If you don't know the letter, double-click My Computer on your desktop and see what letter is listed for your CD-ROM drive.)

   Your browser opens, and the license agreement is displayed. If you don't have a browser, Microsoft Internet Explorer and Netscape Communicator are included on the CD.

4. **Read through the license agreement, nod your head, and click the Agree button if you want to use the CD.**

   After you click Agree, you're taken to the Main menu, where you can browse through the contents of the CD.

5. **To navigate within the interface, click a topic of interest to take you to an explanation of the files on the CD and how to use or install them.**

6. **To install software from the CD, simply click the software name.**

   You'll see two options: to run or open the file from the current location or to save the file to your hard drive. Choose to run or open the file from its current location, and the installation procedure continues. When you finish using the interface, close your browser as usual.

Note: We have included an "easy install" in these HTML pages. If your browser supports installations from within it, go ahead and click the links of the program names you see. You'll see two options: Run the File from the Current Location and Save the File to Your Hard Drive. Choose to Run the File from the Current Location, and the installation procedure will continue. A Security Warning dialog box appears. Click Yes to continue the installation.

To run some of the programs on the CD, you may need to keep the disc inside your CD-ROM drive. This is a good thing. Otherwise, a very large chunk of the program would be installed to your hard drive, consuming valuable hard drive space and possibly keeping you from installing other software.

Using the CD with Mac OS

To install items from the CD to your hard drive, follow these steps:

1. **Insert the CD into your computer's CD-ROM drive.**

   In a moment, an icon representing the CD you just inserted appears on your Mac desktop. Chances are, the icon looks like a CD-ROM.

2. **Double-click the CD icon to show the CD's contents.**
3. **Double-click `start.htm` to open your browser and display the license agreement.**

   If your browser doesn't open automatically, open it as you normally would by choosing File➪Open File (in Internet Explorer) or File➪Open➪Location in Netscape (in Netscape Communicator) and select *CSS For Dummies*. The license agreement appears.

4. **Read through the license agreement, nod your head, and click the Accept button if you want to use the CD.**

   After you click Accept, you're taken to the Main menu. This is where you can browse through the contents of the CD.

5. **To navigate within the interface, click any topic of interest, and you're taken you to an explanation of the files on the CD and how to use or install them.**
6. **To install software from the CD, simply click the software name.**

What You'll Find on the CD

The following sections are arranged by category and provide a summary of the software and other goodies you'll find on the CD. If you need help with installing the items provided on the CD, refer back to the installation instructions in the preceding section.

Shareware programs are fully functional, free, trial versions of copyrighted programs. If you like particular programs, register with their authors for a nominal fee and receive licenses, enhanced versions, and technical support. *Freeware programs* are free, copyrighted games, applications, and utilities. You can copy them to as many PCs as you like — for free — but they offer no technical support. *GNU software* is governed by its own license, which is included inside the folder of the GNU software. There are no restrictions on distribution of GNU software. See the GNU license at the root of the CD for more details. *Trial, demo,* or *evaluation* versions of software are usually limited either by time or functionality (such as not letting you save a project after you create it).

Style Master by Western Civilisation ptd. ltd.

Demo Version, Windows and Mac. Style Master Pro 1.8 is a Cascading Style Sheets editing tool by my friends over at Westciv. You can also visit them at `www.westciv.com`.

TopStyle Pro by Bradbury Software LLC

Trial Version, Windows. Nick Bradbury is a legend in the Web development community. Well, at least he is to some people I know. Anyway, check out the latest version of TopStyle at `www.bradsoft.com`. If you don't like the nagging evaluation version, you can always download TopStyle Lite, which is freeware.

Author-created material

Windows and Mac. All the examples provided in this book are located in the Author directory on the CD and work with Macintosh, Linux, Unix, and Windows 95/98/NT and later computers. These files contain much of the sample code from the book. Here's what each of the files on the disc are:

Chapter 1

original_html.html	Shows the original HTML styles
ch1_P_style.html	Shows how a style rule can be applied to a P element

Chapter 3

ch3_salad_ugly.html	The recipe with no styles
ch3_salad.html	The recipe with the styles applied

Chapter 4

ch4_leaps.html	Nothing exciting, just a style rule being applied to a P element
ch4_leaps_large.html	That same set of elements, with a large SPAN element applied
ch4_news.html	The basic news journal HTML file
ch4_news_revised.html	The news story with an ID selector
ch4_news_with_pseudo.html	The news story with two pseudo elements

Chapter 5

ch5_em-1.html	Em height example number one
ch5_em-2.html	Em height example number two
ch5_indent.html	The indent rule at work
ch5_pixels.html	An example of padding and pixels working together
ch5_x-height.html	The different default fonts and their X heights

Chapter 6

ch6_absolute_size.html	The absolute sizes in CSS
ch6_copperplate_test.html	A test to show what happens when you don't have a font installed
ch6_generic.html	The generic fonts in CSS
ch6_indent.html	The CSS indent property at work
ch6_length_size.html	Using the various length sizes for font height
ch6_percentage.html	A percentages example for font height
ch6_relative_size.html	A relative size example for font height
ch6_spacing.html	The spacing text property at work
ch6_text-decoration.html	The different values for text-decoration
ch6_textstyles.html	Some text style examples
ch6_transform.html	Small caps, all caps, and initial caps all in the same HTML file

Chapter 7

ch7_background.html	The background summary property at work
ch7_background_image.html	A repeating background image
ch7_background_position.html	An absolutely positioned background image
ch7_backgroundcolor.html	An example of background color
ch7_border.html	The double border value in action
ch7_h1.html	A simple H1 element on display
ch7_height.html	An example of how a small height value will be overridden by the size of the content
ch7_line.html	The line height property being used
ch7_padding.html	How padding works, using CSS
ch7_visibility.html	An example of a disappearing headline
ch7_width.html	Fixing the width of an element with the width property
ch7_zindex.html	Showing depth using the z-index property

Chapter 8

ch8_fixed.html	An example showing how fixed positioning would work if it were implemented on a browser
ch8_float.html	Two different float examples, in the same HTML file
ch8_genericbox.html	How to create a generic box using the four corner properties
ch8_middle.html	An absolute positioning demonstration
ch8_overlap.html	An example of two elements overlapping using abosolute positioning
ch8_relative.html	Some elements offset from one another using relative positioning (contains multiple scenarios in the code)
ch8_relativediv.html	More relative positioning, though this time using DIVs
ch8_tablebasic.html	A basic table in HTML
ch8_upsidedownL.html	The upsidedown L design using gifs and absolute positioning

Chapter 9

ch9_basicinheritance.html	An example of basic inheritance using Arial
ch9_default.html	The default styles of HTML

`ch9_h1test.html`	An example of how the user agent can override inheritance
`ch9_important.html`	Showing how the important value works
`ch9_inherit.html`	Another inheritance example with the H1 element
`ch9_inheritance.html`	A lot of HTML elements combining to show the differences in inheritance
`ch9_moreinheritance.html`	Instead of an H1 example, this is P element example of inheritance

Chapter 11

`ch11_font.html`	A layout using only HTML font tags
`ch11_font_notags.html`	More examples of using CSS to replace the font tag
`ch11_fontsize.html`	A comparison of font tage sizes and equivalent CSS font sizes
`ch11_link.html`	Putting the pseudo elements to work on links
`ch11_oldhtml.html`	Old HTML and CSS side by side for comparison
`ch11_tables.html`	A basic table in HTML
`ch11_tables_css.html`	A basic table in CSS

Chapter 12

`ch12_counter.html`	A counter example
`ch12_list.html`	An example of a CSS list
`ch12_list_image.html`	A list using an image instead of a bullet
`ch12_list_position.html`	An example of different list positions using CSS
`ch12_markertest.html`	A simple test of the marker property that doesn't work on any browser
`ch12_pseudos.html`	Some pseudo elements that work on Netscape but not IE
`ch12_pseudos_after.html`	Similar to the above pseudo example, except using the `:after` rule
`ch12_quotes.html`	An example highlighting how the CSS quote properties don't quite work yet

Chapter 13

`ch13_caption.html`	An example showing how to apply CSS to a `CAPTION` element

`ch13_table.html`	An example showing right aligned caption on a table
`ch13_table_decimal.html`	This is a vain attempt to show the decimal value working for the text-align property

Chapter 14

`ch14_xml.xml`	This is the living room example for XML and CSS. This is viewable only in Netscape 6.
`ch14_xml2.xml`	This is the kitchen example for XML and CSS. This is viewable only in Netscape 6.

Chapter 16

`ch16_page.xml`	This is an example of how to create page breaks using CSS

Troubleshooting

I tried my best to compile programs that work on most computers with the minimum system requirements.

The two likeliest problems are that you don't have enough memory (RAM) for the programs you want to use, or you have other programs running that are affecting installation or running of a program. If you get an error message such as `Not enough memory` or `Setup cannot continue`, try one or more of the following suggestions and then try using the software again:

- **Turn off any antivirus software running on your computer.** Installation programs sometimes mimic virus activity and may make your computer incorrectly believe that it's being infected by a virus.
- **Close all running programs.** The more programs you have running, the less memory is available to other programs. Installation programs typically update files and programs; so if you keep other programs running, installation may not work properly.
- **Have your local computer store add more RAM to your computer.** This is, admittedly, a drastic and somewhat expensive step. However, if you have a Windows 95 PC or a Mac OS computer with a PowerPC chip, adding more memory can really help the speed of your computer and allow more programs to run at the same time. This may include closing the CD interface and running a product's installation program from Windows Explorer.

If you still have trouble installing the items from the CD, please call the Hungry Minds, Inc. Customer Care phone number at 800-762-2974 (outside the U.S.: 317-572-3993) or send e-mail to `techsupdum@hungryminds.com`.

Index

• Symbols •

• A •

• C •

• F •

• G •

• H •

• I •

• J •

• K •

• L •

• N •

• Q •

• R •

• T •

• U •

• V •

• W •

Notes

Notes

Notes

Notes

Notes

Notes

Notes

Notes

Hungry Minds, Inc. End-User License Agreement

READ THIS. You should carefully read these terms and conditions before opening the software packet(s) included with this book ("Book"). This is a license agreement ("Agreement") between you and Hungry Minds, Inc. ("HMI"). By opening the accompanying software packet(s), you acknowledge that you have read and accept the following terms and conditions. If you do not agree and do not want to be bound by such terms and conditions, promptly return the Book and the unopened software packet(s) to the place you obtained them for a full refund.

1. **License Grant.** HMI grants to you (either an individual or entity) a nonexclusive license to use one copy of the enclosed software program(s) (collectively, the "Software") solely for your own personal or business purposes on a single computer (whether a standard computer or a workstation component of a multi-user network). The Software is in use on a computer when it is loaded into temporary memory (RAM) or installed into permanent memory (hard disk, CD-ROM, or other storage device). HMI reserves all rights not expressly granted herein.

2. **Ownership.** HMI is the owner of all right, title, and interest, including copyright, in and to the compilation of the Software recorded on the disk(s) or CD-ROM ("Software Media"). Copyright to the individual programs recorded on the Software Media is owned by the author or other authorized copyright owner of each program. Ownership of the Software and all proprietary rights relating thereto remain with HMI and its licensers.

3. **Restrictions on Use and Transfer.**

   (a) You may only (i) make one copy of the Software for backup or archival purposes, or (ii) transfer the Software to a single hard disk, provided that you keep the original for backup or archival purposes. You may not (i) rent or lease the Software, (ii) copy or reproduce the Software through a LAN or other network system or through any computer subscriber system or bulletin-board system, or (iii) modify, adapt, or create derivative works based on the Software.

   (b) You may not reverse engineer, decompile, or disassemble the Software. You may transfer the Software and user documentation on a permanent basis, provided that the transferee agrees to accept the terms and conditions of this Agreement and you retain no copies. If the Software is an update or has been updated, any transfer must include the most recent update and all prior versions.

4. **Restrictions on Use of Individual Programs.** You must follow the individual requirements and restrictions detailed for each individual program in Appendix C of this Book. These limitations are also contained in the individual license agreements recorded on the Software Media. These limitations may include a requirement that after using the program for a specified period of time, the user must pay a registration fee or discontinue use. By opening the Software packet(s), you will be agreeing to abide by the licenses and restrictions for these individual programs that are detailed in Appendix C and on the Software Media. None of the material on this Software Media or listed in this Book may ever be redistributed, in original or modified form, for commercial purposes.

5. **Limited Warranty.**

   (a) HMI warrants that the Software and Software Media are free from defects in materials and workmanship under normal use for a period of sixty (60) days from the date of purchase of this Book. If HMI receives notification within the warranty period of defects in materials or workmanship, HMI will replace the defective Software Media.

   (b) **HMI AND THE AUTHOR OF THE BOOK DISCLAIM ALL OTHER WARRANTIES, EXPRESS OR IMPLIED, INCLUDING WITHOUT LIMITATION IMPLIED WARRANTIES OF MERCHANTABILITY AND FITNESS FOR A PARTICULAR PURPOSE, WITH RESPECT TO THE SOFTWARE, THE PROGRAMS, THE SOURCE CODE CONTAINED THEREIN, AND/OR THE TECHNIQUES DESCRIBED IN THIS BOOK. HMI DOES NOT WARRANT THAT THE FUNCTIONS CONTAINED IN THE SOFTWARE WILL MEET YOUR REQUIREMENTS OR THAT THE OPERATION OF THE SOFTWARE WILL BE ERROR- FREE.**

   (c) This limited warranty gives you specific legal rights, and you may have other rights that vary from jurisdiction to jurisdiction.

6. **Remedies.**

   (a) HMI's entire liability and your exclusive remedy for defects in materials and workmanship shall be limited to replacement of the Software Media, which may be returned to HMI with a copy of your receipt at the following address: Software Media Fulfillment Department, Attn.: *Cascading Style Sheets For Dummies*, Hungry Minds, Inc., 10475 Crosspoint Blvd., Indianapolis, IN 46256, or call 1-800-762-2974. Please allow four to six weeks for delivery. This Limited Warranty is void if failure of the Software Media has resulted from accident, abuse, or misapplication. Any replacement Software Media will be warranted for the remainder of the original warranty period or thirty (30) days, whichever is longer.

   (b) In no event shall HMI or the author be liable for any damages whatsoever (including without limitation damages for loss of business profits, business interruption, loss of business information, or any other pecuniary loss) arising from the use of or inability to use the Book or the Software, even if HMI has been advised of the possibility of such damages.

   (c) Because some jurisdictions do not allow the exclusion or limitation of liability for consequential or incidental damages, the above limitation or exclusion may not apply to you.

7. **U.S. Government Restricted Rights.** Use, duplication, or disclosure of the Software for or on behalf of the United States of America, its agencies and/or instrumentalities (the "U.S. Government") is subject to restrictions as stated in paragraph (c)(1)(ii) of the Rights in Technical Data and Computer Software clause of DFARS 252.227-7013, or subparagraphs (c) (1) and (2) of the Commercial Computer Software– Restricted Rights clause at FAR 52.227-19, and in similar clauses in the NASA FAR supplement, as applicable.

8. **General.** This Agreement constitutes the entire understanding of the parties and revokes and supersedes all prior agreements, oral or written, between them and may not be modified or amended except in a writing signed by both parties hereto that specifically refers to this Agreement. This Agreement shall take precedence over any other documents that may be in conflict herewith. If any one or more provisions contained in this Agreement are held by any court or tribunal to be invalid, illegal, or otherwise unenforceable, each and every other provision shall remain in full force and effect.

Installation Instructions

The *Cascading Style Sheets For Dummies* CD offers valuable information that you won't want to miss. To install the items from the CD to your hard drive, follow these steps.

For Microsoft Windows users

1. **Insert the CD into your computer's CD-ROM drive.**
2. **Open your browser.**
3. **Click Start⇨Run.**
4. **In the dialog box that appears, type** D:\START.HTM.
5. **Read through the license agreement, nod your head, and then click the Accept button if you want to use the CD — after you click Accept, you'll jump to the Main Menu.**
6. **To navigate within the interface, simply click any topic of interest to take you to an explanation of the files on the CD and how to use or install them.**
7. **To install the software from the CD, simply click the software name.**

For Mac users

To install items from the CD to your hard drive, follow these steps:

1. **Insert the CD into your computer's CD-ROM drive.**

   In a moment, an icon representing the CD you just inserted appears on your Mac desktop. Chances are that the icon looks like a CD-ROM.
2. **Double-click the CD icon to show the CD's contents.**
3. **Double-click** `start.htm` **to open your browser and display the license agreement.**

   If your browser doesn't open automatically, open it as you normally would by choosing File⇨Open File (in Internet Explorer) or File⇨Open⇨Location in Netscape (in Netscape Communicator) and select *Cascading Style Sheets For Dummies*. The license agreement appears.
4. **Read through the license agreement, nod your head, and click the Accept button if you want to use the CD.**

   After you click Accept, you're taken to the Main menu. This is where you can browse through the contents of the CD.
5. **To navigate within the interface, click any topic of interest, and you're taken you to an explanation of the files on the CD and how to use or install them.**
6. **To install software from the CD, simply click the software name.**

For more information, see Appendix C "About the CD."

FOR DUMMIES BOOK REGISTRATION

We want to hear from you!

Visit **dummies.com** to register this book and tell us how you liked it!

- Get entered in our monthly prize giveaway.
- Give us feedback about this book — tell us what you like best, what you like least, or maybe what you'd like to ask the author and us to change!
- Let us know any other *For Dummies* topics that interest you.

Your feedback helps us determine what books to publish, tells us what coverage to add as we revise our books, and lets us know whether we're meeting your needs as a *For Dummies* reader. You're our most valuable resource, and what you have to say is important to us!

Not on the Web yet? It's easy to get started with *Dummies 101: The Internet For Windows 98* or *The Internet For Dummies* at local retailers everywhere.

Or let us know what you think by sending us a letter at the following address:

For Dummies Book Registration
Dummies Press
10475 Crosspoint Blvd.
Indianapolis, IN 46256

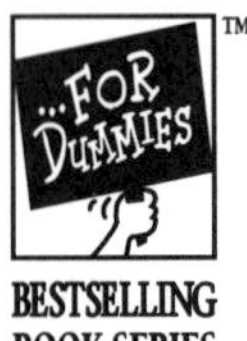